The Bizarre

£2·00

1·50

£1

The Bizarre Leisure Book

From the Alan Whicker Appreciation
Society to Zen Archery – a fun, A–Z guide to 150
off-beat leisure pursuits

Stephen Jarvis

Robson Books

First published in Great Britain 1993 by Robson Books Ltd, Bolsover House, 5–6 Clipstone Street, London W1P 7EB

British Library Cataloguing in Publication Data
A catalogue record for this title is available from the British Library

ISBN 0 86051 878 7

Cover photographs, clockwise from bottom: Alan Whicker Appreciation Society, by courtesy of the Society; Punch and Judy, by courtesy of Christopher Jones; Snail Farming, by courtesy of Dave Williams; Human Torch, author's photographs; Escapology, by courtesy of Nick Janson; Lewis Carroll Society, author's photograph.

Printed in Finland by WSOY

This book is dedicated to my mother, Joan Jarvis

Acknowledgements

The extracts from 'When I'm Cleaning Windows' (music by George Formby, words by Harry Gifford and Fred Cliffe, © 1937) and from 'Matchstalk Men and Matchstalk Cats and Dogs' (music and words by Michael Coleman and Brian Burke, © 1977), are reproduced by permission of EMI Music Publishing Ltd, London WC2H 0EA, in the latter case trading as Parrott Music.

The extract from 'The Generation Game' is reproduced by permission of Bruce Forsyth.

Contents

Preface

This book has its origin in my boredom.

Fed up with the nine-to-five at a major industrial company, I was determined that my leisure time should be as varied and as interesting as possible. So I walked on red-hot coals, swung on the flying trapeze, was sent back under hypnosis to my previous lives, etc., etc. All I wanted was the *experience* of these activities; it didn't bother me whether I was the best fire-eater in the world, or an outstanding Punch and Judy man. I just wanted to have a go – to be it, to do it, to try it. If I had a role model, it was John Noakes, the *Blue Peter* man; but I wanted to go beyond Noakes . . .

After a while, colleagues at work would ask on Monday mornings, 'Well, what did you get up to *this* weekend?' Suddenly, it struck me: if people were interested, maybe I could *write* about unusual leisure – not only to recount the experiences and anecdotes, but also to act as a guide, to give people the contacts so that they could try out the activities for themselves.

So, I started to write about the world of unusual clubs and societies, teachers of peculiar skills, strange sports and so on. Many of my articles on off-beat leisure were subsequently published in the London listings magazine *City Limits* and, more recently, in the *Daily Telegraph*. In time, I realized that there was enough material to put together a book: the complete guide to unusual leisure.

You might wonder if I had problems deciding what to include. The vast majority of the activities that follow would be classified, without hesitation, as both unusual and leisure, but there are borderline cases. For instance, should one include an activity with therapeutic implications, like the use of ear candles? What about a society with underpinnings in religion, like the Institute of Pyramidology? Do pressure groups count, like the Monarchist League? Is barbershop singing unusual enough? There are no definitive answers to these questions, but the activities I have covered seem to me to be of a piece. They all represent out of the ordinary possibilities for using one's free time.

The way I tracked down the contacts is a story in its own right. Looking back, simply asking people whether they knew of an unusual club or society has produced a surprising number of these entries. One man I engaged in casual conversation on a train even found out my address to tell me of an unusual society he had heard of shortly after our encounter! Searching small-ads columns was another research method. But I am always hearing of new activities – which means this book can never really be complete.

The contacts I have listed are mostly representatives of national societies or are the only people in the country who teach a particular skill. In some cases, a regional group may be covered (as with the London Earth Mysteries Circle), but the contact given will still be a valid source of information about other groups around the country. So use the book for networking. I have also included a few societies from North America when I believe that a person from Britain could benefit by joining (by receiving a club's magazine, for example).

As I come to the end of this project, I feel that I should sum up my findings. A book like this prompts a big question: why? Why exactly do people watch the test card as a hobby? Why would anyone publish a specialist magazine about counting backwards? Time and time again, I have been told of an event in childhood that sparks off a lifelong interest. Obviously, though, there are also cases when a chance occurrence in later years – perhaps something as simple as looking down and seeing an object on the pavement – can start a fascination.

It is worth stressing that just because an activity is off-beat does not mean it should be ridiculed. The work of the Dozenal Society, for example, may seem very eccentric, but members do have sensible points to make. They may be out of tune with the times, but perhaps the times are wrong and not them.

What I really hope is that this book will encourage people to set up more of these unusual societies. If you're interested in something, no matter how obscure, there is probably someone else who is interested too.

Stephen Jarvis

The Alan Whicker Appreciation Society

There are times when a word or two of explanation cannot be avoided. 'Look,' I said to the taxi driver, 'I'm going to put on a false moustache.'

So I chatted away as I peeled off the backing paper and stuck the brush to my face. The bristles were jet black, several shades darker than my natural hair, and reminded me of those draught excluders that people put in door jambs. Taking out a pocket mirror, I checked my upper lip. Hmmm ... lopsided. Still, not necessarily a bad thing – just as a bow tie needs *some* imperfection to show it's not a ready-made on elastic. I changed the angle of the mirror. Yes, I was satisfied with the spectacles too. As for the rest of me, that was smart yet casual – blazer, club tie, pressed grey trousers.

'We're here,' said the driver. He stopped at the pub.

Losing no time, I walked up to the bar and addressed the landlord. 'Could you tell me where the Alan Whicker Appreciation Society is holding its meeting, please?'

It was not just the laughter, it was the comments. Like, 'Where's your microphone?' Or, 'I hope you've got your Barclaycard.' When the pub had settled down, the landlord told me that I was a bit early, that so far I was the only Whicker on the scene. So I bought myself a pint – I wondered whether it would be more in character to go for a G and T with a slice of lemon – and I leant against the bar. But as new customers entered, I couldn't help noticing the sideways glances. I didn't need to be a lipreader to know that a woman was whispering to her husband, 'That man over there – I think he's wearing a false moustache.'

Before long, Whickers started to arrive. There were fifteen in all. One or two even had real whiskers and genuinely defective eyesight, but most took spectacles out of cases and then stood at the bar, spirit-gumming their facial hair. And then they began to speak in that slightly staccato delivery, that stream of nasal alliteration, subtle innuendo and dreadful puns, which is known as Whickerspeak, Whickeric or Whickerese. Hence, 'Here, amongst the flotsam and jetsam of human existence, lapping the shores of the urban paradise ...' And, 'Here, in a village at the foot of the Sussex Downs, not a stone's throw from rigor mortis ...' A few were estate agents and, talking shop, spoke of those

1

'panoramic views across enviable countryside' and 'lawns of bowling-green quality'. I myself had a go, repeating phrases like 'a typical run-of-the-millionaire', but somehow I didn't sound anything like the real Whicker, until one member gave me advice on the necessary vocal modulations. 'You have to go a little bit up . . . and then a little bit down,' he said. Pretty soon I had that meander in my sentences, and I started chatting to the chairman, John Ferdinando. It was not so much man to man, as interviewer to interviewer.

'It just happened,' he said, when I asked about the society's origins. 'It was 1973. About the time of the *Monty Python* Whicker Island sketch.'

Ah yes, I remembered that one. 'The trouble with Whicker Island is that there are just too many Whickers,' I said, with that special world-weariness of one who has seen the whole globe and found nothing but Shangri-Las.

John nodded. 'There were some of us in a pub and we started lapsing into Whickerspeak . . .' Soon after that, a letter was written to Whicker, who replied saying, 'If you've gotta be appreciated, relax and enjoy it.'

In the twenty years since, membership has tended to hover around the thirty mark. There are no women – they have a bit of a problem with the moustache – though there have been Whickers and Tarts parties. And all the members are professionals: solicitors, surveyors, accountants. I asked John whether Whicker was something of a role model for the professional classes. 'Very much so,' he said. 'He could easily be your personal financial consultant.'

As we tucked into a three-course meal – the society has a lunchtime meeting on the first Tuesday of every month – John boasted of a five-year waiting list for membership. (Though one member chipped in with, 'That's five years to get out!')

Thus, as the aroma rose from tureens as large as swimming pools, as meat and vegetables went down like a Lear jet landing under a setting sun, and as we tasted a dessert as rich as the sultan of a small petroleum-producing protectorate, we tried to understand the essential appeal of television's most travelled man. 'It's that suave staccato,' said John, doing it himself, 'it's his constant search for the improbable dream . . .'

CONTACT
John Ferdinando
Chairman
The Alan Whicker Appreciation Society
2 South Street
Ditchling
East Sussex BN6 8UQ
Tel: 0273 842554

The Alphorn

When I'd tried all the music shops in the *Yellow Pages*, when I'd been told endless times, 'No, that's one instrument we don't stock,' and, 'No, we don't know anyone who plays,' or even, 'You're joking,' I was left with just one last hope: I phoned the Cultural Section of the Swiss Embassy. 'Yes,' came the reply, 'I think I know of one man in this country you could contact.' Soon, I was on my way to Cheltenham to meet Niklaus Walliman, architect and alphorn player.

Now, many a musical instrument is made out of wood. It's just that in the case of the alphorn, they use the entire tree. You will gather, then, that the instrument is big. But I wish I spoke German, like the Swiss players of the horn, for you need those compound words, piling noun upon noun, to convey the instrument's by-law-breaking size. 'You get people trying to make the longest horn they can,' said Niklaus. 'I heard of someone who made a horn maybe 20 feet, maybe 30 feet long.' His own horn was therefore something of a shorty, being only a 12-footer, but it was still long enough to stretch all the way from his lips to the other side of the room. 'Would you like to try?' he asked. I walked to the horn's narrow end. Then, looking forward – it is as if you are about to smoke the biggest clay-pipe in the world – I filled my lungs and, well, blew.

Somewhere in Africa, an elephant stirred in its sleep.

'If you've got some facility in playing a brass instrument, it's a big help,' said Niklaus. He went on to demonstrate how the horn *should* be played, how minute lip movements are required for

3

the different notes. 'An awful amount of practice is needed to build up the mouth muscles,' he remarked, 'but it's a lovely sound when you hear it echoing across the hills ...'

Traditionally – as well as with the active encouragement of the neighbours of alphorn players – it is indeed to the hills that the horn belongs, used by Swiss farmers to call in the cattle. 'I have played in a field of cows,' said Niklaus, 'and it's true – they did all flock towards me and they formed a semicircle around the end of the horn. And the cows in the adjoining field were straining at the fence, trying to get to me. Whether it sounds like a bellowing bull to them, I don't know.'

Yet somehow, in spite of hearing some masterly playing – full of trills and runs and what Niklaus called 'flutter-tonguing' – I am not quite convinced that the alphorn is the instrument for me. It's not just the problem of finding a carry-case. You see, I keep on thinking of 'Edelweiss'. It's a pleasant enough tune, one I'd like to learn, and it's the most apt of all for the alphorn, but still ... wouldn't the song's delicate wild flower get a little pressed? I can't imagine Vince Hill putting an alphorn in his mouth for an instrumental break.

CONTACT
Niklaus Walliman
Tel: 0242 571317

Alphorns and tuition manuals can be purchased from:
Josef Stocker
Alphornbau
Wichlernstrasse 1a
CH-6010 Kriens/Luzern
Switzerland
Tel: 01041 41452106
Fax: 01041 41452116

The Ancient Astronaut Society

Look at the clouds for long enough and you can see anything you like: the sails of a yacht, or the horn of a unicorn, or simply a very large sheep. Similarly, if you're a patient in analysis, you may be handed an inkblot; take another look and it's the breasts of your mother, or the nose of your father, or your girlfriend with spiders in her hair. Do I mention this for a reason? Well, if you're a member of the Ancient Astronaut Society, you will be sent photographs of antiquities, mainly weathered statues or crumbling buildings, and you will be asked to see *things* within their designs. I am afraid, though, that you will not have free choice, as with the clouds or the inkblots. Instead, there will be a suggested interpretation. Look at that picture of an old carved slab from Guatemala. It could be a bear, or a warrior, or . . . wait, isn't it . . . isn't it a *spaceman?* There's the helmet and there's the back-pack and there's the breathing apparatus. Evidence that thousands of years ago, visitors from beyond the skies came down to our earth, to kick-start civilization. Evidence that God was an astronaut . . .

'I can remember the vicar in my church saying it was blasphemous.' A friend of mine had called round for coffee. When I told him about the Ancient Astronaut Society, we started discussing the man who had been its inspiration, Erich von Daniken, author of *Chariots of the Gods.* It turned out that both of us had bought the book as schoolboys – though that isn't much of a coincidence: 50 million copies were sold twenty-odd years ago, round about the time of the first moon landing, and long before my friend and I had developed critical faculties. 'I was a choirboy then,' said my friend, 'and when I heard the vicar attacking *Chariots of the Gods,* I thought, "That's a load of crap. Von Daniken's got all the evidence."'

Evidence: Mexican bas-reliefs that show a man piloting a possible space capsule; a Peruvian plain, marked strangely, that could have been the landing strip for other-worldly craft; artefacts such as ancient electric batteries.

It seemed to me that von Daniken had gone away. Or maybe I'd just grown up. So I was nostalgic when I opened the booklet that The Ancient Astronaut Society sent to me and saw a photograph of two tracks cut into a mountain at El Fuerte, Bolivia. Each track, I read, is 100 feet long, 1 foot wide and 4 inches deep. 'The site could have been used as a catapult-type launch for spacecraft.' Well, yes, that is a possibility. Then there is the Mayan carving which shows a man's head framed in a rectangle. Could this be a TV set? And I liked the sound of one of their book offers: The *6,000-year-old Space-suit,* by Vaughn M. Green. It analyses the incredible 6,000-year-old Dogu statues found in Japan and 'shows over thirty points of similarity with the modern Apollo space-suit'.

5

I look up at the clouds as I type these words and I see a rather fluffy version of the *Starship Enterprise*.

CONTACT
The Ancient Astronaut Society
1921 St Johns Avenue
Highland Park
Illinois 60035–3105
USA

See also UFOs 2: The International Raelian Movement, page 266

Anglo-Saxon (Conversational)

In a corner of a City of London wine bar, three men sat talking about the weather.

> *'Hu is thæt weder todæg?'*
> *'Thæt weder is sciene.'*
> *'Nis nan regn.'*
> *'Ond seo sunne scinth.'*

Being the least fluent of the three, I needed to have the words translated as we went along. ('How is the weather today?' 'The weather is fine.' 'There's no rain.' 'And the sun is shining.') I repeated everything, and that was enough for me to feel included in the conversation. And when I said, *'We sittath on inne, ond we drincath ond we hliehhath,'* ('We're sitting in the inn, drinking and laughing'), I was praised for my accent. For the hell of it, I asked, 'How do you say, "The cat sat on the mat?"'

'That's easy,' said Stephen Pollington. '"*Se catta sæt on thæm mætte.*" It's not a different language, is it?'

In a way, that's true. It would be stretching things to say we were speaking our *mother* tongue, but it would not be unfair to call it our *grandmother* tongue. Old English, or Anglo-Saxon, was the form of the English language spoken up to about the year 1100; a language whose grammar and vocabulary unravelled when the Bayeux Tapestry was woven. Stephen and the third man at the table, Alan Haymes, are members of Tha Engliscan Gesithas, or The English Companions, a group of enthusiasts for 1066 and all that. Some members even re-enact the warfare – I wondered whether they gave their battle orders in Anglo-Saxon.

'No,' said Alan. 'I'm afraid that the ones who are good at the fighting tend not to be so good at the linguistic side.'

It was the linguistics which particularly appealed to me. Much of Old English is incomprehensible and then you encounter phrases like '*ic eom*', which evolved into our 'I am', and '*he sæde*', our 'he said'. The combination of the unknown shot through with the familiar leads to some of the keenest pleasures of learning a language. As you achieve fluency – which you can do by purchasing a Linguaphone-like course from the Companions – hidden treasures are to be found in modern words: 'werewolf', you discover, contains the the old word '*wer*', meaning 'man', while 'nightingale' contains '*galen*', meaning 'to sing'.

'Old English is different enough to be challenging and yet homely enough to be reassuring,' said Stephen. And he admitted that his private diary was written in nothing else.

CONTACT
The Membership Secretary
Tha Engliscan Gesithas (The English Companions)
BM Box 4336
London WC1N 3XX

Arm-wrestling

Ernest Hemingway's *The Old Man and the Sea* contains the best description of an arm-wrestling contest you will ever read. In a crowded tavern, by the light of a kerosene lamp, two men squeeze and push till the blood oozes from under their fingernails. It is a contest that goes on for a day and a night, for *twenty-four hours*, without a victor – such a test of endurance that the referees have to work in shifts in order to snatch some sleep. Nobel Prize-winning writing, and deservedly so.

Nothing to do with reality, though. For real arm-wrestling is an explosive sport, not a marathon, and has much in common with cobra bites and praying-mantis strikes. Often won within a second, some contests are so fast they're impossible to time with a stopwatch. You might as well try timing a mantrap's jaws.

'Arm-wrestling is going to get into the Olympics in the next ten to twenty years,' said David Shead, one of the most respected arm-wrestling referees in the world. We walked to the regulation table, with its grips for the non-wrestling hand and its pads for the touchdown. 'We know for a fact it was in the original ancient Greek games,' he remarked. Then, to give me a taste of the intricacies of the sport, he introduced me to Katherine Monbiot, the 1990 British Women's Heavyweight Arm-wrestling Champion.

Now, as I write the words 'British Women's Heavyweight Arm-wrestling Champion' I just know you're going to have a false image of what Katherine looks like. I have to tell you that by any standards, Katherine Monbiot is a very attractive woman. 'Most of the women on the circuit are glamorous,' she told me as we faced each other across the table and squeezed hands. 'I think in a funny way, arm-wrestling makes women more feminine. It builds confidence.'

David ensured that the grip met all the rules and we were ready to go. OK, I thought, I'm a man, she's a woman, I'll try not to hurt her too much.

There's a time to laugh, a time to cry and a time to rid oneself of sexist assumptions; the time to do all three is when Katherine Monbiot takes about half a second to send your arm crashing to defeat. Afterwards she told me that she once issued an arm-wrestling challenge to the men dancing in a Bath nightclub. Lots came forward, all left beaten.

'She knows about technique,' said David. 'She's using the right muscles, big muscles, while you're using small muscles. Though of course she is very strong.'

Arm-wrestling, I now know, is a technically difficult sport, with moves and counter-moves all performed at high speed and under continual pressure. Consider the single problem of trying to change your position while maintaining your arm's strength: if you relax just a little, you've lost. With such a sport, training does not mean simply working out with weights, important though that is. 'You do things to improve reflexes,' Katherine told me. 'Things like playing computer games and snap.'

You also have to approach the sport with the right mental attitude. 'I don't think I hate my opponents enough,' she said worryingly.

CONTACT
David Shead
The British Arm-wrestling Federation
Unit 4 Gym
Nettlefold Place
West Norwood
London SE27 0JW
Tel: 081 761 0597

Art from Within

You have heard of painting by numbers. Well, you might call Art from Within painting by random numbers. If it's rules, guidelines and instructions you seek, this isn't the art for you. Sketching nudes? Following perspective? Copying bowls of fruit? They too are out. What's left is simply you, your brush and your inspiration. As in a free period at school, you can do whatever you want, painting anyhow – splash it, dab it, daub it. Whether your fancy is circles or squiggles, moons or horses' manes, emptiness or meaningfulness, the 'what' doesn't matter. Neither does the 'how'. If you're right-handed, why not hold the brush in your left? Or even paint with your eyes closed? Or, as I did, see whether your masterwork is improved by crumpling and unfolding the paper while the paint's still wet? As Avril Wigham, who runs the class, says, 'Lack of technical ability could be an advantage.'

All of this is reminiscent of the Abstract Expressionist school of painters, particularly Jackson Pollock, the notorious 'Jack the Dripper', who produced entire canvases of drips and flicks. His paintings range from the explosive to the spidery. Sometimes they resemble the toppings of pizzas.

I myself find Pollock's technique most congenial. In Avril's class, I wielded my brush like a whip, curling out my tongue with the sheer violent joy of it all as I made weals of green and purple and black. What did it matter if a drop or two landed on the nose of the person opposite? I was into my work, creating those pieces I would later christen 'Entrails', 'Maelstrom', 'The Creation of the Universe' and 'Nebula'.

Now, you may laugh at all this. Many do. Tony Hancock even made a movie mocking Abstract Expressionism – have you ever seen *The Rebel*, in which he plays an untalented buffoon who persuades the world and himself that he's a genius? And a couple of years ago, Paul Hogan advertised lager against the background of an art exhibition, mishearing 'They're Pollocks' as 'They're bollocks'. But for all this, it has to be said that there is a serious side to Art from Within.

Pollock once described his works as 'memories arrested in space'. He also wrote, 'When I am *in* my painting, I'm not aware of what I'm doing. It is only after a sort of "get acquainted" period that I see what I have been about ... the painting has a life of its own. I try to let it come through.' Avril Wigham makes a similar point: 'The first time I painted and forgot to "think about" what painting should look like, I got lost in the process, allowing another part of my mind to take over for a while. When I eventually stood back my response was, "Did I do that?" The message of my picture was multi-levelled and took time to come through. Art can allow half-forgotten memories or nameless, labelless feelings to emerge.'

Similarly, in the class I heard a woman painter of silvery rectangles and fish-like forms say that the colours had suddenly made her recall an imaginary playmate of childhood times – a long-lost friend, this see-through pal, unthought of for years. Another woman began to cry, saying she felt 'separated'.

Though my own memories were not stirred quite as forcibly as this, I did notice that I became more and more focused upon my own pictures, scarcely casting a glance at the other work in the class. I was being sucked into a quicksand world I was painting . . .

CONTACT
Avril Wigham
119B Grosvenor Avenue
London N5 2NL
Tel: 071 354 1603

The Artillery Association

For emphasis and a sense of history – two things I need to discuss this subject – let me use a plural that takes no 's': these people fire cannon. I do not mean scale models – or, if I do, that scale is one to one. What I am saying is that members of the Artillery Association own and fire full-size field-pieces, either reproductions or genuine items, but always a weapon that makes the appropriate noise.

'In a lot of ways,' said Ron Hill, one of the association's founders, 'I don't like myself for liking guns.' He and I were in an Essex pub, chatting over a pint, as he considered the distastefulness of instruments of misery. Set against the objections, though, he knew that he'd given a lot of pleasure with public displays and that his guns had raised money for charity. And since no shells or cannonballs were actually fired, the guns were harmless. 'The occasional burnt finger is about the worst that can happen,' he said.

As he spoke of how he wouldn't have minded living at the height of Britain's imperial power, of how he would have relished being a sergeant in a Victorian artillery battery, I wanted to know when his passion had started. Now in his fifties, Ron told me that his parents had taken him to Windsor Castle when he was seven. There was a large cannon on the outer terraces. 'That was it,' he said.

As we drank, he took me through a brief history of big guns – for the association is interested in firepower regardless of era. We began with medieval cannon, which Ron saw as psychological weapons, frighteners. 'Can you imagine what it was like to hear a gun suddenly go off? There was no heavy machinery in those days, no cars. The loudest noise was the clip-clop of a horse.' In other words, guns were a way of saying 'Boo!' with a boom. He spoke also of a seventeenth-century Swedish weapon, merely a copper tube wrapped round with ropes, to be thrown away after use – or, a disposable cannon, which the association has actually reproduced in modern times. Then it was on to the eighteenth century, when weapons became manoeuvrable. 'Why do you think Ordnance Survey maps are called that?' he asked. 'It's for moving guns.' He added that there is still a statute under which British Rail is obliged, for the princely sum of five shillings, to move guns anywhere around the country. 'It might even be worth owning a cannon to get cheap fares,' he said.

We finished our drinks and Ron drove me to Fort Coalhouse, in nearby Tilbury. Resembling an amphitheatre, this is an historic fort which is open to the public. Once inside, I was introduced to members of the Artillery Association. They were in full Second World War battledress. Oh, and they had brought a gun: a genuine 25-pounder. I remembered that as a boy I had a model of one of these that fired matchsticks; a direct hit from the real weapon on a fully grown tree would leave you with *nothing but* matchsticks.

After we'd shaken hands, the members of the association gave me the opportunity of sitting in the gunner's seat and turning the wheel that made the barrel traverse. Then Ron and I stood aside as a blank cartridge was loaded. The commander gave the order to . . .

Onomatopoeia: a word that sounds like the thing it describes. 'Bang' is a miserable attempt. Ron told me to open my mouth –

11

an old artilleryman's trade-secret for dissipating the effects of shock. Meanwhile, a member of the public, a mother with a child howling in her arms, was complaining to the artillery commander that insufficient warning had been given, that her little girl was seriously frightened.

I thought back to Ron's own childhood and the effect a single experience had had on his future life. I then looked at the little girl, and I wondered whether we had started the career of an anti-war campaigner.

CONTACT
Ron Hill
The Artillery Association
3 St David's Drive
Leigh-on-Sea
Essex SS9 3RQ
Tel: 0702 558743

Astral-projection Techniques

'You go to sleep,' he said, 'and suddenly you find yourself in another world.'

I was at a public lecture at Hemel Hempstead. The subject: astral projection. You've probably heard of this. Otherwise known as the out-of-body experience, in this state the consciousness is supposed to unshackle itself from the flesh and wander as a living ghost. Dr Douglas Baker, the lecturer, claimed to have had thousands of these trips outside himself – it seems he's hardly ever in! Furthermore, the lecture covered the *techniques* of astral projection, because Dr Baker believes that anyone, with the right training, can project a phantom duplicate of themselves. And it's not all done with mirrors.

He described the astral world as being very like our own, with people, places and traffic. And the two worlds interpenetrate, so in your astral body it is possible to visit a sister in Canada, travelling 4,000 miles in ten to fifteen seconds. 'As you fly along, you may see icebergs, or the astral equivalent of Quebec,' he said. I put up my hand and suggested that all this might be a dream, but Dr Baker disagreed most firmly.' 'You have no control over a dream,' he said.

In a short article I cannot go through the range of astral-projection techniques taught by Dr Baker, but he sells books, cassettes and videos, runs correspondence courses and gives numerous public lectures if you want all the details.

He recommends that you start by trying to project yourself within your own home; you shouldn't try to conquer the universe overnight (though this is not impossible – some astral projectors say they have been to Alpha Centauri and back). In the lecture hall, Dr Baker held up a Schweppes lemonade bottle and said that the first step was to choose some object – it could be a bottle, a statuette or anything else – and then memorize its every detail. 'Emblazon it on your mind so that you can call up a detailed image at will,' he said, 'and when you're in bed, be determined that you will go to it. It should be the last thing in your mind before you fall asleep.' With any luck, in the middle of the night, you will leave your body to seek the object – you might walk downstairs, you might even go straight through the walls.

Well, I have tried. The first object I chose was a toy galleon on my windowsill. I soon realized that its rigging was too complex to remember. I switched to a chessman, the knight, but even this I could not memorize to my satisfaction. The object I settled on was a key.

Dr Baker would undoubtedly comment that projection takes practice, that I shouldn't expect it to happen straight away. But every night, that key lies on the table in the lounge . . . while I remain inside myself, firmly locked up.

CONTACT
Baker Publications
'Little Elephant'
High Road
Essendon
Herts AL9 6HR
Tel: 0707 646115

Avengers-location Spotting

There is a road in Old Hatfield I have been down many a time. Charles Dickens used to take his quill there; the road's inn, the Eight Bells, makes an appearance in *Oliver Twist*. Perhaps I

shall go for a Dickensian pint again soon, only next time Bill
Sykes and Nancy will have to compete for my attention with
another fictional pair: Steed and Mrs Peel. Without knowing it, I
have been setting foot in Avengerland.

I put down the booklet 'A Guide to Avengerland' and asked its
authors, Tony and Annette McKay, exactly why they spent their
weekends driving along the roads of Herts and Bucks trying to
find the locations where the outside scenes of the *Avengers* were
filmed. 'It's another facet of being a fan,' said Tony, 'and no one
else was doing it.' (Though he did know of one man who was
doing extensive research on the *times* of the shooting schedules
– the days, the dates, the hours – in contrast to his own interest
in *space*.) But regardless of the appeal, what is life like if you're
trying to find the very patch of land where Joanna Lumley once
performed ju-jitsu on a master criminal's henchman?

Let us suppose Joanna (Purdey) is hand-chopping a windpipe
in the foreground. Tony and Annette will have their faces
pressed to the screen, looking for clues in the background: it
could be a glimpse of an outbuilding, or a public footpath, or a
hill, or a junction. Ordnance Survey maps and textbooks on local
architecture will be consulted. Then it's into the car, with no
stopping until a match is found for a photograph taken from the
screen. It could be that Tony and Annette are seeking a church
with a spire; but with equal enthusiasm they will look for a bend
in a road. And while many of the locations are to be found within
a certain radius of the Borehamwood and Pinewood studios,
there are others farther away. 'When we went on holiday to
Paris,' said Annette, 'we found some *New Avengers* locations in
the backstreets around Sacré Cœur.'

Tony got up to put on a videotape of *Avengers* clips, and it
illustrated how a single location could be used in different
episodes, playing different roles. First on, a scene from an early
black and white episode – a man with a rifle, walking up a
building's external stairs. 'That's Shenley Lodge,' said Annette,
'and those banisters are still there.' We then switched to a colour
episode of *The New Avengers*. Shenley Lodge again, with
Gambit. Then black and white once more, with Steed in army
uniform driving a tank towards you-know-where. 'In some series
it got really cheap,' said Tony. 'The same place would crop up
three or four times. There's even one episode where they use the
front and back of a house and they say it's two different houses.'

Apart from producing 'A Guide to Avengerland', which gives

details of how to find locations, and a description of what happened at them – Steed, I learned, was handcuffed to someone called Merlin when he was walking in Old Hatfield – Annette and Tony hold yearly *Avengers* treasure hunts. At these, hardcore fans follow clues that lead to *Avengers* locations. Tony put on a home video of last year's event. It showed forty or fifty fans gathered around the British Rail Training Centre, near Watford – a dour building which appeared in several televised stories. As the camera panned, Tony drew my attention to a stretch of road. 'At the end of the black and white episodes,' he said, 'Steed and Mrs Peel would finish the show by driving off in odd vehicles, like Hansom cabs or go-karts. Well, that's the road they went along.'

The conversation continued. I heard of the search for the village in Norfolk which featured in the episode 'The Village of No Return'; of the treasure hunt that started at the hotel where Tara King sent a postcard to Steed; and of the unfinished quest to find Steed's house. 'It's a real downer,' said Tony, 'when you drive around and you don't find a location.' It would really help, he admitted, if someone could lend him a helicopter.

CONTACT
Time Screen
88 Edlington Lane
Warmsworth
Doncaster
South Yorks DN4 9LS

Backwards Counting

Six minutes to ... five minutes to ... At the o'clock I started climbing the stairs. Four floors to go ... three floors to go ... When I got to the top, I entered the passage. Two doors to come ... one door to come ...

And I was face to face with Cedric Smith. Though the countdown to our meeting may have ended, the theme of countdowns in general was to dominate our discussion. Because Cedric – the Emeritus Professor of Biometry at University College London – is interested in challenging the assumption that, when we count, the numbers have to go forwards. Why can't they go backwards? Since I'm not backward about coming forward, I decided to open the interview by asking the Professor how his interest in reform of the number system began.

'When I was six,' he told me, 'I was taught how to do subtraction. And I was revolted by it. I knew it wasn't right.'

As an adult, he is still seeking to take revenge on his primary school teachers, for he advocates nothing less than the total abolition of subtraction as an arithmetical operation, as well as the extinction of the numbers six, seven, eight and nine.

Now, you're probably thinking that all this is crazy. It sounds like something from the looking-glass world of Lewis Carroll, or one of the fantastic stories of Jorge Luis Borges, such as his account of the land of Tlön, where people use 'indefinite numbers' based upon the notions of greater and smaller. But just a moment. Are you quite *sure* that the way we count really is the most efficient way of using numbers? It may *seem* natural to count forwards, but what if this is just a custom or a convention, a mere tradition?

Let's have an example. Take a number like eight. You might consider this as eight units counted forward from zero, but you can also see it as two units counted backwards from ten. So why not write eight as two digits: 1 (for the ten) followed by an upside-down 2, to indicate that two should be counted backwards. This is the Professor's approach. He points out that he is doing nothing unnatural, because we already use some backwards notions, such as when we remark, 'There are just ten shopping days to Christmas', or when we tell the time and say, 'It's twenty to four.' And such is his conviction in backwards counting that he has even had his typewriter modified, so that it will type the numbers upside-down.

'But what's the point?' I hear you say. Well, it turns out that arithmetic using the Professor's system is actually much, much simpler and faster. For example, the highest multiplication you ever have to do is 5 × 5, because six, seven, eight and nine are expressed as numbers counted backwards from ten. As for subtraction – well, that just vanishes, because it's the same as adding a backwards number. And to demonstrate the benefits of the system, the Professor publishes one of the strangest recreational magazines I've ever seen: *Colson News*, named after an eighteenth-century mathematician who first advocated turning arithmetic on its head. In its pages – which are numbered, not surprisingly, using the upside-down keys on Cedric's typewriter – there is an extraordinary range of articles on all aspects of radical reform of the number system. Only here will you find features on the history of backwards counting (the great mathematician Cauchy used it), as well as advice on how to teach children the elements of the new sums. (A lesson using snakes and ladders is described, played with two dice, one for forward and one for backward counting.) Then there are titbits about the advantages of backwards numbers. For instance, with our present system you often see prices in the shops like £399, which don't sound as high as they really are; in backwards counting, in which the same price would be £400 plus an upside-down £1, people wouldn't be so easily fooled.

But even if backwards is better, isn't it Utopian? Not according to Cedric Smith. 'I'm pretty sure that someday the penny will drop,' he told me.

'But don't you think you might be wasting your time?' I asked.

'No.'

'Why?'

'It's such a good idea . . .'

CONTACT
Professor Cedric Smith
141 Portland Crescent
Stanmore
Middlesex HA7 1LR
Tel: 081 204 5540

See also The Dozenal Society, page 67

The Bagpipe Society

So then it was my turn. Puffing hard on the mouthpiece, I inflated the bag till it was like a hot-water bottle fit to burst. I squeezed it against my ribs. Blowing again and squeezing some more, out came a sweet sound, a remarkably sweet sound. 'You've done this before,' David's wife said. David himself confirmed that, for a first attempt, I had played unbelievably well. 'Most people make the noise of a dying cat,' he said. Strange, because until then the nearest I had been to a set of bagpipes was a picture on the lid of some Scottish shortbread. Mind you, as David was to explain, it's wrong to think that the pipes belong to Scotland. 'In fact, the biggest manufacturer of bagpipes in the world is Pakistan,' he told me. 'You can buy a set of Pakistani pipes in London for thirty-five quid ... though they're not much good.'

And David VanDoorn should know. Stretched out on his sofa were different pipes that he had made, based upon investigations of drawings, paintings and texts from many cultures. His collection ranged from a reproduction English medieval pipe – whose shaggy bag and various drones made it bear an astonishing resemblance to Rod Hull's Emu – to an enormous construction with multiple cowhorns, called the Grosser Bock, German for 'the bigger goat'. 'The term goat is used throughout the world to describe bagpipes,' he said, 'but traditionally only billy goats are used for the bags. The air comes out of the female's nipples.'

David is the founder of the Bagpipe Society, a group of some 500 enthusiasts worldwide, aiming to promote the instrument in all of its forms – Breton, Czech, even Iraqi. Oh, and we certainly mustn't forget English regional pipes, for there was once a time when the different counties had their own distinctive bags and drones, though most have now died out. 'We're putting a lot of research into Lincolnshire pipes,' David said. 'There is speculation about a possible radio broadcast of Lincolnshire pipes as recently as the 1930s, though they were thought to have died out in the 1850s. We're hoping to send a member down to the British Library, to see whether we can find an old issue of *Radio Times* confirming it. There could even be a genuine set of Lincolnshire pipes in someone's attic if there really was a broadcast.' I remarked that it was a bit like tracking down coelacanths.

Yet David is not interested in historical authenticity for its own sake. For him, the bagpipe is a living instrument; although his creations are based upon traditional designs, he won't hesitate to add the odd extra goat's head for decoration or the occasional extra drone for the sound – anything as long as it feels right. He has even invented an instrument, 'The Hornchurch Pipe', named after the town where he lives. It incorporates a bag made from a combination of a pondliner and an old goatskin rug. Cowhorns also feature in his work, and I wondered about his source of supply. 'Normally Oxfam shops,' he said, as he squeezed a few dying notes out of the bag – eerily, because with a full bag you can play a little without blowing. 'The cowhorns are often attached to a wooden plinth with "A souvenir of Switzerland" written underneath.'

I was still wondering, though, about the traditional Scottish pipes. What was David's view of the pibroch, the classic Gaelic skirl? 'We do have members who are into the Scottish instrument, but Scottish music tends to be very conservative. You can be drummed out of a band simply for doing a vibrato.' He proceeded to tell a story about the dangers of the Scots' inflexible approach to the pipes. 'In Canada, there is actually a large Gaelic-speaking community, descended from Scottish immigrants. Even the Red Indians round there speak Gaelic. In the 1930s, a band from Gaelic Canada toured Scotland. They used vibrato and received such a terrible reception that they abandoned their playing techniques. An entire tradition was wiped out overnight.'

Suddenly, the lid of a shortbread tin had sinister undertones.

CONTACT
Val Woolard
Membership Secretary
The Bagpipe Society
33 Beaconsfield Avenue
Colchester
Essex CO3 3LY
Tel: 0206 47830

Barbed-wire Collecting

Why was there an ad offering a gift set of 100 pieces of barbed wire? Why was there a notice about a mail auction for a commemorative coin celebrating 100 years of fencing?

When I received my copy of the American publication *The Barbed Wire Collector*, I took a brief look at the contents and immediately the hobby seemed one of the more inexplicable of those I have encountered. The regular features set the tone: there was the photograph of a married couple, both wire collectors, introduced as 'The Prickly Pair of the Month'; and the box called 'Fence Facts', on this occasion stating that there was enough barbed wire to circle the earth with a three-wire fence twenty times over – and this was the output of just one company. As for the editorial, that covered the recent find of a full roll of G278 planter wire on an original reel with cast-iron spokes. So, once again, I could only ask: why?

I knew it would be difficult to find the answer. The magazine's editor had already written to me, saying he knew of no wire collectors in Britain, so there was no one I could interview, nor any collection to examine. I could only guess that the appeal of a barbed-wire fence was similar to that of a laid hedge or a dry-stone wall, which I cover elsewhere in this book. Maybe every culture throws up an attachment to its own traditional livestock enclosure?

The magazine lay around untouched for a long while, but a few days ago I opened it again. This time, I took a closer look at the illustrations, and I now know the truth. I am tempted to buy myself a pair of cutters, put on leather gloves and become the magazine's first subscriber in Britain.

It's all to do with the patent system. Any manufacturer entering the market has to offer a barb that's completely original. This means that barbs cross their legs, wind like spaghetti, splice like a mariner's knot, coil like a spring and curl like a lock of hair. If you were to take a length of fencing and clench it tightly in your palms, the stigmata would be different for every manufacturer. You start to wonder how many more types of prickle there can possibly be. Hence the urge to search and to collect.

The magazine contains a letter which reads: 'I have a few pieces of barbed wire, but none to speak of. But I started collecting fence posts some fifteen years ago and have collected seventy-seven so far.' This time, before I ask why, I'd better go out and have a look at some.

CONTACT
The Barbed Wire Collector
1322 Lark
Lewisville
Texas 75067
USA
Tel: 0101 214 317 7999

Barbershop Singing

It's easy to imagine the barber getting carried away, scissoring in time to the music. To the rhythm of 'Swannee' ('How I love ya, How I love ya'), you can imagine, 'How I – snip – ya, How I – snip – ya.' Sixty years ago it must have been like this, when American hairdressing salons laid on singing quartets to entertain the customers.

Nowadays, barbershop singing survives as the name of a musical style and has nothing to do with short-back-and-sides – although, I am tempted to add, it is a style demanding such discipline and conformity that not a musical hair must be out of place. That was my discovery when I went to Sheffield to meet a choir of barbershoppers, the Sheffield Barbershop Harmony Club.

The discipline of barbershop was brought home to me when I heard a man criticized for his pronunciation of the third syllable of the single word 'memories': it didn't quite conform, being a little too short, a little too much like mem*oriz* rather than mem*oreez*. 'It's not a witch-hunt,' whispered Tony Foster, the club's chairman, when he took me aside, 'but we have to make certain that we're all singing precisely the right vowel.' He mentioned that the club would soon be visited by an American trainer, whose approach was like a drill-sergeant's. 'He goes up close to whoever's going wrong, like this –' He pointed a finger right in my face, imitating the intimidation. 'They're frightened to death of him,' he said, withdrawing the finger, 'but at the same time they love him to death. It's what we need if we're going to win competitions.'

Competition is what modern barbershop is all about. When

the club goes on stage, wearing their team strip of tuxedos – the cuffs are false, pinned to the sleeves, so that every singer has precisely half an inch showing – it's them against the rest. It is generally agreed that Sheffield is the most outstanding club in Britain, though that position is never guaranteed. 'The Bristol Chorus are really gunning for us this year,' one barbershopper remarked. He went on to describe the emotional tensions of the national championships. 'It's like a cement mixer in the stomach, when you're waiting for the judges to announce one, two and three,' he said. That final judgement isn't simply based on musical harmonies, for barbership singing is a harmony of *everything* – dress, movement, even the facial expressions of the fifty-strong chorus. 'If you move an eyeball,' said Tony, 'it will be noticed by the judges.'

Eyeballs are the responsibility of the club's choreographer. Sitting on the sidelines, I watched him take command of the dance steps and other stage movements, and when it came to a line in a song where that word 'memories' was used – 'Where has that old gang gone, those memories linger on' – he instructed the members of the chorus to see old faces passing before their eyes. So fifty men reminisced in four-part harmony.

Later that evening, a new song was added to the club's repertoire, and I was invited to be a part of the chorus. The first performance of 'The Irish Blessing' was – by the club's exacting standards – somewhat ragged, but that raggedness was my only hope of fitting in. I sang, 'May the road rise to meet you, may the wind be always at your back . . .', but I knew that before long excellence would be established and the need for conformity would squeeze me out. For that matter, I don't think I could conform, even if I had the talent. It takes a special attitude to be a barbershop singer.

'It's a religion, not a hobby,' said Tony. He told me of one chorus member, now deceased, who was so committed that he had an arm tattooed 'British Association of Barbershoppers'. Unfortunately, two weeks later, the name was changed to British Association of Barbershop Singers. So he had the other arm tattooed as well.

CONTACT
British Association of Barbershop Singers
Little Orchard
Manor Road
Claybrooke Magna
Leics LE17 5AY
Tel: 0455 209555

The Bed of Nails

It is 6 feet by 2 feet. It is a porcupine rectangle, it is where fakirs are horizontal and it is my oblong of pain. I had come to learn the technique of lying on the bed of nails.

In the room with me was Terry Cole, who describes himself as the 'Greatest One-man Circus on Earth'. Amongst his achievements is the world record for balancing milk-crates on a chin: Terry has held twenty-five in a single pillar so weighty that his teeth were left shattered. As he let go of his lower lip, after showing me his shipwreck of a mouth, he simply said, 'It's the price I pay.' Because Terry Cole – stage performer and teacher of circus skills – has devoted his life to a philosophy: be different, feel proud. 'Doing what your neighbours do might be wise, but it's not clever,' he said. All very well, but my own worry was that I'd be left smarting in the endeavour to be smart, for Terry was about to teach me the rudiments of lying on the hardest mattress of all.

He took me to his bedroom, where for a joke he had placed his nailbed under the duvet. 'Do you ever actually sleep on the bed of nails?' I asked.

'Sometimes I do, if I fancy forty winks in the afternoon,' he said, and he proceeded to strip to the waist.

I watched as Terry lowered himself on to the points – in my imagination, they seemed to gleam all the more, as if they were welcoming him.

'Is that comfortable?' I asked.

'Absolutely,' he answered, and smiled. Then he turned over and lay on his front.

Now, since I'm a man, it is only natural that I was a bit concerned about what a sharp, 6-inch nail would do to masculine characteristics. 'Doesn't that get a bit . . . awkward . . . around the crotch?' I said.

'I suppose you could always wear a condom,' he replied.

Terry lifted himself off the bed and offered me the opportunity of taking his place. He emphasized that attitude is the key: you have to confront the nails, you have to almost talk to them, you have to say, 'Okay, you're nails, you're pieces of metal, you're nothing else. I'm going to lie on you.' He also advised me on the correct method of distributing bodyweight. I spread my legs on either side of the board, getting into a crab position, and lowered first my nether regions and then the rest of my world.

Every pain is specific. Kicking your toe is a different experience from a stinging in the eye. All I can say is that the bed of nails is unique and unpleasant: like a migraine of the back, or a toothache of the spine, or rheumatism in your very pores. As I lay there, I realized the absurdity of this self-inflicted agony. Why was I doing it? I could only grin at my ridiculousness. Grin and bear it – the facial muscles employed in making a grimace are not so dissimilar to those for a grin . . .

I stayed for a few minutes. Yet Terry aims to go for the world record and spend 400 hours on the nails. To do that, you would need psychological preparation: you'd have to be completely involved with yourself, you'd have to forget your surroundings and enter a semi-meditative state. Sometimes, to psych himself up, Terry returns to the house of a now-dead circus performer, Albertino Alcole, the man who taught him the art of lying on the bed of nails. 'I go there and feel the vibes,' he said.

I left Terry's house feeling certain vibes myself: silliness mixed with self-esteem; thoughts of comedy, pain and pride. Beds are often where we are born, often where we die . . . And the nails? A bed in between. But at the time I felt like saying to myself, yes, this is experience, this is what it's all about – as if, until I had lain on a bed of nails, I hadn't lived at all.

The points don't make an impression only on the skin.

CONTACT
Terry Cole
6 Acacia Rd
Walthamstow
London E17 8BW
Tel: 081 520 2063 or 0831 550688

The Boomerang Society

The wind was too strong: When it moves the leaves, and only the leaves, then it's fine. But the branches as well? No.

I waited till the trees said yes and then I drew back my hand. With the sun behind me, I cast a long shadow ahead – like an Australian discobolus? Or a sort of falconer? Who knows? By then, I'd stopped looking down and I was watching only the spinning in the sky.

Dammit, too far back. It went over my head, to be lost in the sun. When the boomerang landed, it lay in the tall grass far away, like a teacher's tick.

The other man in the field, Sean Slade, was actually a teacher by profession. He also runs the British Boomerang Society. Did his return? Return his did. 'I like to see a big symmetrical circle,' said Sean. 'There's something very satisfying about that.' He remarked that boomerang is the perfect slob sport: you don't have to be athletic or macho – once you've mastered the throw and the catch, you stand still. 'And how many other sports can you play on your own?' he said.

Just why boomerangs are so satisfying is a puzzle. They simply are. Dogs like to chase sticks; human beings like something more sophisticated. You might be tempted to say that if we knew all the scientific laws involved, the boomerang would be banal, would lose its wonder. Yet Sean is a teacher of physics, so he knows precisely how they work.

When we returned to his house, he explained that he is willing to experiment in constructing boomerangs in any known material. 'I had one member of the society phoning me up,' he told me, 'and he said, "Have you ever thought of making them out of old LPs?" The ridged surface could have interesting effects on the airflow.' He also spoke of the adjustments, the slight twists to the shape, that affect the aerodynamics. 'There are different approaches to tuning them,' he said, as a pile clattered down on his kitchen table. 'I put the wooden ones in the microwave for ten to fifteen seconds.'

Surprisingly, many boomerangs are not, well, boomerang-shaped. There are thousands of types. I saw a 'water molecule', consisting of three circles, a big 'hydrogen' and two smaller 'oxygens'; a 'cat', to be tossed by the tail; a 'tomahawk'; a 'tennis racquet'; and a 'Gurkha knife'. One of the aims of the society is to keep members supplied with blueprints for new designs.

The society's other function is to organize the British boomerang championships. There are numerous events, including 'fast catch', in which the boomerang is thrown 20 metres and has to be caught in the fastest possible time. The world record for this event is less than fifteen seconds, and because the boomerang is travelling at 50–60 mph, contestants have to wear gloves. Another event is 'endurance', which involves throwing and catching as many times as possible, until the boomerang is

dropped. The endurance world record is 800 catches – and could
have been even more. 'The bloke doing it got bored,' said Sean.

CONTACT
Sean Slade
1 Berkeley Ave
Mapperley Park
Nottingham NG3 5BU
Tel: 0602 604992

Bowling: *The Baby Split . . . News*

By now, you should have an understanding of the theme of this
book. Why, then, am I including a section on ten-pin bowling?
After all, bowling is a pretty ordinary kind of leisure activity,
isn't it? Well, *isn't* it?

The reason is that I have been reading the magazine *The
Baby Split Bowling News*. This isn't simply a hobby journal;
instead, it offers a variation on this book's entire theme – it
takes an ordinary activity and writes about it in an extraordinary way. For in its pages, any conceivable subject, from the
trivial to the profound, is examined from the perspective of a
ten-pin bowler. In short, life is a bowling alley.

Let me step out of the way and give you some examples.
Remember the old TV western series *Rawhide*? Remember the
theme tune? Well, try singing this little number:

'Rawpins' (to the tune of 'Rawhide')

Ya (*whip crack*),
Bowlin', bowlin', bowlin' (*whip crack*),
Ya (*whip crack*),
Bowlin', bowlin', bowlin',
Keep movin', movin', movin',
Though they're disapprovin',
Keep them maples movin', raw-*pins*.
Don't try to understand 'em,
Just roll one down and blam 'em,
Soon we'll be livin' high and wide.
Rawpin's calculatin',
My true love will be waitin',
Be waitin' at the end of my game.

Bowl 'em down, set 'em up,
Set 'em up, bowl 'em down,
Bowl 'em down, set 'em up, rawpins.
(*Whip crack*) Sweep 'em up, clear 'em out,
Clear 'em out, sweep 'em up,
Set 'em up, clear 'em out, raw-*pins*.
Bowlin', bowlin', bowlin' . . .

Choose another subject. What about phrenology, the attempt to discern character from the bumps on a head? This inspires an article on 'Bowling Phrenology': the bowler has his bowling ball examined by an expert who, from the number, size and length of the nicks and scratches on different areas of the ball, can tell the bowler what he is doing wrong in a game and can suggest corrections.

Still more examples required? Consider, then, the terracotta warriors of China – or rather, the terracotta bowlers. Many of the figures are shown mid-stride, arm out, after ball release.

Too narrow a choice of subject? OK, let's take food. One of the back issues has a recipe for 'Bowling Pins with Hidden Ball Salad', where the pins are represented by pears stuffed with cream-cheese balls. (It is recommended that the dish be served on a lettuce-lined platter with a real bowling pin in the centre.) What about modern history? Interested in bowling parallels to the Gulf War? Or what about the assassination of Jesse James considered as a 7–10 split?

This goes on for issue after issue. It isn't exactly funny – if the joke were a carpet, you'd be walking on underfelt, it would be worn so thin – but this only serves to make the magazine even more of a curiosity. Anyone could come up with a humorous magazine, but *The Baby Split Bowling News* is unique, a one-off from one-track minds. I wrote a letter to its editor, Julian Davis, asking what was the magazine's purpose. He replied in this way: 'We don't really have a stated aim. I guess you could say it's to spread the word of deviant bowling around the world. A few of us started bowling once a week and one day I said, "Hey, let's start a magazine!" I think most people don't really get it. They just like it and feel better thinking they get it. It was a weird enough idea and I figured no one else was doing it.'

I looked at a biological article, 'Zombie Bowling Ants'. Some hours after their death, these ants will start to move again and in minutes begin to create their bowling equipment. To make the bowling ball, the ant will start with a small particle of dust and cover it with layers of a secretion which hardens quickly. (This particular issue of the magazine included a small polythene bag containing a genuine dead ant. It was suggested that it might be a Zombie, in which case eating it will mean the transference of its bowling spirit into your aura and improve your scores.)

Turning from ants, I found a section on bowling-ball hygiene. It recommended cleaning the ball with hand soap, then swabbing the holes with alcohol and putting the ball in a patch of sunlight – orienting it so the light would go into the holes. (The technique utilizes the ultra-violet component of sunlight to further sterilize the insides of the holes.)

And finally, to romance. Seeking a husband? Then choose a man who has pins in his eyes. Looking for a wife? Then search long for a girl who loves polished balls.

CONTACT
Baby Split Bowling News
PO Box 7205
Minneapolis
MN 55407
USA

Brick Collecting

Life, the biologists say, has building blocks. And building blocks are Henry Holt's life.

The event that changed the course – should we say the *damp*course? – of Henry's life occurred twenty years ago. 'A factory was being knocked down opposite our house,' he told me. Walking past the demolition site, he happened to look on the ground . . . and he saw an old brick with his name upon it – HOLT – imprinted into the clay. Could the brickmaker be a relative? After research, Henry found out that this was not so. But in the kiln of his head a passion had started to be fired . . .

On his front-room table, seventy-nine-year-old Henry and his wife Mary, eighty, had spread out some of the collection. There were bricks with holes, bricks with lugs, bricks with manufacturers' names. The Holts have amassed over 5,000 different specimens – one of the largest collections of bricks in the world. I mention the world, for I do not want you to think they are alone. There is an International Brick Collectors' Association, in whose journal you will read of bricks that are 'real gem discoveries that turn up the adrenalin,' as well as finding articles like 'A Brief History of Ceramic Drainage and Masonry Tiles', and slogans like 'Happiness is the smile of a child, the wag of a puppy's tail, the swap of a brick.'

Henry and Mary reminisced about how they used to travel all around Lancashire, visiting a different demolition site every Sunday. In some cases, they would watch a condemned property for years – like masonry vultures, hovering – just waiting for the arrival of the wrecking crew. 'But why?' I asked. 'What's the attraction?'

Henry simply shrugged. 'We haven't got any children,' he said. 'What else can we do?'

Mary said that every brick told a story. Like the time when Henry picked up one that was frozen to the ground and he lost two fingernails; or when they braved an encounter with a demolition site's three Alsatians; or when they found some embossed bricks very deliberately placed near the bodies of dead rats – a children's game of funerals. 'I think the world of my bricks,' said Henry, 'and I handle every one of them with care.'

Henry showed me some of his favourites. Like an 1860s American pavement brick marked 'DON'T SPIT ON THE SIDEWALK'; or a Romanian brick, so plain it was just a block – as drab as Ceausescu's regime; even a fake rubber brick, which he tossed at me, shouting, 'Catch!'

Later, when he took me to a garage containing rack after rack of carefully catalogued bricks, I quoted to him a slogan I'd seen in *The International Brick Collectors' Journal*: 'Should we have our lives to live over, we still would collect bricks.' I put the question to Henry: 'Do you think you'd do the same, and collect bricks, if you had your time again?'

'I don't think,' he said. 'I know.'

CONTACT
Ken Jones
Treasurer
The International Brick Collectors' Association
100 Manor Drive
Columbia
MO 65203
USA
Tel: 0101 314 445 7171

The Bruce Forsyth Social Club

A street in Plymouth, late at night, the pubs all closed. One of the members was still doing an impression – albeit a bit slurred – of Bruce Forsyth. 'All right, my loves? Marvellous.'

'You've got all the facial expressions,' I said.

'I've studied him on video.'

Maybe I was drunk, but his very chin seemed to have grown during the course of the evening.

Just hours before, I had been on one knee in the Barbican Arms. The initiation was under way. Fifteen men formed a circle around me and began singing the song most sacred:

> Life is the name of the game,
> And I want to play the game with you.
> Life can be terribly tame,
> If you don't play the game with two ...
> *And I want to play the game with you!*

Whereupon the object that all their hands were holding – a cream-coloured square of carpet, attached to a strip of double-sided double-strength carpet tape – was pressed down upon my head. At last I was given the official greeting into the organization: 'Nice to see you, to see you – *NICE!*' It was time for game number one.

The Bruce Forsyth Social Club was formed five years ago by Mike Colwill, a bank employee with an admiration for the all-round entertainer and king of the game shows. 'He's great with people,' he told me. Now, with a nationwide membership of fifty, the Brucies meet every two months in Plymouth, touring the pubs and playing their own version of *The Generation Game*. What's more, the meeting always has a theme: there was the Robert Maxwell evening, when the members wore body-padding and attached pension books to their toupees; the pro-celebrity golf evening, when they tucked their trousers into their socks; and – the theme when I attended – the *Dad's Army* evening, when every so often someone would shout 'Take cover' and all the Brucies would make the noise of an air-raid siren.

But let me say a little more about those wigs. Because of the generosity of a local carpet-fitter, the club is kept well supplied with offcuts, which are then trimmed to the size of a mortar board. Any colour or design is acceptable – bright red, striped, even fluorescent – although if someone in a pub asks about the material used, there is an official club reply: 'They're real hair.'

The real question, however, is this: what does Brucie think? 'We met Bruce in 1990,' said Mike, 'when he came to Plymouth to play golf. We told him that we'd formed an appreciation society – and at first he thought that Ronnie Corbett had set him up and was taking the piss. We eventually convinced him that we were serious – and he was *absolutely marvellous!*' Here, on 'absolutely marvellous', a phrase much used throughout the evening, Mike returned to Bruce-mode. 'We didn't wear our rugs, though, when we met him,' he said.

As the hours passed, we went from pub to pub, always saying hello to the customers with a 'Nice to see you, to see you – *NICE!*' Other catch-phrases from Bruce's career had their uses too. Barmaids were greeted with, 'Come on, dollies, do your dealing'; a fruit-machine player heard shouts of 'Higher, higher'; and an offer of a pint led to, 'You're too kind, you really are.' Best of all were the games: putting the toupee on the bald landlord (a variation on putting the tail on the donkey); one-legged arse-kicking (combining the athleticism of Long John Silver with the viciousness of Thai boxing); and hunt the carpet tape. At every round of every game, Mike was the perfect Bruce, putting his arms around the contestants' shoulders. 'Do you want to go first or second? First? Yes, get it over with.' Then, when a game was finished, he would offer the appropriate commiserations to the runners-up. 'We're sorry to lose you, we really are . . .'

The evening was marvellous, it really was.

CONTACT
Mike Colwill
2 Cranbourne Ave
St Judes
Plymouth
South Devon PL4 8RT
Tel: 0752 674349

Bus Enthusiasts

The train-spotters will come later. In the meantime, let us consider this: when a spotter feels he's seen one loco number too many, when it's time to leave the track, to get up, grow up and cultivate sophisticated new tastes, then where does he go? What is the train-spotter's equivalent of the transition from rock to jazz?

An obvious move is into buses. 'In the case of London Transport,' said Peter Courtenay, 'there are about 8,000 vehicles in the fleet. There are certainly people who have seen every single one of those buses.' As he started to talk about the marital problems that can result when a woman marries a bus-spotter, I suddenly recalled a famous headline. 'Do you remember that piece in the *Sunday Sport* about the London bus found at the Antarctic?' It's difficult to forget the icebergs, the penguins and the big red double-decker. 'Yes,' said Peter, 'but unfortunately the photo wasn't clear enough to get the fleet number. Lots of enthusiasts were disappointed by that.' I am not certain whether he was joking.

Peter and I were surrounded by stationary buses at the Transport Museum in Manchester. Here, enthusiasts like himself volunteer to restore old vehicles. It's the little touches that count, like the pristine decals that say 'Lower your head when leaving your seat', in defiance of the human instinct to scratch out such words. Indeed, the enthusiasts immerse themselves in all aspects of bus culture. Some are concerned with the museum's collection of tickets and ticket machines; others study timetables of the 1930s.

As Peter and I climbed the stairs of an 1890 horse-bus, as we took a seat in its open-top upper deck, I could understand the appeal of a bus that old. Especially if it were attached to a horse. But an *ordinary* bus? The French avant-garde novelist Raymond Queneau once wrote a book called *Exercises in Style*, in which he described a short sequence of events, including a bus journey, in 99 different ways: he chose a bus *because* it was so mundane – the perfect vehicle, as it were, for his stylistic experiments. But what could cause a *passion* for a bus? An admiration for the comic genius of Reg Varney?

Peter found it difficult to say. Nostalgia for childhood, he thought, was part of the appeal. He pointed towards a London Routemaster. 'I can remember visiting my grandmother on one of those,' he told me.

Unfortunately, Peter had a lot of work to do, so we were forced to bring our conversation to a halt. His priority was the preparations for the next day: the annual bus rally, the high point in the bus enthusiast's calender, when the vehicles would be on the road. 'I'll be wearing my conductor's uniform,' he said, and went on to describe how he'd be rushing up and down the aisles, taking fares at 60p a time.

CONTACT
Greater Manchester Transport Society
Museum of Transport
Boyle Street
Cheetham
Manchester M8 8UL
Tel: 061 205 2122

Camel Racing

The twelve dromedaries that live in Longleat Safari Park are hired out in the summer months to entertain the guests at private functions and the general public at fêtes – an alternative to a donkey derby. Though you can imagine a wealthy man hiring one specially to shout out, 'Where's a needle? I want to take on the eye.'

When I met up with four of the camels – Topsey, Nicky, Amanda and Wobble – I soon realized they were placid, soppy creatures. They roll over on the ground; they stare at you with their big brown eyes; they flutter their 3-inch eyelashes. Up close, you can see that they have the most peculiar mouths, with only a bottom row of teeth: they grind their food against a hard palate. But do they spit? Their trainer told me that some camels do, but these don't. Their only unfortunate habit is revealed on hot days: when the temperature soars, they cool down by piddling on their tails and splashing it all over themselves.

In Saudi Arabia there would be nothing unusual about sitting astride such a beast, for over there camel racing is a serious matter. The animals are prized like racehorses, and the boy jockeys rarely fall off – not only because of their skill but also because they are Velcroed to the hump. Racing the Longleat camels is a more relaxed affair. You mount, either with the assistance of a leg-up from someone else or when the creature is on the ground, and then the trainer simply releases the reins and the camels run, motivated by the desire to get first snout in the feeding bucket. I held on tight to Wobble and was pounded on alternate buttocks. Camels run in a different manner from horses, moving the two left legs, then the two right – which is why they sway.

Wobble finished a poor third on the 100-yard course. I patted her neck – the hair was like stroking a doormat – and I heaved one of my legs over and slid off.

My groin ached for three days afterwards.

CONTACT
Mary Chipperfield
Tel: 0264 781233
or
Roger Cawley
Tel: 0985 844328

The Carnivorous Plant Society

The fly is drowning. The mouth-parts are trumpeting. It is more than drowning; it is dissolving. The wings are becoming a cape of threads; the eyes are loose, like buttons. It will be the flavour in fly soup.

How did this insect find itself here? Play back the tape. See it tumble into the tall, green wine-glass – but no, it is the hollow stalk of a plant. Rewind more. See the fly at the top, at the rim. How slippery it is, like a floor that has been deliberately polished. The fly's feet, magnified, are like six doormats. Further into the past now. See the fly lapping at the sugary stuff, the honeydew, that makes a trail all the way up the outside of the plant. If a sunbeam strikes the trail, you can see it glisten.

Maybe one day a species of insect will evolve called the Houdini fly. Until then, the cobra lily and its kindred carnivorous plants will never be short of a meal.

My own introduction to the feeding habits of the cobra lily – which even looks like a cobra, with two stiffened leaves hanging down like fangs – occurred in the greenhouse of Dudley Watts, the secretary of the Carnivorous Plant Society.

'You get some people feeding carnivorous plants bits of beef and cheese,' he said, as a Venus fly-trap's jaws closed around my finger. It's an eerie sensation, being gripped by vegetable teeth, and it's not surprising that Darwin called this 'the most wonderful plant in the world'.

But although the Venus fly-trap is widely known to the public – it has even been used to advertise Peperami sausages – most people are not aware of the 500 other types of killer blooms. Some species are indigenous to Britain, such as *Drossera anglia*, which has sticky, spiky protuberances, like medieval maces dipped in glue. Many more species are to be found in Dudley's menagerie-cum-greenhouse . . .

Take the bladderwort. On its stems are tiny bubble-like sacs, containing water under pressure. Each bubble has a trapdoor mechanism and a sensitive hair. Pity the poor insect that touches that bristle, for the trapdoor is immediately flipped inwards, sucking in the water and the prey. Dudley said that he'd heard a recording of the sound made by the bladderwort's trap: death comes with a pop.

Let us not forget charmers like the huntsman's cap, a pitcher plant whose nectar contains a mild narcotic: insects become very happy, stagger around, lose their footing and fall into a digestive hell. Then there is the sundew – a rosette of overlapping leaves: an insect alights, gets caught in slime, struggles, becomes completely trapped and then suffocates. Eventually, all its goodness is absorbed into the plant. And what about the Portuguese dewy pine? Its leaves are long, red-tipped tentacles that exude a sticky solution for catching flying prey. 'Some of these sticky ones,' said Dudley, 'can become black with flies in the summer.' He then told me about certain species of butterwort whose paste-pot leaves roll inwards to protect victims from being washed away by the rain.

Joining the Carnivorous Plant Society offers an excellent way of finding out about the real-life *Little Shop of Horrors*. In the society's beautifully illustrated journal is a mixture of scientific articles, tips on cultivation and accounts of field trips to find rare, or perhaps undiscovered, species. As I turned the pages and learned more about the marvels of carnivorous plants, I began to wonder whether that Houdini fly could ever evolve. I think the plants are just too damn clever. In some pitcher plants, for instance, it is *conceivable* that an insect could take advantage of the surface tension of the digestive juices to crawl out . . . if it were not for one problem: the plants produce their own surfactants which destroy even that means of escape.

CONTACT
Dudley Watts
The Carnivorous Plant Society
174 Baldwins Lane
Croxley Green
Herts WD3 3LQ
Tel: 0923 779767

Carry On Appreciating

A rock cake? A ploughed field? Old potatoes in a sack? I have been considering these as comparisons to the face of Sidney James. A face so wickedly wrinkly and funny, it's a bashed-up warm-up act in its own right. Actually, I've also been looking in a book of photographers' pictures. When I came to the portraits by Yousuf Karsh – his famous studies of Hemingway and Churchill – I thought: how anaemic, how insipid. They are as nothing compared to the flesh-coloured prune that was Sid.

I have also been hunting phenomena analogous to the nostrils of Kenneth Williams. A couple of French horns, maybe? Or two uncovered manholes? Or a view down a double-barrelled shotgun? Ah, but Kenneth would have called a halt to this business, just using three simple words: 'Stop messin' about!' And that catch-phrase just happens to be the title of a magazine produced by the Kenneth Williams and Sid James Society, a group of 400 people devoted to the appreciation of *Carry On* films. When I went to the home of the group's chairman, Carl St John, the video was soon running and I couldn't resist a snigger at dialogue like this, from *Carry On Abroad*, featuring Sid and Barbara Windsor:

BABS: (*Asking for a drink*) Have you got a large one?
SID: I've had no complaints so far.

Then I had a chuckle at the interplay between Sid and Joan Sims, in *Carry On Camping*. They find themselves in a typical *Carry On* situation, in a cinema showing a film about a nudist colony:

JOAN: I suppose you'd like it if we all sat here stark naked.
SID: Wouldn't bother me.
JOAN: It would if your ice-lolly fell in your lap.

All right, the humour may lack a certain dinner-party sophistication, but the thirty *Carry On* films defined a universe, a sex 'n' lavatories nether-world populated only by people with names like James Nookey, Gladstone Screwer and W. C. Boggs. And some of the lines are comic jewels. Remember Bernard Bresslaw's dismissal of an Indian fakir in *Carry On up the Khyber*: 'Fakir – off!' Or Kenneth Williams's cry of betrayal in *Carry On Cleo*: 'Infamy! Infamy! They've all got it in for me!' Perhaps it's the sort of infantile nonsense one should apologize for liking – but I'm not going to. The *Carry On*s captured a part of the British soul on screen; and as long as the British are British, we're going to find this kind of sauce a source of amusement. Carl, indeed, believes that the *Carry On*s were just about the best humour that Britain has ever produced, and in his society there are members who nowadays never go to the cinema or watch TV because they find nothing else entertaining – people who won't hear a word against the films, whose greatest passion is still the *Carry On*. 'People can relate the films to their lives – hospitals, holidays abroad, the police and so on,' he told me.

As I read *Stop Messin' About*, I realized just how firmly Ken and Sid have embedded themselves in my mind. One look at their photos made me want to imitate Sid's lusty laugh – hyah, hyah, hyah – or Kenneth's nasal whine – oooooonnnnhhh. No written symbols in any language can reproduce the sounds, but if you've ever seen a *Carry On*, and of course you will have, you'll know precisely what I'm referring to. Who can forget moments like Barbara Windsor losing her bra in the exercise scene of *Carry On Camping*? Or Jack Douglas getting out a magnifying glass in a urinal in *Carry On Dick*? Or the daffodil used as a thermometer in *Carry On Nurse*?

Scenes, though, that are just memories and celluloid now. Sid died in 1976, Kenneth in 1988, Bernard in 1993. These days, if you watch one of the films, there's just that hint of grief, a knowledge of times past. In 1992 there was the attempted revival, with *Carry On Columbus*, but it wasn't the same. The carrying on is over.

As I slowly close the magazine, it occurs to me that the death of a comedian is one way of defining poignancy.

CONTACT
Carl St John
27 Brookmead Way
Orpington
Kent BR5 2BQ
Tel: 0689 833711

The Celtic Re-enactment Society

It's difficult sitting down when you're wearing chain-mail. It's even harder standing up again.

The 26,000 washers that made up my singlet were not only heavy enough to make me overbalance and then totter like a wino; they also did a fine job of chilling my skin. Imagine 26,000 doctors applying stethoscopes all over your front and all over your back and all at the same time – get the idea? As I sat in that lounge in Fareham, I was getting some ideas myself; like maybe those doctors would have to be summoned – and would my mail give me total protection against the swipe of a sword? 'No, not total protection,' said a man in a helmet. 'But it's better to have a couple of broken ribs than your lungs on the floor.'

All around, people were finger-painting their bodies blue, adding snaking designs to faces and arms. Some had rinsed their hair with a dye and stiffener known as limewash, which gave a bleached, punkish look. And as I prepared to go into battle along with the members of the Celtic Re-enactment Society – a group devoted to re-creating the lives of the ancient Britons – the talk was always of the invader. 'What did the Romans ever do for us, except build a few viaducts?' said a member called Karl (though he preferred to be known as Lucetius). 'In the Rhineland, the Celts wiped out 12,000 of them,' said another of the limewashed. Adding, 'It was brilliant,' he told of how, sometimes, he dresses up as a legionnaire, because 'everyone loves to beat up the Romans'. As for the fight on the menu today, that was to be an inter-tribal skirmish, Celt against Celt. A lot of this went on twenty centuries ago, and if one tribe managed to kill the chief of another tribe, his head would probably end up pickled in cider, kept for years and brought out at parties. 'Doesn't that strike you as a bit barbaric?' I asked. 'No,' replied Paul, one of the youngest members, 'it's just like collecting football trophies.'

With the woad still wet upon our cheeks, we took a car, not a chariot, to the war zone, which happened to be the football pitch of the local school. Before long, the swords were windmilling through the air and all the members were exchanging shouts, smiles and death rattles.

In the art of mock warfare, spears have to be blunt and punches have to be pulled. 'Anyone can pick up a sword and hurt someone,' said Jane Smith, the group's organizer, as she gave me my first lesson in combat. Our blades clashed in slow motion. 'It takes real skill,' she said, 'to fight someone so that they leave with their arms on.' That is not to say that the members emerge unscathed from their meetings: the force of a sword crashing on a shield will take the skin off the knuckles of the defender's hand – everyone I saw had bloody fingers. To this must be added the risk of stray blows. 'I'm proud of this one,' a Celt said, as he showed me a healed-up gash on his brow. 'I had blood going all down the side of my face.' A colleague-in-arms told me that he sometimes allowed his dog to lick his knuckles, because of the antiseptic in canine saliva.

Now, you may be tempted to dismiss all this as play-acting, like the antics of some amateur dramatics group. I have to say, though, that during the time I spent with the society, I came to realize that theirs is a passion for the past much deeper than mere drama. All of the members admitted that they would have preferred to have lived in the warrior era, away from the pressures and regimentation of the nine-to-five. 'All I want,' said one, 'is a job that pays enough money to buy my swords.' He went on to describe a yearning to hunt boar and wolf and stag: 'Think of the glory . . .'

When we were back in the lounge, I removed my chain-mail and someone said, 'The Romans couldn't match our metal-workers.'

'*Our?*' I asked. 'You speak as if you really are Celts.'

'We are.'

CONTACT
Jane Smith
44 Iron Mill Close
Fareham
Hants
Tel: 0329 842055

The Cheese Club

Take a moment to imagine the colours: Sage Derby with its branches of green; then the Windsor Red, streaked with port wine; and then the blue-veined Stilton and the yellow Gaperon and the gold and black wrappers of the Brie de Meaux ... This is the world of Paxton and Whitfield of Jermyn Street, cheesemongers since 1797, suppliers of the Royal Family's Cheddar. It is rumoured that here, behind a façade of respectability, lies the headquarters of a secret society known only as the Cheese Club. Rank and file members receive the said substance in sealed packages, by mail; at their inner core is a shadowy group of curd-connoisseurs, led by one Mr Berard Nichols, the managing director of Paxton and Whitfield. I needed to know the truth ...

What can I say about Mr Nichols? Well, for some men, their passion is art; for others, it's sport; for Berard – we are on first-name terms now – it happens to be cheese. 'I don't hide, or apologize for, my enthusiasm for the product,' he told me, as I sampled an Innes Button. The taste was so wonderful, it reminded me of abstract emotion: joy, madness, conviviality, noble loneliness ... Was I being indoctrinated? Had I been slipped the cheese equivalent of a Mickey Finn?

But back to Berard. I tried to induce him to talk about his clients, though all the time I was being distracted by the subtle and soulful aroma from the shelves. 'We have people coming in who treat Paxton and Whitfield as a hallowed temple,' he said. 'It makes me feel very humble sometimes.' I seem to remember him commenting that people travel hundreds of miles just to purchase the Dorset Blue. And that there is a senior member of the legal establishment who comes into the shop and spends a fortune on curd-related products. 'We've got a healthy country as long as that happens,' he said. But by now, my senses were swimming. One of the shop's assistants, David of the bacon counter, brought forth a small cone-shaped cheese, half goat and half cow, called a Boulette d'Avesnes, coated in chilli powder – apparently it has been dubbed, for some reason, the Devil's suppository. What happened next, I do not recall ...

And though my mind was in a haze – that delicious mental fog brought about by the sight of the British farmhouse selection and the double-smoked double-cured bacon – I seemed to hear Berard's charming voice rising above it all. He was touching upon themes, coming out with phrases, using words that somehow I felt I would soon be repeating to others. Such as ...

Cheese and self-liberation: 'As the world gets more and more safe and bland and controlled in whatever sphere, how are we going to express ourselves? One way is through dinner parties.'

Cheese and the supermarkets: 'Our *bête-noire*. They're selling industrially produced, forkliftable cheese, made when Fred of Dagenham punches a few buttons. No individuality whatsoever.'

Cheese and morality: 'Why should an industrial producer bother with properly maturing a cheese? There's a whole generation of consumers who know Brie only in its supermarket form, just three months old. That's infanticide – too young to be eaten.'

Cheese and patriotism: 'Why are we so besotted with French cheese when we've got so much choice in this country?'

Berard gave me a little brown bag to take home, containing one more Innes Button and yet another cheese, whose name I no longer know but which he described as 'wickedness on a biscuit'. Well, what else could I do but accept this package? When the will has gone, there's nothing left but surrender ...

CONTACT
The Cheese Club
Paxton and Whitfield
93 Jermyn St
London SW1 6IE
Tel: 071 930 0250

The Cheirological Society

'I just happen to have a couple of hand-prints of mass murderers,' he said.

Christopher Jones opened a ring binder containing dozens and dozens of pictures of hands – as if an entire tribe of Native American Indians were saying 'How!', one after another. 'Here,' he said, when he reached the page.

They were unusual mitts, right enough. The palms were too large, suggesting an ape, or perhaps some ancestor of *Homo sapiens*, not a man; one finger was so abnormal it looked like a crooked chimneystack.

Years ago, people believed in physiognomy: that it was

possible to relate behaviour, and in particular criminal tendencies, to the narrowness of the brow or the closeness of the eyes. Is it rather *the hand* that reveals a man's character – when the knuckle-dusters are off, can we still identify the man who wore them? The Cheirological Society says yes. And they would only need sight of an empty hand to know the policeman who swings the truncheon, the judge who wields the gavel and the gaoler who turns the key.

Taking its name from the Greek word *cheir*, meaning hand, the society was formed as long ago as 1889, with the intention of studying and teaching the link between hand and person. Yet cheirologists are second to none in opposing palmistry. 'I went to a palmist for a joke,' said Christopher, the society's current secretary, 'and I ended up reading *her* hands.' Cheirology examines the whole hand, not just the palm; and, more importantly, cheirologists do not predict the future. 'Palmistry comes out of the Middle Ages,' said Christopher, 'when life was short and people were looking for immediate signs. Like an "M" in the palm is supposed to represent money, marriage and good fortune.' I checked my own palm. There was an 'M' there. 'But everyone has one of those,' he said.

Now, you will probably agree that up to a point a hand says something about a person: a navvy is unlikely to have the fingers of a violinist. Yet can analysis really go any further? In spite of the cheirologists' dismissal of the palmist, do they belong in the same booth?

There is some evidence to indicate that the hand *can* be used for medical diagnosis. A good example concerns Down's Syndrome, in which there is a so-called simian line, or single crease on the palm. Sufferers also have distinctive hand-shapes and unusual fingerprint patterns. If genetic disorders are mirrored in the hand, then so might be genetic components of personality. Yet cheirology goes beyond this. It claims that in the hand are not only the moles of nature but also the calluses of nurture. How can that be?

'The lines in the hand aren't static,' said Christopher. 'Broken lines can join up. Or lines can diminish and lose definition.' He brought forth another of his ring binders and showed me two hand-prints belonging to the same woman, but at different periods of her life. At the time of the first print, she was having problems with her husband. When the second print was taken, a few months later, she had found happiness with a new man. The two prints were entirely different.

Then it came to the real test: Christopher carried out a character analysis of my hand. I have to say, he was uncannily accurate. I suppose he could have gleaned a lot about me from our conversation – I would like to see a more rigorous test – but he made me believe that cheirology shouldn't be, shall we say, dismissed out of hand. The key to my character? The whorls on my fingertips. Most people have a couple – I have five. People with those extra whorls have a strong unconventional streak; and I've certainly done one or two things off the beaten track.

What's more, he pointed to a feature called a 'writer's fork'. Just think: if it hadn't been for those snake-tongue lines on my palm, you wouldn't be reading this now.

CONTACT
Christopher Jones
Secretary
The Cheirological Society
16 Bridge Street
Osney
Oxford 0X2 0BA

The Chocolate Society

Chocolate, if the quality is fine, should melt at the temperature of blood. So test it. Break off a square – noting, in passing, that it makes a crisp snap and there is the texture of tree bark at the break – and then put the piece in your palm. If you do not need to be feverish before it liquefies, then rest assured. Place the square upon your tongue and let it spirit itself away deliciously. You must never . . .

'No, don't chew it, or suck it,' said Nicola Porter. Once again, I had shown my lack of breeding. Until I met the Chocolate Society, it had not occurred to me that there was a proper way of eating sweets. Though I should perhaps have guessed that rituals of connoisseurship would apply – for I had been offered a square of a *grand cru* chocolate, a piece of Valrhona, which has a

45

very high cocoa-butter content: about 70 per cent, compared to the 20 per cent you will find amongst TV-advertised brands. 'We are scouring the world, looking for super high-cocoa-content chocolate,' said Nicola. 'It's good for you. It's got less sugar.' She went on to condemn manufacturers who over-roast beans, so as to achieve a strong and bitter taste, while keeping cocoa-content low.

Although the Chocolate Society obviously has the aim of eating confectionery, any member will soon start to learn about what might be called chocolate culture and chocolate history. You will hear how the Aztec emperor Montezuma drank cup after cup of chocolate – a drink so precious it was served in golden goblets that were thrown away after use. You will hear too about the different types of bean, like the criollo, the king of the beans, which has a characteristic fruity flavour with some acid – it corresponds to the Chardonnay grape, used for making champagne. The society will also send you chocolate recipes, including one for a chicken dish; and from time to time, there are chocolate-related outings – perhaps a tour of upmarket sweetshops, perhaps a visit to Kew Gardens to look at the pods on a cocoa tree.

Whilst on the subject of gardens, it is worth mentioning that you can obtain garden mulch from the society. It turns out that the mulch is made from the cocoa shell and is a by-product of chocolate manufacture. As I read in a society hand-out, the mulch 'adds nutrients, controls weeds, retains moisture and repels insects and most cats'.

CONTACT
The Chocolate Society
Norwood Bottom Farm
Otley
Nr Leeds
West Yorks LS21 2RA
Tel: 0943 851101

Clog Dancing

'So we rolled back the proggy mat and we danced on the lino next to her sink.'

If you manage to find a proggy mat – a carpet made from sacking and rags – you'll probably be visiting a pensioner's house in a working-class district of Tyneside. I heard a lot about trips to see sixty-, seventy- and eighty-year-olds at the Maidenhead Festival of Clog Dance. Collectors of rare clog-dance styles know that dead heels don't click, and that they'd better make some notes before the grim reaper takes to the floor. Hence, at sixty-three, Mrs Ivy Sands, owner of the opening sentence's mat, was asked to give a performance – something she hadn't done since the age of nine. 'It took her two years to remember all the steps,' I was told by a collector, 'and then we had to write them all down. Here, have this, free of charge.' He handed me a booklet marked 'Mrs Ivy Sands's Double Hornpipe'. 'We have notation for well over 100 dances in triple-time hornpipe rhythm alone,' he added. I turned the pages and saw instructions like click heel, tip tap, step, shuffle, hop.

Clogs, as you well know, are shoes with wooden soles. But sometimes irons are attached, like horseshoes for people, and if you scuff them against flagstones, you might be lucky enough to get a spark with your dance. Remember Brian and Michael?

> And he painted matchstalk men
> And matchstalk cats and dogs,
> He painted kids on the corner of the street
> That were sparking clogs . . .

You can also scuff someone's shin: in the sport of 'purring', two competitors kick at each other's shins till they bleed, with the first to give in being the loser. A case for manslaughter was brought in the 1920s.

Above all, clogs are working shoes, still worn in some heavy industries, and out of the mimicry of the rhythms of machines, the first dances emerged. It is said that if you listen carefully to the tapping of a heel, you'll hear the grinding of a mill, or the chugging of a boat, or the shuttling of a loom. From these beginnings in the workplace, the clog dance has travelled. There is apparently a gumboot version in Uganda, and in a French-speaking Irish community in Quebec there is believed to be a caller who calls in an Irish brogue to dancers who can't understand.

As the festival proceeded, there was some of the trickiest dancing I have ever witnessed. When Pat Tracey – known as Britain's best dancer – tapped along to the tune of 'Oh, Susanna', you could almost hear the words in her heels:

> Don't you cry for me,
> I'm going to Alabama
> With a banjo on my knee.

For to every syllable of that lyric, she fitted a decisive click. Then along came a French Canadian who danced such a difficult hornpipe that the MC remarked: 'You've seen it done – so now you know it's possible.' And I was especially lucky to meet the veteran champ Sammy Bell, now seventy-eight, who first started to dance when he was fourteen. 'My old teacher, Jimmy Ellwood, charged me 2/6 a lesson when beer was 4d a pint,' he said. 'And even when I won a competition, Jimmy used to get the prize-money – all I had was a bag of sweets.'

Surrounded by little girls, and a few brave adults, I joined a clog class for beginners. I shuffled and I tapped and sometimes I was in rhythm. Then I heard a woman of my own skill standard whisper behind me, 'Forget beginners – is there a remedial class?' At the first coffee-break, she and I escaped. You couldn't see our heels for dust – or should that be our wooden heels for sawdust?

CONTACT
Chris Brady
Flat 31
Felbridge Court
311 High Street
Harlington
Middlesex UB3 5EP
Tel: 081 897 1700

Conkers

If I talk of a sea of leaves, it is merely to mention the sea mines. Remember, under horse-chestnuts, kicking aside most of autumn's waves, looking only for the green and prickly shells? I wanted to relive it all; I wanted to enter the world conker championships in Ashton.

That's what I wanted. The dream was shattered like a defeated twenty-fiver by adulthood's commitments and appointments. So John Hadman, the secretary of the Ashton Conker Club, very kindly agreed to meet me on the Monday after the competition, in Ashton's Chequered Skipper pub. We started a game and I soon rediscovered one memory that nostalgia had filtered out: how painful it is when you miss and the conker continues its trajectory towards your own body. 'Some people wear a cricketer's box,' said John, 'and you can tell from the sound when they've been hit.'

The origins of the game of conkers are difficult to trace. It is known that *Aesculus hippocastanum*, the horse-chestnut tree, was first brought to England in the sixteenth century and the first recorded use of its fruit in combat was in 1848, on the Isle of Wight. But the game may go back much further, perhaps to the Middle Ages, when boys would amuse themselves by, among other things, pressing snail shells together till they broke. It is also known that by the seventeenth century their descendants were using hazelnuts threaded on a string. In modern times, though, the most significant place and date in the history of conkers is Ashton, 1965. 'Some locals were sitting in the Chequered Skipper,' said John. 'They had planned to go to sea on a fishing trip, but it was cancelled because of bad weather. One man looked out on to the village green and challenged another to a game of conkers. They agreed to hold a knock-out competition the following week.'

That was the very first of the world championships. The world was smaller then.

John explained the rules used in the championships of the 1990s. Contestants take three alternate strikes, and the length of lace in play must be no less than 8 inches. Furthermore, competitors are not allowed to bring their own conkers. 'So there's no baking and no pickling,' he said. 'And no passing them through a pig ... as one ex-champ said he did as a boy.'

CONTACT
John Hadman
22 New Road
Oundle
Peterborough
Cambs PE8 4LB
Tel: 0832 272735

Contemporary Legend Research

This actually happened to a bloke I know ... He's on a business trip, and in the evening he gets talking to this woman who's sitting in the hotel bar. Anyway, she's very attractive, one thing leads to another, and that night they end up in bed together. But when he wakes up in the morning, he finds he's on his own. He calls her name; no answer. Then he sees her clothes aren't there. So he shrugs and goes to the bathroom. And written on the mirror in red lipstick he sees: WELCOME TO THE AIDS CLUB, SUCKER!

'You can find a similar story in Daniel Defoe's *Journal of the Plague Year*,' said Dr Gillian Bennett. In Defoe's version, hundreds of years before Aids, a man kisses a gentlewoman and then tells her that she might as well have the plague as he has.

Gillian is one of the founders of the International Society for Contemporary Legend Research, an organization devoted to the study of urban myths: those nasty stories, reflective of the fears of their times, which people claim to be true. Such as:

This man, a friend of a friend of mine, was offered a drink by this stranger in a pub. Next thing he knew, he was waking up on Wimbledon Common. His stomach felt sore. So he lifted his shirt and there were these stitches, like he'd had an operation. So he went to a hospital, they examined him – and one of his kidneys had been removed.

There are hundreds of myths on the society's database. They

range from accounts of pet dogs (poodles normally), soaked in a downpour and dried off in a microwave, through to tales of restaurants which serve up rats in batter – stories that play upon people's anxieties and are told with utter conviction. 'People are narrative artists,' said Gillian. 'They'll improve a tale to make it more plausible.' She mentioned one of her favourites, the legend of the vanishing hitchhiker. Unlike many urban myths, this is often told as a direct personal experience, rather than something that happened to a friend of a friend. I once heard the following version of the story from the lips of an apparently trustworthy taxi-driver.

One night, driving along a deserted road – he even named the road! – the taxi-driver saw an old woman by the roadside. Next instant, she vanished. He looked in his mirror and there, on the back seat behind him, was the same woman. She stayed a few seconds, then vanished again. 'I was in such a state, I had to stop the car,' the driver said to me. I had shivers up my spine. I believed him.

But this story is very old, and exists in many forms. In the nineteenth century, a horse and buggy took the place of the car. Prior to that, the ghost would appear on the horse, behind the rider. 'I even know of a pedestrian version,' said Gillian, 'where a beautiful woman walks beside the narrator, then vanishes.'

The point about urban myths is that they appear to be modern but in fact are old. You find them in Boccaccio's *Decameron*, or *The Arabian Nights*. In some cases, myths go back even further, perhaps several thousand years – the death and resurrection of a hero is an example, a theme continuing today with the many sightings of Elvis Presley after his death. And not just Elvis. Gillian quoted a list of the risen: 'JFK, Che Guevara, Jim Morrison . . .'

'John Lennon?' I suggested.

'John is most certainly alive,' she said with a smile. 'They're all alive.'

Since I had been gullible enough to believe the tale of the vanishing hitchhiker, I wondered whether Gillian had ever been caught. 'You develop a nose for it,' she said. 'You hear a story and you think, oh-oh, that doesn't sound right.' She recalled an edition of *That's Life*: Esther Rantzen and the team told of a couple who were in their car, on the way to the rubbish tip, when beside the road they spotted a brand-new microwave. Since no one was around, they picked it up and put it in the car boot. A little later, they were flagged down by a police car. The policeman got out and said: 'Would you mind opening your boot? You've just taken our speed trap.'

Like many urban myths, this could conceivably be true. But one has one's doubts. Especially when one hears about microwaves confused with speed traps in America, Europe and the rest of the world. Indeed, the confusing of one thing with another is a standard motif in urban myths. 'Have you heard,' said Gillian, 'about the couple who mistook a tube of superglue for a tube of KY jelly?'

CONTACT
Professor Paul Smith
Department of Folklore
Memorial University of Newfoundland
St John's
Newfoundland A1C 5S7
Canada

The *Crossroads* Appreciation Society

Yes, I was aware of its failings – the wobbly scenery, the fumbled acting – but when it came to the transmission of that very last episode ... well, I'd be lying if I said there wasn't poignancy. To realize that after twenty-three years it was gone. No more Meg, no more Benny, no more Miss Diane. Although in reality all of those characters had long ago left the series and what remained was just a husk of what had been. Watching that last episode of *Crossroads* was like spending the last ever day at school: time to go out into the big world ... and suddenly you're not convinced you want to go.

So when I travelled to Bournemouth to meet Simon Cole and John Kavyo, the founder-members of the *Crossroads* Appreciation Society – a group dedicated to keeping alive the memory of television's most famous motel – it was a marvellous opportunity to turn back the clock. There on the video was little Amy Turtle, played by the late Ann George, who more than anyone else in the cast was responsible for the *Crossroads* tradition of forgotten lines. 'But that's what *made* her character,' said Simon, as we watched her at work in the motel kitchen, peeling vegetables and repeating words which had already been spoken by another character. John remarked that the society had acquired a portrait in oils of little turtle-like Amy. 'Imagine that hanging above your bed,' he said. 'It would put anyone off.'

Of course, many people would mock an enthusiasm for a series which had the reputation of being the *Plan 9 from Outer Space* of soaps – a series dubbed by the critics: 'The worst television drama in the world.' But one also has to bear in mind the sheer achievement of *Crossroads*: at the height of its popularity, the programme was broadcast *five times a week*, and actors were given almost no opportunity for rehearsals or retakes. Peter Barkworth, in a tribute to the series, called it 'the rep of television'. What resulted was a programme endearingly imperfect: where a well-placed cough would cover a forgotten line; where a studio microphone boom would be caught reflected in a mirror; where you could actually *hear* the sounds of cast members running from one set to another. Yes, *Crossroads* was savaged by the critics, but its popularity was undeniable. It regularly achieved audiences of over 16 million, and for a period in the 1970s its viewing figures even outstripped those of *Coronation Street*.

But back to that room in Bournemouth. Another video had started and there was that Tony Hatch tune: Ding dang dang ding daaaang dang . . .

'I've always told everyone that if I was in a coma the *Crossroads* theme music would bring me out,' said John.

'You know, we own the sign,' said Simon, 'the one that says "Crossroads Motel – Bar, Restaurant and Swimming Pool open to non-residents". We got it for £75 at a props auction.'

I wondered what had become of the motel's register and was informed that it too had been sold off, to an unknown buyer – though apparently it contained nothing meaningful, just doodles and jottings. 'We'd love to get hold of that register,' said John. 'I bet Tish scrawled a lot in there.'

Meanwhile, there on the screen was slow-in-wits, wool-in-hats, big, lovable Benny. John and Simon reminded me that in 1979 there was a story which featured the murder of a girl – and everyone thought that Benny did it. This sparked off a nationwide 'Benny is Innocent' campaign, complete with T-shirts, badges and graffiti. And who can forget Benny's relationship with Miss Diane, the woman who taught him to read? Diane was a fascinating character in her own right – a woman who somehow managed to take plenty of trips to America to see her son ... on a waitress's salary. What's more, when she returned, she always got her job back.

But, then, *Crossroads*'s strength was that it never tried to be realistic. If Jill, for example, opened a trendy boutique, the shop would be a meeting place for everyone – including the vicar. Or if someone was in a serious car accident, they would emerge with just a few smudges of dirt on their face. In the world of *Crossroads*, almost *anything* could happen: Benny could develop ESP powers; the Hunters' son, Chris, could become an international terrorist; the motel could be haunted by a poltergeist. In the Christmas shows, the characters would even burst into song or talk directly into the camera. 'This,' said John, 'is true cult TV.'

Yet at the very heart of the plot, whatever its ups and downs, was always one character: Meg, the queen of the motel; Meg, who cared, who cried, and who would always somehow carry on. Meg, as you will recall, was played by Noele Gordon, who died in 1985. Every year John, Simon and the other members of the society make a pilgrimage to her grave. These days, it is perhaps too easy to forget just how popular a star Noele was: she won the ITV Television Personality of the Year award six times in succession – and was eventually taken out of the running so as to give other personalities a chance. Most *Crossroads* fans regard the decision to write Meg out of the series in 1981 as unforgiveable; following her sacking, the show lost almost half its viewers. Still, Meg's great scenes remain in the memory, like the time she delivered Sheila Harvey's baby on a kitchen table. 'I was twelve at the time,' said John. 'I felt sick. I was sweating. I felt really ill.' Or what about when she was being poisoned by Malcolm Ryder (using a lurid pea-green potion)? That episode ended with Meg lying on her bed with her eyes closed and her mouth open. Anxious viewers had to wait until Monday to discover her fate. 'It was terrible,' said John. 'I thought she was really dead.'

But when it came to Meg's final cliffhanger – it was implied that she had been burnt in the motel fire but she had in fact gone to the *QE2* to set sail for America – at least the script-writers gave Meg a definite farewell: they told the viewers she had gone. This was at odds with the normal *Crossroads* practice, where characters would simply vanish without explanation. For instance, Benny would go into a workshop to fetch a spanner . . . and would not be seen for six whole months. Or Mr Booth would spend ten months looking for vegetables in a freezer; or, worst of all, Shughie McPhee would vanish for ever, taking with him the entire kitchen set.

Though, of course, the likes of Shughie McPhee do not vanish from the minds of the viewers. One of the great joys of meeting John and Simon is to reminisce about long-gone characters, particularly the minor ones. Just hearing their names again is something to be treasured. People like Carlos the chef, or Vince Parker the postman, or Miss Tatum the postmistress. To think that someone else remembers them . . .

So I have considerable sympathy for the work of the *Crossroads* Appreciation Society. I may not go quite as far as Simon and John – they have, on occasions, dressed up as Meg and Diane for a comedy drag double-act – but I certainly approve of one of their ventures: to continue the storyline of *Crossroads*, in their magazine *Crossroads Chronicles*. So far, Jill and the Hunters have set up a new motel (after the original was destroyed in a gas explosion) and also Jill has found her mother's lost diary. What is needed are more members to share the workload. I wish the society well.

Because, in the end, what's left is my affection for *Crossroads*. It was a show that went out of its way to offend no one. There were no expletives – you couldn't even call someone 'an old basket' in the world of the motel; the worst thing you could say was 'ruddy'. It was very clean, very comforting; it was always there. 'It was something you could rely on,' said Simon. 'It was like a part of the family.' And somehow, I know I would like the motel's story to continue, even if only in the pages of a small-circulation magazine. I hate the thought of writing '*Crossroads*

1964–88, RIP'. Dammit, I grew up watching that show. It shouldn't just fade away and die.

CONTACT
Simon Cole and John Kavyo
The *Crossroads* Appreciation Society
Flat 8
Harewood Apartments
9 Undercliff Road
Bournemouth
Dorset BH5 1BL

Cryptozoology

Do elephants exist? Of course. Do pink elephants exist? Of course not. Do pygmy elephants exist?

I'll terminate the paragraph there, make a gap in my words, for the only answer is no answer. It boils down to whether you can trust explorers. They do claim to have seen pygmy elephants. They say these creatures have tusks and trunks, and are neither dwarfs nor babies nor normal elephants shrunk in the wash. Pygmy elephants, it is said, are an undiscovered species, and if you cannot afford to travel to Africa to see one, they do have another habitat – the pages of the journal of the International Society of Cryptozoology. I assure you its writers have not been influenced by *The Adventures of Babar*.

Cryptozoology. Let me give you a definition: 'The scientific study of hidden animals, that is of still unknown animal forms about which only testimonial and circumstantial evidence is available, or material evidence considered insufficient by some.'

Obvious examples of cryptozoological phenomena are Nessie and the Abominable Snowman. Less well known is Mokele-Mbembe, the dinosaur which is reputed to inhabit the swamplands of the Congo. 'I actually think that's one of the most likely to exist,' said Dr Karl Shuker, a leading British cryptozoologist, when I spoke to him on the phone. 'That part of Africa has been totally unchanged for millions of years. There's hundreds of square miles of lagoons and impenetrable jungle. It's like an island that is cut off from the rest of the continent.'

According to eyewitnesses, the dinosaur is about the size of a non-pygmy elephant, with a long serpentine neck. Are there photographs? 'There are some blurred photographs,' said Dr Shuker. Ah, blurred. 'But photographs are never satisfactory evidence even when they're very clear. There are many faked pictures. And the fakes are getting better.'

I have a suspicion that some of you are thinking that Mokele-Mbembe is about as likely to exist as King-Kong. But hold on.

'Yes, Miss, it is a strange fish. I have been trawling for over thirty years, but I have never seen its like.' Words spoken by a trawler captain when his nets brought up the first coelacanth. That was fifty years ago, but as recently as 1986 the society published a list of over 100 unconfirmed animal forms – and since that time three on the list have been confirmed by specimens and the case for several others strengthened by evidence. The most spectacular of the recent discoveries is the Onza, a long-legged puma-like beast, rumoured to exist in Mexico for five centuries.

The fact is, many species have been discovered throughout the twentieth century and are still being discovered. 'As recently as 1990,' said Dr Shuker, 'a new species of marmoset was discovered near São Paulo – near a centre of population! And the creature had orange, red and yellow fur! How could people have missed it?'

CONTACT
The International Society of Cryptozoology
PO Box 43070
Tucson
Arizona 85733
USA

The Decimal Time Society

Time itself went out of fashion.

At least, the way of telling it did. I can still remember the steeplejacks at work on the face of Big Ben. And how someone brought out a new version of 'Rock Around the Clock'. There was a bit that used to go 'Nine, ten, eleven o'clock, twelve o'clock rock' and it was changed to 'Nine, zero, one o'clock, two o'clock rock'. I didn't think the new lyrics fitted as well as the old. I guess that's what you'd call a sign of the times.

As I understand it, the new system was based upon the work of a man called Mike Pinder, who in the early 1990s set up the Decimal Time Society. It was difficult to escape his logic: we'd already decimalized everything else, so why not have a ten-hour day and a 100-minute hour? Mind you, it wasn't just the clocks he had in his sights; it was the whole calendar – so that's how we got the ten-day week. No more Mondays and Tuesdays; we had Oneday and Twoday instead. Getting rid of Sunday caused a hoo-hah, I can tell you. 'God created the world in six days and rested on the seventh' – all that stuff. In the end the government gave the different religious groups their own special days – so that days zero and five were for the Muslims, one and six for the Jews, two and seven for the Christians and so on.

Our lives certainly changed. There was no such thing as the weekend any more. (Funnily enough, people still talk about a 'dirty weekend' – though it's come to mean any assignation.) Anyway, once we were rid of the seven-day week, we all started working five days on, five days off. That had some consequences. Firms started to have two internal hierarchies: a first half of the week team and a second half of the week team. West End plays had two casts. And it was then that we introduced two leagues for every major sport. For a while, youngsters used to call someone a 'twenty-five-hour man' – which meant that he was not only old-fashioned, believing in the old twenty-four-hour day, but also stupid because he didn't even know how many hours the old day had.

And me? I sit here writing my memoirs. I look at the top of the page and see it says Wednesday. Old diaries are worth a bit of money now because quite a lot of people – for example, yours truly – like to use them as notebooks.

CONTACT
Mike Pinder
The Decimal Time Society
6 Hamble Close
Warsash
Hants SO3 9GT

Decoy-duck Carving

Like the bingo-caller who has reached the number 22, I am going to talk about representations of little ducks. For in the village of Farrington Gurney, not far from Bristol, is the country's only school of decoy-duck carving. It is here that you will learn how to make a mallard out of sugar pine or, if you prefer, a red-breasted merganser out of Bornean jelutong. I went along, ready to make anything that wouldn't sink in the bath.

And then the Stanley knife slipped. Sophie Ridges, who runs the school, fetched the first-aid box and applied an Elastoplast to stop my finger staining the wood – blood does not run off a decoy duck's back.

The school was founded by Sophie's late husband, Bob, who took a course on duck carving in the USA. Originally, the Americans used art to attract life: poor old Donald (or whatever the duck was called) would waddle along, thinking he'd found a quacking pal, only to see a shotgun barrel poking out of the reeds. Nowadays, with stricter controls on hunting, decoys are carved as a sport in their own right – for the Americans hold a world championship, in which entrants strive for total duck realism. The painting of these models is virtually a matter of applying DNA on a brush: one competitor has described world championship decoy art as 'mixing paints with infinite subtlety to achieve black which is not black, but a soft feather tone which identifies the crimson sparkle of the chest'.

'At the championships, you hear people saying, "He's really got the *jizz* there",' said Sophie, 'jizz' meaning the spiritual essence of a flapping, swimming bird. Sophie's husband once achieved this, with a wooden mallard: he was carrying the bird under his arm and a stranger came up to him and asked, 'Is it injured?' It was all a little daunting. I doubted that I would have the patience to apply seventeen washes of colour to make the plumage seem as soft as real down.

I decided to ask Sophie a question, partly because it was bothering me, partly because, with all this talk of jizz and accuracy, I felt I needed to appear half observant about waterfowl. 'How do you get the metallic effects you see on certain birds?' I asked. Sophie produced a tube of acrylic paint which would give the appropriate iridescence. 'You only want to use a tiny amount,' she said. If you put too much on, the duck glows like something out of a nuclear holocaust.

My finger sealed, I picked up duck and knife. Whittling the corners from the bird is dangerous but unfortunately necessary, for unless we are dealing with some mutant strain, evolution does not seem to have developed a waterfowl with angles. However, I had noticed, in a catalogue of the school's merchandise, a chain-mail carver's glove. Just as falconers wear a gauntlet, I thought. As I whittled, I reflected upon the idea of buying protection against the claws of a bird that was lifeless, unmoving and had webbed feet anyway . . .

CONTACT
The Decoy Gallery
Hollow Marsh
Farrington Gurney
Bristol BS18 5TX
Tel: 0761 452075

The Dental History Society

School history lessons used to be about kings and queens; the history I have been studying is more concerned with crowns – *dental* crowns. Specifically, I have been looking at the magazine *Dental Historian*. The cover illustration is of beautifully decorated dental probes – silver gilt, with fleurs-de-lis. And many are the subjects this journal explores: '150 Years of Anaesthesia', 'Dentists in Seventeenth-century Holland', 'The History of Dentistry in Western Painting', etc. To find out more,

I went to meet the publishers of the magazine, the Society for the History of Dentistry – a club for those intrigued by the evolution of drills, extraction equipment, amalgams and the rest of the armoury used in the battle against decay. Some of the members actually collect dentists' chairs.

My appointment – I think we should call it that – was with Julia Marsh, the society's secretary. She also happens to be the curator of the museum of the British Dental Association, and so she took me on a guided tour of the exhibits. We stopped at an array of X-ray equipment and a spittoon that looked like a font. Then it was on to 'anaesthesia corner', with its many machines devoted to numbness; followed by a display of dentures, including the black ones made for habitual chewers of betel nuts; and finishing at the cabinet of probes, rootscrews and other instruments of torture. I asked Julia whether working amongst all this equipment had changed her attitude towards dental hygiene. 'I floss now – I didn't before,' she said. 'I've seen too many journals describing the nasty things that can happen if you don't care for your teeth.' She claimed that she wasn't frightened of dentists. 'They've never hurt me,' she said. 'Not even when they did my root canal work.'

We moved to a cabinet of tooth-powder pots. Julia said that over the years, there had been many pet recipes for powders and pastes. Everything from chalk to urine has been used to give that ring of confidence, because until fairly recently dentists would manufacture their own. 'Unfortunately,' she said, 'some of the dentists' powders contained sugar.'

This led me to ask who were the greats of the dental profession. Julia showed me a print of an eighteenth-century British dentist called Martin Van Butchell: he was shown riding his pony . . . which he had painted purple. If that wasn't enough, he also had something to amuse his patients while they were in the waiting room. No, not old copies of *Punch*, but something almost as horrible: the embalmed body of his wife.

But as Julia was about to move on to the history of the toothbrush (the first mention was apparently in 1649) I wanted to know whether there were any controversies in the field; other branches of history are notorious for reinterpretation and debate. It turns out that one of the most disputed questions is whether the ancient Egyptians knew how to make dentures. 'Some sets of false teeth have been found in mummies,' said Julia, 'but did the owners have them in life or only in death?'

I wonder whether Howard Carter found a tumbler beside Tutankhamun's sarcophagus?

CONTACT
Julia Marsh
The Society for the History of Dentistry
64 Wimpole Street
London W1M 8AL
Tel: 071 935 0875

The Didgeridoo

Mr Ant had a slogan. To describe his faddish songs like 'Dog Eat Dog', 'Prince Charming' and 'Stand and Deliver' he used the expression 'Antmusic for Sexpeople'. In the early 1980s, you'd find it biroed on lavatory doors, ring-binder covers and human skin.

Pop music cannot last, but there are musical traditions that do – like the didgeridoo. Emerging from the 40,000-year-old culture of the Australian Aboriginal, the 'didge' produces the only sound that really matches Adam Ant's description.

What? You didn't realize that didgeridoos are made by *ants* and not by men? Well, it's true . . . termites, to be precise. They feast on the softwood of stringybark trees, but like miniature Jack Sprats, they're choosy, these ants, never touching the hardwood and the bark. When they've eaten their fill, all that's left of a branch is a tube, and there's your instrument.

I discovered the truth about the production process when I met Cyrung, the former didgeridoo player with the band Lights in a Fat City. As an aside, he told me that there is an Australian artist who practises 'termite sculpture': by coating a piece of wood with patterns of honey and poison, little jaws can be made to chomp to order, thus creating bas-reliefs. Cyrung added that, as far as the didgeridoo is concerned, you're only talking quality if it's genuine termite.

The tones of the didge are, of course, familiar to everyone because of Rolf Harris. What isn't widely known is the knack to playing. Ask a layman to pick up a didgeridoo and you'll have a re-enactment of the Sword in the Stone sequence of Arthurian legend: person after person will come forward and try to make the sound, without the slightest success. The trick is to vibrate the lower lip with a constant stream of breath. Your mouth has to make a noise a little like a motorbike, a little like a horse.

But that is just the beginning. Over several weeks, my lessons with Cyrung led me to explore the versatility of the instrument. When the basic sound has been learned, you can move on to harmonics, toots, wah-wah effects and, if so desired, bird-song, barks, shouts and squeaks. At the highest levels of skill, it becomes possible to tell stories, using a vocabulary of sounds to represent animals, people and aspects of daily life; this is one of the most important roles for the didgeridoo in Aboriginal society.

There is another role, though. Which brings me back to Adam Ant's Sexpeople. When your eyes alight on a didge, you can't help noticing that there's something, um, *male* about the instrument. That is the point, so to speak. For the act of playing is a deliberate flaunting of masculinity – indeed, in most Aboriginal tribes, only men are *allowed* to play, while women are supposed to listen. And most didgeridoos are over 4 feet long.

Think of that next time you're listening to 'Sun Arise'.

CONTACT
Ray Man Eastern Music
64 Neal St
Covent Garden
London WC2 9PA
Tel: 071 240 1776
(Sells didgeridoos)

Dog-sled Racing

Really, you need to be in Alaska. But the lack of snow in England has never deterred Sally Leich. All you do is put wheels on your sled, harness together ten Siberian Huskies and say . . .

Well, actually dog-sled racers don't say 'mush'. That was one of the myths to be shattered when I met Sally and her dogs at Thetford Forest in Norfolk. The real commands are 'Haw' and 'Gee', which mean left and right, and 'OK', which means . . .

We were hurtling forward through the forest, Sally driving, though I had a contribution to make, being required to shift my weight at corners. Dog-sled racing without the snow is not exactly comfortable – as we went over the forest's ruts, it was like resting my bottom on a pneumatic drill – but the dogs do make it worthwhile.

Huskies may look like wolves, but they'll lick you rather than bite you. They're all loveable, but the cutest make you aware of their eyes: it's quite common for huskies to have irises of two different colours, one ice-blue, the other brown.

They don't forget their nature, though. As we emerged into a clearing, a tiny muntjac deer stood there, exposed, and ten heads changed angle by several degrees. They were teeth and hunger; they were back in the wild.

The deer bolted. There was no chase, but only because Sally was in charge, the leader of the pack. Indeed, dog teams owe their existence to the huskies' pack urges; the skill in racing is to control and, of course, harness those urges. And skill there is. For several years, there has been talk that dog-sled racing will become an event in the Winter Olympics, with teams competing in timed trials. Even so, should the event happen, it is unlikely that British dogs will take part: our quarantine laws will see to that.

Sally and I couldn't speak much *en route*, but I do recall her words just as we were about to go round for a second time. The dogs, you see, have acquired the talent of eliminating waste-matter on the move. Sally's command still lingers in my head: 'Pogo, this is no time to stop for a pee.'

CONTACT
Mrs P Evans
The Siberian Husky Club of Great Britain
The Old Post Office
3 High Street
Lamport
Northampton NN6 9HB
Tel: 0601 28281

Dowsing

It was saying yes, no, yes, no, and I hadn't even asked a question. There's nothing that goes up and down quite like a novice's V-rod.

Walking about the room with a dowsing tool alive in my hands, maybe I should have been astonished, but I am afraid I was not. I attributed no magic to the V-rod. It was just an unstable structure: two lengths of plastic, each straining like an archer's bow, meeting at a single point. Something has to give. But people who *are* serious about dowsing say that when it 'gives', the rod can be used to answer questions: not just the traditional, 'Is there water here?' but any kind of query for which a yes/no is required. So does that mean you could find out the winner of the 3.30 at Haydock Park? Surely you'd just have to hold the V-rod over a list of runners and riders?

'No,' said Deidre Rust, of the British Society of Dowsers. 'You have to sincerely want to find the answer to a question, but you mustn't want it *too* much.' She explained how you might use the rod to predict twenty winners in succession – but as soon as you put money on a horse, it would probably come in last or break a leg. She gave me an example of a legitimate use. 'You sometimes see a gas repair-man with a dowsing rod, trying to find where a leak is in a pipe.'

So how does dowsing work? 'No one knows,' she said. 'People used to think that the things you are dowsing gave out invisible rays. But today it is generally believed that there is a sort of universal mind that knows everything. It gives answers which are acknowledged by twitches in your nervous system. That's why the dowsing tool moves.' For this to happen, you don't need the V-rod, or even that other popular tool, a pair of L-Rods. 'You can dowse with anything,' she said. 'You can put a button on a piece of string and still get results.'

The interplay of these two propositions – that you can dowse with anything and that you can answer a host of questions – provides the content for the society's magazine. I liked the article written by a woman who uses her *arm* to dowse, dangling it like a pendulum, and depending on whether it swings to and fro or in a circle, she gets her answer. If she doesn't do that, she uses the blink method – one quick blink after asking a question means yes. These forms of dowsing are very convenient when in supermarkets. The woman goes up the aisles, swinging her arm and blinking, asking whether this food or that contains additives. When she gets home, there are more precise questions, such as asking an individual egg whether it was laid by a hen that suffered.

But before I can put any questions to the contents of my own shopping basket, I shall have to learn to control the vacillations of my V-rod. Deidre told me to be patient. 'You can't expect to play a concerto the very first time you sit down at a piano,' she said. She passed me some literature on dowsing courses run by the society.

Hmmm ... Talk of tuition and courses makes me think of schooldays and exams. Here's a poser: if dowsing works, surely a kid could take a tiny pendulum out of his pencil case and use it to dowse for the right answers in a GCSE multiple-choice paper. The question is: would it be cheating? I think the Board of Examiners should give us clarification on this issue. I keep on asking my rod, but it keeps on changing its mind.

CONTACT
The British Society of Dowsers
Sycamore Barn
Hastingleigh
Ashford
Kent TN25 5HW
Tel: 0233 750253

The Dozenal Society

A couple of extra fingers, one more on each hand, and we would have counted in twelves, not tens. There would be no decimal system, no metric measures. Base ten? Madness. Anyone counting in tens would probably also believe he was Napoleon.

The physiology of the hand being what it is, together with the real Napoleon's role in spreading metrication, means we're landed with ten as the norm. This is the problem, according to the Dozenal Society, and twelve is the solution. Membership of the society is not large – less than a gross – but I must tell you that I have signed up. When I spent a couple of hours with the society's secretary, Donald Hammond, I could see the apostles of twelve had a point.

And let us consider the decimal point. Anyone who has tried to divide one by three ought to have qualms about the decimal system. A third is a most important fraction, yet decimals express it as an unending series, namely 0.3333 ... and so on, for ever. If a third really is a worthwhile fraction to have – if a third is an integral part of life – then in some sense isn't the decimal system out of harmony with the way things are? Do not decimals fail to reflect reality?

'The trouble is,' said Donald, 'the decimal system goes in twos and fives. Everything else goes in twos and threes.' He spoke about his experiences as an engineer: the geometrical shapes used are triangles, rectangles, hexagons and circles – how often does the (five-sided) pentagon occur? It begins to look as if twelve *might* be a more rational basis for a number system. Maybe we should preserve feet and inches and oppose metrication? Perhaps we should have hung on to shillings and pence?

The society's magazine, *The Dozenal Journal*, is an exposé of ten's failures. A good example is the housebrick. If bricks are measured in a twelve-based system like feet and inches, the factors of twelve allow you to say straight away the size of any wall built. Donald has penned a poem on this subject:

> ### The Writing on the Wall
> I am a brick: a house-proud brick –
> > My proportions are six–three–two
> In English, plain or Flemish bond,
> > I'll build a home for you.
> Four courses to a foot I lay
> > And four lengths to a yard:
> A wall at the back? A chimney stack?
> > Nothing is too hard
> The secret lies in my handy size
> > And my ratio of two–three–six
> Set me on edge, or even on end –
> > I still fit with the other bricks.
> Metricate me? They can't, you see
> > To metres I pay *no* regard:
> Four courses to the foot I lay,
> > And four lengths to the yard!

Metric bricks can never work, for the number ten does not have the right factors. (If you doubt this, consider the following: in Europe the metre is not used as a building module; instead, 1.2 metres is used – a twelve-based unit!)

There are plenty of other examples to show the superiority – the naturalness – of twelve. Cylindrical tin cans are much more cheaply packed by the dozen than by the ten. (A twelve-pack with two empty spaces actually costs less than a ten-pack completely filled.) In music, there are twelve semitones in a scale. And if you consider the factors of twelve, still more examples come to light. After all, bees build honeycombs with hexagons.

'Twelve is something you can believe in and can prove to be superior,' said Donald, 'and it's not all faiths you can do that with.' He spoke about 'the decimal dark age' we live in, and how the idea of twelve has to be kept alive. 'We've got to keep the lamp lit,' he said. There is always hope, always a new example to find of twelve's inherent power. He referred me to an issue of *The Dozenal Journal* – latest research indicates that the universe consists of not ten but *twelve* fundamental particles.

I still wondered if the fundamental problem was not the quantity of fingers. Donald disagreed. The hand, he told me, isn't really based around the number five: there are four fingers and one thumb. Such a system is eminently suitable for counting in twelves: instead of counting individual fingers of one hand with the opposite hand, one should count the segments of each finger with the thumb of the same hand. 'Apparently,' he said, 'this is how people count in certain parts of northern Iran.'

I knew I had to join.

CONTACT
Donald Hammond
Millside
13 Mill Road
Denmead
Hants PO7 6PA
Tel: 0705 262907

Dracula versus the Wolfman

Is it dark now? Does the wind howl? You, you out there, sitting comfortably, reading your book – quite sure, are you, that your windows are shut? And your back door, is it locked? Not that any of this will help you when the full moon shines – for the lock is not yet made that will keep me out. And I can assure you, I am no vegetarian … I tell you, there are things that live in forests and subways and dark places, things not really alive but cursed to walk with the living. Such as that split thing who talks to you now: I, not quite a man, not quite a beast …

If myth I am, then you are safe; but if I am real, beware. Is that the wind a-howling, or is it something more? Could it be me? You may have guessed my genus: *Homo lupus*. Man-wolf, werewolf – call me what you will, I exist.

And yet I hear you scoff. Mere make-up, you say. I tell you, when you feel the hot breath on the nape of your neck, when you turn your head and see the fangs, when your flesh is torn and being chewed, you will not say make-up then, oh no.

Even if I, like an actor, were not real but made up, would it make you safe? Go to your dictionaries and find the word lycanthropy. There are men afflicted with a madness who think themselves wolves. Strong they are and teeth they have. You are certainly not safe with a lycanthrope. Indeed, it occurs to me now that some of you readers may be lycanthropes yourselves. So let me tell you that there is a place you can go where you can live out your wretched fantasies to the full. Recently, during the daylight hours, when my own five o'clock shadow was still waiting to grow, I sampled their services. For who else but a real werewolf could judge the quality of the wares?

At the Dawn Cragg College of Make-up, they suspected nothing. I was introduced to two students, Nicky Harrison and Sharon Goldsmith, who would do their best to change me from man into wolfman, ha-ha.

For three hours I sat still. The spirit gum was slapped on and the false hair applied. To pass the time, I indulged in small-talk – for I wanted to put them all at ease till I could bite. I soon learned that this is a school where the pupils transform anyone into anything. A man can leave with one eye hanging out, a woman can be turned into an amputee.

But I had had enough. Patience was wearing thin. As the students leant over me, I looked at their soft, succulent necks and I began to growl. They thought it was just a joke, the fools. 'You're really getting into the part,' they said. I bared my teeth – and they laughed. Tonight, when the moonbeams break through the clouds, I will make certain they laugh no more. I will kiss their jugulars and caress their throats, I will make them pay, I ... No! No! Get away from me!

Bang.

In most cutlery sets, you will find an equal number of knives and forks. In my family's set – which, I hasten to add, has a very fine hallmark – there is a disparity, with one less in the number of the forks. I am afraid I had to melt it down.

Now, you may say that it violates all the canons of aesthetic sense simply to dispatch a leading character, as I have done to that poor chap with the hormonal problem. You may tell me that it destroys all sense of artistic unity. And I would agree. But on this occasion there is a very good precedent. Did you ever see the old Universal film *The House of Frankenstein*? It features a titanic tussle between Frankenstein and the Wolfman, but it also has a stand-alone prologue about Dracula, tacked on to the film for no reason other than to incorporate yet one more monster. Prologue and main plot are as distinct as life and death. I therefore feel justifed in terminating the intro and turning my attention, without warning, without justification, to Count Dracula.

Or rather, to the Dracula Society. 'I should make it clear that we've got a rule that prohibits our members from dressing up as the Count,' I was told by founder-member Bernard Davies, when I attended the society's annual general meeting. 'There was an embarrassing incident once on *The Russell Harty Show*. Media people just love us to dress up and put in fangs.' However, the society does own one item of clothing of special significance – the actual cloak of Dracula. At least, it has the one worn by Christopher Lee in all the Hammer films. At the society's little museum – where there are rubber masks of Bela Lugosi, and bottles of red liquid marked 'Dracula Elixir from Romania', as well as assorted stakes – I had the privilege of trying on that cloak. I was amazed by the weight. The museum's unofficial curator, Robert James Leake, told me that the cloak was made heavier in certain places, 'so that it would billow just right'. So now you know.

The Dracula Society is a group for all those with a serious interest in Gothic horror. Its members range from skinheads in Alice Cooper T-shirts to silver-haired pensioners. One of its aims is to promote discussion about Bram Stoker's masterpiece. 'Pre-Stoker, the returning dead had always been treated in a Byronesque, romantic manner,' Bernard Davies told me. 'The Victorians were very interested in the beauty of death. So many people in those days died young, and the Victorians used to think of the returning dead with pale, marble faces.' Stoker's treatment, though, was totally anti-romantic. 'Dracula was a filthy, stinking creature,' said Bernard. 'He had halitosis. Stoker told vampirism like it was.'

Like it was? But aren't we talking about fiction? I pressed

Bernard on the point: do vampires really exist? 'I have an open mind on the subject,' he told me. 'I firmly believe there are more things in heaven and earth ... I certainly don't pooh-pooh the idea of vampires.'

Getting a bit worried, I asked Bruce Wightman, another founder-member, whether he had ever met anyone who genuinely believed in the undead. 'Yes, there was one woman who was a member for a short while,' he told me. 'She used to frighten her room-mate by getting up in the middle of the night and, in only her nightdress, throwing open the bedroom window and shouting, "Take me, Dracula, I'm yours." Of course, she didn't really want Dracula. She wanted Christopher Lee in his underpants.'

One of the society's activities is organizing tours of Transylvania. Long-standing member Peter Swindell reminisced: 'It's a fascinating place. You get the same sort of farm-carts as in Stoker's book. They're still horse-drawn or bullock-drawn.' He said that he had been to the very house where Vlad Dracula – the fourteenth-century tyrant from whom Stoker took the name of his vampire – was born. 'It's now an inn,' he remarked, 'so I can actually say I've had lunch in the house of Dracula.'

But having killed off a werewolf with a silver bullet, I was naturally interested in the vampire's nemesis: garlic. Would it work if I ever needed to write a longer version of this piece, killing off Drac and bringing in, say, Frankenstein's monster or the Mummy? Peter had the last word: 'When we return from the tours of Transylvania, we say to everyone back home in England that the Romanians still believe in vampires because they string up garlic outside their houses. What we don't tell people is that the Romanians also string up carrots and cabbages. It's simply their vegetables drying out ...'

CONTACTS
The Dawn Cragg College of Make-up
58a Bridgegate
Retford
Notts DN22 7UZ
Tel: 0777 707371
and
The Dracula Society
c/o Julia Kruk (Membership Secretary)
213 Wulfstan Street
East Acton
London W12 0AB

Dry-stone Walling

Some years had passed since I last built a wall – and, to be honest, I had doubts that an acquaintance with Lego would be of much help in piecing together a dry-stone structure. Still, the three-day course in Halifax, 'Dry-stone Walling – A Beginner's Guide', seemed to summon me. So, off I went to Yorkshire, to a fine seventeenth-century hotel, Holdsworth House, in the hope of becoming Hadrian.

A dry-stone wall is a structure in which skill replaces mortar: nothing bonds the pieces, except the way they are placed. It's often called a three-dimensional jigsaw puzzle, though really the comparison is inappropriate, because the parts of the wall are not pre-cut and, except by chance, do not slot snugly together. The other characteristic is the material used: naturally occurring stone, unshaped except by hammer-blows, lacking altogether the geometry and uniformity of bricks. One might be tempted to say – if it is not too irreverent for such an ancient craft – that building a dry-stone wall combines the qualities of two television programmes: the manual dexterity of *The Krypton Factor* and the visuals of *The Flintstones*.

On the Friday evening at Holdsworth House, eight novices, including myself, met Paul Webley, a master craftsman in dry-stone walling. By means of a video, and by informal conversation, we learned that the formula for ensuring strength is to place two stones on top of one, alternating with one stone on top of two, as much as the shapes allow it, as you build the layers of the wall. Then there were discussions on safety, such as being careful to look away from the stone when using a hammer. Plus advice on the secret lore of the craft: wallers, I discovered, have pet recipes for trying to encourage green algae to grow upon the stone. 'A mixture of sheep's muck, cow's milk and soil seems to work quite well,' said Mr Webley. All this was the theory; the practice was to come next day.

A few miles from the hotel, in the village of Wainstalls, Mr Webley led us to a wall which, apart from a certain amount of droop due to land subsidence, was in good condition. It was about 1½ yards in height and had probably been around since the 1830s. Our first task was to dismantle this antique – or anyway a 9-yard section of it. To use again the jigsaw comparison, we would put the pieces back in the box having seen the completed picture.

As we started heaving off the top stones, it all seemed to me rather sad, adding a sense of pointlessness to the task – why knock down only to rebuild? However, there were advantages. For one thing, we knew that in the accumulating pile there was a potential wall ... we just had to find it. And we wouldn't be troubled by a shortage of stone; at least, that's what we thought.

So, we stripped the wall down to nothing. Joshua and his trumpet, or the Berlin Wall protesters, could not have done a better job.

I was already feeling worn out. Some of the heavier stones, the so-called 'throughs' – flat slabs which go from one side of the wall to the other, for added stability – weighed as much as a bag of cement. I saw a drop of sweat from my forehead fall on to the earth we had by then reached – or was that the rain starting? Rain meant shelter and shelter meant precious rest ...

As we sat in the nearby farmhouse drinking tea, I noticed that Mr Webley was not wearing gloves, contrary to the advice he had given us. Was it a question of his skin being tougher through frequent use? 'You can get a better feel of the stones without gloves,' he said stoically, and added that some professionals dripped wax on their fingers. 'But you don't realize how much of your fingertips you've worn away,' he said, 'until someone hands you a mug of hot tea and you take it without using the handle.'

The tea was drunk and the rain was over; it was time to work on the foundations. I realized one thing: I was not enjoying myself. I found it hard to believe that *anyone* could enjoy the foundations – you are at the farthest point from the goal, you're bending over all the time, you're working in mud. I suppose the best strategy is to keep thinking to yourself that it's all part of the job, a necessary means to an end. Since Mr Webley owned up to being hooked on dry-stone walling, I reasoned that there had to be *something* enjoyable about it.

With the foundation stones down, we started the real building: large stones on the outside, smaller ones filling the interior, trying always to keep the layer level. The problem is that none of the stones is perfect for the task, and so it is always a matter of doing the best you can. If a stone wobbles, you have to lock it in place, using a smaller stone as a wedge; if a stone is not right, perhaps it will be if you turn it over. Gradually, a psychological shift occurred in each of us: we started to worry about the wall. There were concerns about appearance: 'I've got a number of thin ones there and it looks odd.' And concerns about strength: 'I've got a weak spot. Broken the two-one-one, one-on-two rule.' There were also many moments of quiet satisfaction: as when two stones fitted as perfectly as if they were parts of a broken vase. We were absorbed into the stone. Mr Webley remarked that although everyone had been chattering away at the start, there were now long periods of silence. By the end of the day we had restored the wall to three-quarters of its former height.

Sunday dawned, and after breakfast we were out in the fields again. We now had a couple of problems. First, we had already used the best stones and were left with the more awkward and difficult-to-anchor pieces. Second, we did not have enough stone to complete the task. Mr Webley said that this always happens when rebuilding a wall – over the decades, some stones simply crumble to dust. Two of the team then went back and forth, fetching armfuls and bucketfuls of fresh stone from the far side of the field. These new stones tended to be flatter than the others. 'It's easier with these flat stones,' said one waller. 'But it's not so exciting,' said another. 'You don't have to wheedle them in.'

Finally, we replaced the top stones which would hold the structure together. But before the last stone was laid, before we stood back and admired, we decided to insert a time capsule. So in went my train ticket to Halifax, together with a 5p coin and a piece of paper bearing our names – all stuffed into a Frank Sinatra cassette box. Perhaps one day, when repairs are being carried out, someone will run an eye down the list of song titles, see 'High Hopes' and look at the wall. And maybe that person will close the box and wonder who on earth Frank Sinatra was . . .

CONTACT
Holdsworth House
Halifax
West Yorks HX2 9TG
Tel: 0422 240024
or
The Dry-stone Walling Association of Great Britain
YFC Centre
National Agricultural Centre
Kenilworth
Warwicks CV8 2LG
Tel: 021 378 0493

Ear Candles

It was soiled foil: a scrap of silver paper and some yellow muck – a wax. Jili Hamilton was about to crumple it, throw it away, but I stopped her. As if I needed to prove that what had happened *had* happened. I said something about a souvenir. 'Oh, I've never had anyone who wanted that,' she said. 'Anyway, we need to do the other side to balance the energies.'

I turned over on the cushions. I was about to have a nice soothing smoke – only I wouldn't be puffing on a Marlboro or a Silk Cut. Oh, and the orifice, yes the orifice, I must mention that. I heard Jili strike a Swan Vesta and then she placed the candle in my ear . . .

I should tell you that this practice is nothing new. If you travel to a distant and arid corner of Arizona, you'll find the Native American Hopi tribe, who centuries ago developed a yearning to insert beeswax candles into their ears. Today, the candles are quite well known in continental Europe and a German factory currently has an output of a million candles a year. As Jili strives to promote their use in the UK, she feels that she has finally found her purpose in life. 'I believe that the universe brought me this idea,' she told me. 'I believe that this is what the universe intends me to do.' She also believes that she was probably a Hopi in a previous life.

But back to me and my burning ears. I have to say that the experience of a Hopi ear candle is relaxing and pleasant. Fortunately, they are not inserted flame-end first, but there is still enough heat to create suction in the sinuses. It is like a chimney: any impurities in your ears are drawn upwards, to be deposited on the silver foil, along with your earwax. As this proceeds, your head is filled with herbal vapours, for every candle contains a mixture of added ingredients: sage, camomile and St John's wort. Overall, the effect may be likened to sucking Tunes.

Jili maintains that the candles can be used to treat all manner of hearing problems, from tinnitus to catarrh to glue ear. And that isn't all. 'It is said that the key to our past life is through the ear,' she told me. She went on to describe a woman who had flashbacks to her youth whenever a candle was inserted. 'Oh, there am I as a teenager,' the woman would say, 'and there are my parents and grandparents having arguments.'

Will ear candles ever catch on in the UK? Jili reports a surge in interest, with some people improvising when they can't get the real thing. 'There's one chap I know who puts rolled-up newspapers in his ear,' she told me. All the same, she concedes that a lot of British people are cautious because of the burning. In fact, she wonders whether this could be a throwback to the days of the Witchfinder General, when so many people were burnt at the stake.

After I left Jili's home, I was determined to find out more about the inventors of the ear candle, the Hopi tribe. I was intrigued to discover in a Reader's Digest book of strange facts that the Hopi language does not distinguish between past, present and future tenses: I was, I am, I will be – it's all the same if you're a Hopi. ('When were you born?' 'Yesterday, today and tomorrow.') If that's the language the Hopi have to understand, well, it's no wonder they stick candles in their ears.

CONTACT
Revital
35 High Road
Willesden
London NW10 2TE
Tel: 081 459 3382 or 0800 252875 (Mail-order hotline)

Earth Mysteries

There is a type of musical composition known as the 'list song'. Cole Porter's 'You're the Top' is one of the finest: 'You're the Nile, You're the Tower of Pisa, You're the smile on the Mona Lisa . . .' Love for Porter is a pot-pourri – hard to define, easy to list – and I feel it's much the same for the members of the London Earth Mysteries Circle. When I boarded the group's minibus, I realized that theirs is a complex, many-sided passion: for archaeology, folklore, dowsing, astronomy, various New Age concerns, investigations into earth energies, explorations of unexplained phenomena and lots more besides. As I discovered when, in the words of another song, off I went on a 'Magical Mystery Tour'.

First stop was the prehistoric hillfort of Old Sarum, in Wiltshire. As I sat on top of this ancient mound, I chatted to the Circle's organizer, Rob Stephenson, and he told me of a typical interest: strange lights in the sky. 'People see will-o'-the-wisps and such like,' he said, 'and they tend to appear above stone circles and other ancient sites. Now why is this?'

His theory: as the moon's gravitation pulls the sea up, it also lifts the land, leading to the chafing of rock against rock. Couldn't this generate electricity? Might not electricity lead to sparks and lights in the sky? Maybe ancient man worshipped natural fireworks? And perhaps that's why stone circles appear on the earth's fault lines, where landmasses rub and electricity is most likely to occur.

It might all be true – or it might not. Like the moon's influence on the tides, one's belief can ebb and flow. But I do not dismiss the hypothesis, not when Rob can tell me about a standing stone in Gloucester, known as the 'Tingle Stone', which, when touched, actually gives an electric shock.

Then there's the case of ley lines. We were at Old Sarum because of a line linking this hillfort to Salisbury Cathedral and to Stonehenge. Leys are alleged to be straight lines in the earth just sizzling with energy. Some group members detect ley lines with dowsing rods. A man and a woman, both dowsers, joined in the discussion. 'We were once in a field at the crossing of two leys,' said the woman, 'and we looked up in the sky and saw some Canada geese. We realized that their flightpath coincided exactly with one of the leys. Then, when the geese got to the point of intersection, they shot off in the direction of the other ley.' The man rubbed his beard and added, 'What's more, there was a horse in the same field that seemed to know about the lines too.'

Soon we were on the bus again, travelling to our next destination, Winchester Cathedral. Time for more talk. 'Have you heard of geopathic stress?' asked one of the group. I confessed that I hadn't. 'They are forces in the ground that affect health adversely,' he said. 'But you can buy a special blanket to put under your bed that will protect you. And if that fails, you can always drive a stake into the bad line to disperse it.'

We reached Winchester, and the female ley-hunter took out her dowsing rods. As we walked up to the cathedral the rods crossed and I asked her how she experienced the sensation of a ley. 'It's a feeling of tightness,' she said. 'And sometimes it can make your head ache.' Another member offered the opinion that the sound of the choristers' singing could actually boost the ley's energy.

On to the bus again, and the climax of the trip: the hunt for cornfield circles. Sure enough, from the minibus window we spotted 360 degrees of flattened wheat, and we stopped for a closer look. Other cornfield-watchers were already there. 'I tell you, there can be no doubt,' said one man we met by the roadside, 'that these circles were caused by the landing gear of a spacecraft.'

The conversation continued: how the ancients deliberately distorted their stone circles, so as to avoid the irrational number, pi; how the standing stones are possibly part of the earth's life-support system; how energies from ancient sites can affect one's dreams, as if they are videos in stone.

So many theories. Maybe too many. Are some of you out there whistling another Porter song, 'Anything Goes?'

CONTACT
London Earth Mysteries Circle
PO Box 1035
London W2 6ZX
Tel: 081 969 3928

Electronic Gem Therapy

There were just the two of us in that room in Woking, or three if you count Valerie's Red Indian spirit guide. 'He's always with me when I'm healing,' she said. The curtains were drawn and everything was dim, apart from the glow of the apparatus.

The apparatus: imagine lying on a couch while, above you and parallel with the body, is a pair of tubes, like strip lights. From these are suspended a number of Perspex drums, each containing a ground-up gemstone in glycerin. So, above the brow, diamond; above the throat, topaz; emerald for the heart; and pearl for the spleen; and, for other viscera, ruby, coral and sapphire. Each drum is connected to a copper transducer and wires lead to a control panel. Here, just like a radio ham, you'll find Valerie twiddling knobs.

She had already made a diagnosis: by moving a pendulum over my body and picking up 'vibrations', she had discovered that certain parts of me were in need of a recharge – so, at her control panel, she turned up the powers of the coral, the topaz and the diamond. From these three drums I detected the faintest shimmer. She started a tape – plenty of flutes and waterfall sounds – quit the room and shut the door. I was left on the spiritual sunbed.

In her publicity material, Valerie extols the powers of the gems. She calls them 'mines of cosmic rays'; they give 'waves of bliss and deep, restful peace'. What did they do for me? Well, I admit I did relax on the couch. But then, people generally *do* relax on a couch.

Occasionally, I would open my eyes and peep at the drums. Valerie describes electronic gem therapy as a combination of ancient wisdom and modern technology. For centuries, precious stones have been associated with healing – some Native American tribes make pills out of gems and swallow them whole. Passing an electric current through the gems is the twentieth century's twist to therapy's old theme; and Valerie claims that her apparatus causes the gems to vibrate at frequencies that are just right for a healthy body. She sees herself as a restorer of natural harmony.

Fifteen minutes passed. I could easily have fallen asleep. Then the door opened and Valerie came in. While I stretched, she told me that some of her psychically powered friends could see the beams of healing energy emerging from the drums. 'I'm told that they make an egg-timer shape,' she said.

But I was concerned about whether I could spare the time to go to Woking whenever I needed electronic gem therapy. Valerie told me not to worry. 'My friend John sells a small pocket machine,' she said. 'So if you're feeling low in the solar plexus you can always give yourself a quick boost.'

CONTACT
Valerie Wood
21 Streets Heath
West End
Woking
Surrey GU24 9QY
Tel: 0276 857243

The English Place-names Society

After a lifetime of studying the origins of Lincolnshire place-names, wouldn't interest start to flag? 'How can it?' said the Professor, and his secretary added her support. 'Why, just a couple of weeks ago,' she said, 'he was like a young lad again because he'd found a new derivation.'

One day, the English Place-names Society will have no good reason to exist. Its mission, which began in 1923, is to uncover the origin of all the place-names in England. Since there is only a finite number of places, one can draw the obvious conclusion. However, it is debatable as to which will come first – the society's final meeting or the Day of Judgement. For let me reiterate: the society hopes to discover the origin of *every* name – every town, every street, every field. 'Here, have a look at this,' said the Professor. He stood by my shoulder and held open a society publication. 'Here are six and a half pages of field names for one parish alone.' And how much time will each of them take to research? It obviously depends, but in the society's journal I have seen a twenty-five-page article devoted to the origin of the name of a single rock off the Cornish coast.

Professor Kenneth Cameron is the honorary director and secretary of the society, and in his study are filing cabinets containing cards on which he has written the development of names, showing how the spelling has altered since the earliest recorded usage. I *almost* suggested to the Professor that, with one card per spelling variant, you could take a handful of cards pertaining to the development of a particular name and, holding them at the corner, flick them, to give an exciting animated version of the etymology. But the conversation had already shifted, and the Professor was talking about some of the more common origins of suffixes in place-names.

I learned that 'field' in Old English meant open country. So Ashfield means 'open land where there are ash trees'. 'Bury', as in Bloomsbury, means a fortification. Other frequent endings from the Old English period are -ton, -ley and -ham (Brighton, Burnley, Tottenham), meaning respectively a fence, a forest and a home. But it is the Viking names that are especially dear to the Professor, with their endings like -by and -thorpe (as in Whitby and Scunthorpe), meaning respectively 'farmstead' and 'outlying settlement' – because as a child he had been fascinated by the invaders from Denmark (this was probably the origin of his interest in name origins). 'As a boy, I could see the longboats sailing up the river,' he said.

But for me the conversation only really warmed up when the Professor began to discuss obscenities. Do the residents of Shatterford in Worcestershire realize that they're living at the ford of the shitter? And let us take a name like Claptongate ... Seems harmless enough, but 'clap' turns out to be an old word for 'fondle', and if you look back in the records, you can find a time when the place was called Clapcuntgate. Discovering this came as a bit of a shock to the Professor. 'For years I looked for a record of a family called Clapton,' he said.

CONTACT
The English Place-names Society
University of Nottingham
Nottingham NG7 2RD

The Ephemera Society

It's funny. I've spent a couple of hours talking about printed matter, yet the image which stays with me is not of any illustration or text, but of their absence. I am thinking of the hole in a piece of paper caused by a filing spike. It seems to be the key, indicating how that piece of paper has survived, yes; yet mainly it betrays how it was treated as part of the general traffic of paper, how it was one of thousands, millions, of documents, only useful and active for the shortest of times, before being sent to the file and ultimately to the dustbin.

Now, imagine the clerk, the agency, the country and the historical period that files without a second thought an order to hang a sixteen-year-old boy. Imagine piercing with the spike a workhouse admission form or a debtors' prison diet chart. Or imagine *not* filing, but crumpling, because it's of no concern, a handbill advertising fumigating ingredients, with the selling-point, 'A whole cargo of Negro slaves may be saved by the moderate use of these ingredients.' I asked Maurice Rickards whether collecting such printed matter of bygone ages gave him a better understanding of the follies of our own era. 'Absolutely,' he said. 'The follies, the deceits, the whole bullshit industry.'

Maurice opened a file containing nineteenth- and early

83

twentieth-century advertisements and product labels. I was immediately struck by their offensiveness. There was the one for Sperm Whale Candles, with a picture of a harpoon entering the white blubber of a Moby Dick. And there was the overt racism of the Pears' Soap handbill showing a Negro child in the bath and the caption 'How ink is made'. Yet the greater the offence, the greater one's realization that this is history undiluted. 'It was the real truth about real life,' said Maurice. He also showed me some notices which were simply quaint: like the sign informing hotel residents that their electric lights should not be lit with a match.

Maurice, a distinguished graphic designer, is the founder of the Ephemera Society. But what is ephemera? Or should that be are? There is confusion about the grammar, the pronunciation (epheemera? ephemmera?) and the scope of the term. Ephemera is defined by the society members, who collect it, as 'the minor transient documents of everyday life'. It includes admission tickets, reward notices, pools coupons, advertising and price tags – everything from an eighteenth-century receipt for the purchase of horse manure to a handbill for a stage show from the 1890s, with its 'startling disrobing scene'.

And talking of disrobing scenes, ephemera also includes the cards which prostitutes leave in present-day phoneboxes. Maurice showed me a selection from this part of his collection, including 'Spanking fun with sexy eighteen-year-old', illustrated with an open-mouthed human Barbie Doll. 'My very respectable friends take great pleasure in bringing me handfuls of these cards,' he said, as we looked at the basques, the fishnets, the whips. He remarked that it was some time before he realized that TV did not stand for television.

CONTACT
The Ephemera Society
12 Fitzroy Square
London W1P 5HQ
Tel: 071 387 7723

Escapology

If the phone had rung, I would have had to pick it up with my teeth. And thank God I didn't want to scratch my nose. Maybe I should have been content to *watch* Nick Janson get out of the straitjacket, rather than attempt it myself . . .

His arms were crossed and secured by straps. There was a padlock under his crotch. He started to jiggle his body like a grub in a cocoon. Then one arm was free, the buckles were undone and he was out. 'I've done it so often it's like taking off a shirt,' he said. Though he preferred to remove the straitjacket when he was upside-down – suspended from a crane 200 feet in the air, with a burning rope attached to his feet. 'You don't get many people buying straitjackets nowadays,' he said. 'It's really only escapologists or people who are into bondage.'

Nick Janson had come to give me advice on the art of escape, and few people are better qualified. Nick, now sixty, has been a professional escapologist for over forty years and he holds the world record for escaping from handcuffs – he has freed his wrists from 1,400 pairs, of many different types, and in all cases the cuffs were supplied by police officers. Even as a schoolboy, Nick wanted to be an escapologist – though his father favoured a career for his son in the insurance industry. 'As a compromise, I became a locksmith,' he said, 'which is actually how Houdini started out.'

Nick's career progressed rapidly. In 1954 he was signed up by Paramount films to help promote the movie *Houdini* – he carried out the first post-war straitjacket escape as part of the film's publicity, and a week later was handcuffed and hurled off Westminster Bridge in a mailbag. He is also probably the only man ever to escape from a padded cell. 'I did it naked,' he said, 'and I was examined by a doctor. He even had a look up my backside.'

For the amateur escapologist, Nick recommends that the first step is to join a magic society. This is not only because escapology has much in common with conjuring but also because you will gain access to the how-to-do-it books that never appear on library shelves – books which give instructions for emerging from locked safes, riveted containers or even welded-down boxes. Nick stressed too that anyone taking up escapology must pay the utmost attention to safety. Twenty people have died attempting the straitjacketed burning-rope escape – most recently, when a man used a nylon rope which melted. In Nick's own career, there was a moment when he came near to death: he was buried 6 feet underground in a coffin, and the coffin started filling up with water. 'I had to be dug up pretty quickly,' he said.

Otherwise, they might just as well have left him there.

But there is one thing from which the escapologist never escapes: the reputation of Houdini. 'I could hang from the moon or be chained to the bottom of the sea,' said Nick, 'and I'd still only be the *second* Houdini.'

CONTACT
George Norrington Magic
36 Lincoln Road
Dorking
Surrey RH4 1TD
Tel: 0306 884538

(George Norrington Magic sells *Who's Who in Magic* – a list of magic societies and useful contacts.)

Straitjackets can be purchased from:
Fetters
40 Fitzwilliam Road
London SW4 0DN
(Visitors by appointment only)

The Eurovision Song Contest Fan Club

'Just as other people like football, so we like Eurovision,' said Perry Robbins. 'I wish people would give it a chance, the music's so varied.'

Keith Foord agreed. He admitted that he had been passionate about Eurovision music since childhood, when, on the night of the contest, he would drape national flags across the lounge and follow the action on his own chalk scoreboard. Keith was about to give me a quote, summing up what the contest means to him, but just when he'd settled on the likes of 'Without it, there would be a big gap in my life', he was interrupted by Lee Colquhoun, the third person present. 'No,' said Lee, 'don't say that. People will think we're weirdos.'

Whatever people may say about the members of the Eurovision Network – a group of nearly 500 people devoted to the critical appreciation of the Eurovision Song Contest – I must tell you that the evening I spent with Perry, Keith and Lee couldn't have been more fascinating. As we settled down to watch a video of Clodagh Rodgers's 'Jack-in-the-Box', we entered a magical world of three-minute tunes, manufactured groups, Katie Boyle . . .

The first thing you realize is that Eurovision music is, well, European, and cannot be dissociated from the history, conflicts and politics of our little continent. Take ethnic tensions. One year, Turkish television decided to black out the Greek entry; the following year the Greeks responded with a charming *chanson* about a Turkish napalm attack carried out during the invasion of Cyprus. Then there are the political bandwagon tunes. Fears about nuclear obliteration led to a Finnish entry entitled 'Don't Drop the Bomb on Me'. The thaw in relations between East and West produced the Norwegian song 'Glasnost', with a chorus about Reagan and Gorbachev. Then the collapse of Communism gave us 'No More Walls' and 'Brandenburg Gate'. The contest's most recent investigation of post-war European history was an inspiring Italian song called '1992', about the creation of the Single European Market.

There are those in the network who lap up the trivia surrounding the contest – Eurovision know-alls who can tell you precisely how many points Austria awarded Germany in the 1958 finals – but for most members the appeal is the music. I settled back in my chair and watched videos of entries like the Greek song 'Socrates – First Superstar', and an effort from the former Yugoslavia in praise of Levi's jeans (chorus: 'Come on, put on your Levi's').

We came to a Norwegian song called 'Oi, Oi, Oi'. As you will no doubt be aware, Norway once achieved the distinction of scoring *'Nul points'*. I was intrigued by the effect of that disgrace upon the Norwegian national psyche: the Norwegians hired a professor of linguistics to write lyrics that would smooth out the more unpleasant of the Scandinavian sounds. When they eventually won the contest, the country went wild: flags waved, horns honked and a national holiday was declared. 'Unfortunately, when the contest took place in Norway the following year,' said Perry, 'the Queen of Norway had her bag snatched.'

On to a moody ballad – something to do with how sweet is the sea – sung in an Italian dialect. With such cosmopolitan fare, I began to wonder whether any of the members were patriotic about British entries like Black Lace's 'Mary Ann' or Samantha

Janus's 'A Message to Your Heart'. 'Yes, we do have patriotic members,' said Lee. 'One girl always cheers on the UK entry.'

'Even if the song's appalling?' I asked.

'I don't think she's ever thought we've put in an appalling song,' he replied.

Someone was singing a chorus which consisted solely of 'la la la'. 'You get so many musical styles,' said Perry.

CONTACT
Joseph Currie
Eurovision Network
1 Byres Road (4/3)
Glasgow G11 5RD
or
Perry Robbins
4 Parkin Street
Alfreton
Derbyshire DE55 7JS

Falconry

Emma Ford lifted the lid of the milk-crate-sized box and at once my nostrils said something's gone off in here, it's old meat. Inside the container was a pile of puffballs: all yellow, all fluffy ... and all gassed. Falconry requires bait, what better than newly hatched chicks?

I asked Emma whether she had any problems with anti-blood-sports campaigners. 'No, because it's in the hawk's nature to kill,' she said. 'It's not contrived, like fox-hunting.' She took a handful of the dead chicks and began pulling the legs from the sockets. 'We may get pleasure from watching a hawk make a kill, but is that any different from a birdwatcher wanting to see a bird on the nest? I even get vegetarians coming to the school and after a few days, it's quite amazing. They develop a bloodlust. They're desperate to see the birds in action.' She handed me some of the baby-pink claws.

The school is the British School of Falconry, run by Emma and her husband, Stephen. Here you will find hawks called Aero and Wispa, Aspirin and Dispirin, and Oscar, who stepped from the perch on to my glove. 'The glove is always worn on the left hand,' Emma said. 'The falconer keeps the right free for his sword, so he can protect his lady.'

So we walked then, Oscar and I. He let me stroke his chest. And as we crossed the grass, I felt his weight on my forearm. He wasn't heavy, just nicely present.

It's a little like using a slingshot, when you 'launch' a hawk. You hold on for a moment to its jesses and then it's free and it flies to a perch. Overcoming squeamishness, you take out a chick's leg. What happens next is unforgettable.

When a bird of prey swoops in to take the bait from your glove, when a hawk spreads its wings and glides ... and glides ... as if following the curve of a valley, when you see it come closer, till its claws grip your skin through the leather of the glove – then you know why Emma does it, you know why people take up the sport.

But this was just the start. Real falconry means going out to a forest and watching the birds hunt.

Hawks wear bells on their ankles, so that if you can't see them while you're in the forest, you can at least track them by ear. So, there's a faint tinkle-tinkle in the distance and you think of

Christmas bells, and all the while you know the bird is seeking to tear the heart from its prey.

I cannot claim to have enjoyed the moment of the kill. I can still see the bird pinning down a rabbit, its hook-beak in the corner of the animal's terrified eye. Yet all too often, people become sentimental about nature. A hawk will soon show you the reality.

CONTACT
The British School of Falconry
Braco Castle Estate
Braco
Perthshire
FK15 9LA
Tel: 0786 880530 or 0227 87575

Feng Shui

'I could tell you had money problems the moment I saw the position of your lavatory,' he said.

He stood in the doorway of my bathroom, looking inwards towards the porcelain and the chrome. 'Though it's not as bad as having the lavatory over there –' He pointed towards the bath. 'If you owned a business and your lavatory was where your bath is now, you'd go bankrupt.'

Now, as far as I am aware, there is no generally accepted principle of financial appraisal which links the state of a balance sheet to a plumbing floorplan. Yet Nik Fernee, my guest, was right: I *was* finding it difficult to make ends meet. He told me that a mysterious life-energy, which the Chinese call *ki*, was not circulating around the flat in the right way. 'Your *ki* is coming in through the front door and going straight down the lavatory bowl,' he said. The solution he recommended was to put a plant on the lavatory's cistern, to encourage the *ki* to move upwards. 'After I've paid a visit, most people go out and spend about £100 on plants,' he said.

Nik Fernee is one of the very few *Feng Shui* teachers and consultants in Britain. Originating in China 4,000 years ago, *feng shui* (which means 'wind and water') was initially a practical approach to finding the best places to farm, taking into account climate and land. Over the course of centuries, this evolved into the belief that environment influences life, health and prosperity. Today, in Chinese communities around the world, *feng shui* experts can earn fortunes by telling companies how to arrange office furniture. Most important of all is the location of the managing director's desk.

Meanwhile, Nik was in my kitchen. 'That cooker will make you feel insecure,' he said. 'You'll be cooking with your back to the doorway. You wouldn't be aware of someone approaching behind you.' The fix? To place a mirror on the wall above the hot-plates. But in the bedroom, it was a mirror itself that posed a problem. Or rather, the matching mirrored doors on the wardrobe. 'Anyone entering the bedroom would be cut in two by those mirrors,' he said, 'which isn't good for health.' He also diagnosed that if I wanted to attract more women, I should put pink sheets on my bed and place a large rock on the floor. 'At least you haven't got a wooden beam crossing the bed,' he told me – that would cause a lot of depression, though it could be corrected by hanging up two Chinese flutes.

I needed more than a stream of comments; I wanted to know Nik's reasoning. So, we sat down at the table in my lounge for my first *feng shui* lesson. Fortunately, the table is not in the centre of the room, which Nik said should always be free of furniture. 'The centre is the emptiness which makes it all work,' he said, as if quoting a line of poetry.

He drew an octagonal diagram, called the *ba gua*. Each of its sides, he told me, represented a different area of life: wealth, fame, marriage, children, knowledge, career, helpful people and family. The diagram also represents areas of a room. Hence, if you put a wastepaper bin in a knowledge area, your insights are not likely to be profound. Likewise, in my marriage area – currently occupied by a television – Nik advised me to bring out the masculine side; a red ornament on top of the television would be a big help in getting me hitched. But *feng shui* is a vast subject and its principles cannot be boiled down to a diagram. There are always complicating factors, like the positions of windows. I happen to have french windows in the lounge, which Nik said I should cover with a net curtain; otherwise, I'd lose any woman I attracted by the red object on my TV.

Does it work? Nik himself has been convinced of *feng shui*'s power ever since he shifted a laundry basket and found that it improved his ability to study. Though even before that, he was influenced by an extended stay in a Tibetan community in northern India. 'Tibetans have an insatiable curiosity about homes,' he said. 'It drives Westerners mad. They're always looking under beds or down lavatories. And if you pull them up about it, they just say, "If you come to our area you're welcome to look down *our* lavatory."'

Which reminded me of my financial problems. Since everyone in my block of flats would have a lavatory in the same position relative to the front door, wouldn't that mean trouble for *all* the residents? Nik said yes. And it was true that I had heard of nine repossessions.

Whether it works or not, I know one thing: a knowledge of *feng shui* would bring a whole new dimension to watching *Through the Keyhole*.

CONTACT
Nik Fernee
Twiglees House Annexe
Castle O'er
Lockerbie
Dumfriesshire DG11 2LU
Tel: 03873 73309

Fictional Languages

If language is the dress of thought, then some people hope to be couturiers. These are the subscribers to *The Glossopoeic Quarterly*, a publication for those not happy with the choice offered by Linguaphone, but who instead try to invent new *fictional* grammars and vocabularies.

In the *Quarterly*, you might find an article on Valrast, which its creator describes as loosely based upon Spanish/Latin, although, as he remarks, 'much of its vocabulary is drawn from those strange areas of netherworld inside my head'. Here is a snatch of Valrast:

> '. . . *hin Nareth jos oshu Olpa Sekel hin smol ve ketil hon jos tur em olpa.*'

Which translates as:

> '. . . *and Nareth saw the three Fallen and, drawing his sword, he slew them.*'

There is an explanatory note that Nareth is the Chosen Warrior and the three are the Fallen Sons of Heaven, for Valrast's creator is also working out a mythology for the speakers of the language, loosely based upon the history of the Byzantine empire.

Like other languages, Valrast has a grammar. In the *Quarterly*, you will find a rule for plurals: add an 'e' at the end of the word, unless it already ends in a vowel, in which case you would drop that vowel and add the e. You will also discover the correct way of stressing syllables: in Valrast, the accent is usually placed on the first syllable, except when there are more than two syllables. Hence, we have tir-an-*em*, *tol*-tra. tren-*o*-sa, ler-e-*tu* and *mi*-reth. However, like any good language, there are exceptions to rules: stress-patterns will tend to differ for words which have been influenced by other fictional languages, like Pezhüzhüm.

What is the point of all this?

There is a role for invented languages in certain works of fiction – Tolkien is the obvious exemplar. But I have heard it said that there are two sorts of glossopoeists: those who invent languages for fun and those who believe it will revolutionize the world.

I have spent a half-hour trying to create a tongue of my own. Or, at least, playing with the idea. For instance, could you have a language with no adjectives? You might have no word for 'tall', so you'd translate 'He is tall,' as 'He is like a tree', while 'He is very tall' could be 'He is like a skyscraper.' I've also been coming up with words like *dwoon*, *frunhile*, *pywith* ... I couldn't be bothered to do much more. Would you have the sticking power to invent a vocabulary of several thousand words? Would you work out detailed phonetics, as for Pezhüzhüm, which has a 'kw' sound lying somewhere between the sound at the start of 'queen' and the sound at the end of 'loch?'

There is also the problem of what others would think. The *Quarterly*'s editor, Steven Deyo, admits that he's become cautious about having people in the vicinity while he tries out various sound-system pronunciations. One of his languages is Bzhaghitakh, which has six or more levels of two-tone aspirants – a kind of mixture of guttural Arabic and tonal Chinese. 'Years ago,' he writes in the latest issue, 'my sister once came into my room while I was practising toned vocalics for certain letters. She said I was weird.'

CONTACT
Steven Mark Deyo
1165 Bidwell Street
West St Paul
MN 55118–2231
USA

First Drop: The Roller-coaster Society

There was a time in Andrew Hine's life when he would see roller-coasters everywhere. Going past a building site, he would notice a crane and think: looks like a roller-coaster. A glimpse of planks of wood on a lorry would lead him to reflect: could be used in the construction of a support lattice. No longer in a state of such obsession, Andrew is none the less still *interested* in roller-coasters. How interested? Oh, he and his wife recently got married on one. (The priest conducted the ceremony at Blackpool's Grand National coaster.) Moreover, with his friend Justin Garvanovic, his free time is spent running First Drop: The Roller-coaster Society of Great Britain.

Andrew, Justin and I met at Chessington's World of Adventures, where we took to the Vampire, Chessington's blood-curdling ride. Along 750 metres of track, as high as the trees and then underground, I was screaming as much as a kettle whistles. There is a specialist vocabulary that First Drop members use for rides – they talk of 'speed humps' and 'double dips' – but I don't think words are good at describing the coaster experience; you need to speak to the accompaniment of your hands.

Andrew and Justin have had thousands of rides on roller-coasters throughout the world. On their first American tour, they went to twenty-three amusement parks in twenty-one days. Did they ever get the willies that a bolt on a coaster might come loose and that, well, they'd die? 'No,' said Justin. 'Never. You just wouldn't believe how safe roller-coasters are. They're reckoned to be the second safest form of transport in the world, after the Otis lift.' Had nothing gone wrong? They confessed that there was one occasion when the society obtained special permission to go on a kid's ride: twenty adults were crammed on a coaster meant for twenty children – and the brakes were only designed to stop passengers of a certain weight. 'It just wouldn't stop,' said Justin. 'We went round four times. In the end, it only came to a halt because we grabbed the structure.' Otherwise they would have gone on all day.

I soon realized the connoisseurship of coaster fiends. A fast ride isn't necessarily the best; you want your stomach all over the place. The materials used in the construction of the coaster are also of significance: a steel ride gives roller-coasters new possibilities, like corkscrews, but steel is also *dead*. Wooden coasters are *alive*. 'Wood flexes, it moves, it's affected by weather conditions,' said Andrew. The true enthusiast also explores the effects of sitting in different cars, searching for the best 'negative g', the momentary experience of being lifted off the seat.

And let us talk more of g-forces. The Vampire can attain 3.5g of force, but Andrew and Justin told me of a German machine which attains 6.5g. It should be borne in mind that at 7g a human being will lose consciousness. In the back seat of the German coaster, you see stars as the blood rushes out of your head.

Andrew and Justin have also walked the tracks of some coasters – at Cedar Point in the States, that meant walking up to a height of 42 metres.

'It was terrifying,' said Justin.

'Would you do it again?' I asked.

'I have done it again,' he replied instantly.

CONTACT
Coaster House
16 Charles Street
Hillingdon
Middlesex UB10 OSY
Tel: Andrew Hine 081 848 4073, Justin Garvanovic 081 561 3192 or, for 24-hour answer phone, 0895 238272

The Flat Earth Society

I think I shall write to the manufacturer. 'Dear Sir,' I shall say, 'I was recently shopping in a novelties store when I noticed an item from your product range: namely, a variation on the Rubik's Cube, consisting of a small blue and green sphere, twistable in many directions – this sphere supposedly representing the world. I have to say that I would have been happier if you had retained Rubik's original shape for this piece of merchandise – and happier still if you had adhered to true principles of geography and produced the puzzle in a two-dimensional format.'

Having met Ellis Hillman, the president of the International Flat Earth Society, I admit I was tempted to write such a letter, because I now have considerable sympathy with the flat-earther's position. As Ellis told me, 'The flat earth hypothesis is more convenient, more useful and altogether more sensible than the spherical hypothesis, which is more complicated and a wholly unnecessary hypothesis at that.'

Now, you may think that you can easily refute this point of view. You may, for instance, say that the earth must be round because ships disappear over the horizon. 'That doesn't prove anything,' Ellis will tell you, for by the laws of perspective, a far-away object gets smaller and smaller, and eventually vanishes. Photographs from space? No, Ellis won't have that: the earth's atmosphere has a refractive index which distorts light and could certainly account for the apparent curvature. Ah then, surely circumnavigation is the trump card . . . But no, that won't do either. The earth could be a disc with the North Pole at the centre and the South Pole distributed around the circumference. You would then travel in circles, just as you would on a sphere; and, as Ellis doesn't fail to point out, a ridge of ice would stop you from falling off the edge.

Ellis Hillman claims never to have lost a debate on the shape of the earth, and as I was speaking to him, the awful truth dawned on my increasingly flat horizon: the earth might not be round. At least, I could not *disprove* the possibility of its flatness.

I knew then that I had been sold sphericalism as a dogma. I had accepted the rotundity of the world without question, without understanding why. Am I any better than those in the Middle Ages who accepted, without question, that the earth was flat?

Start quizzing yourself like this and you'll see the merit of being a flat-earther in the 1990s. It shakes you out of intellectual lethargy; it makes you challenge established ways of thought. I should tell you that Ellis himself does not actually believe the earth is flat, but as a politician – he is London's longest-serving Labour councillor – and as a trained scientist, he is attracted to the in-built radicalism of the flat-earth theory. 'There is a danger of science becoming too axiomatic,' he told me. 'Scientists can easily fall into the very trap they accuse non-scientists of being in. The Flat Earth Society will continue to challenge scientific and astronomical orthodoxies and fashions.'

But I was interested in those people who genuinely believe the earth is flat – do they really exist? I'm afraid they do. The late Sam Shenton, Ellis's predecessor as president of the society, was a true flat-earther, publishing a magazine called *The Plane Truth* and finding biblical support for the hypothesis. 'I saw four Angels standing at the four corners of the earth,' as it says in Revelation, 7. Furthermore, to this day, the Ethiopian Orthodox Church makes the flatness of the earth an article of faith. I remarked to Ellis that it was rather strange more fundamentalists didn't declare their support. 'True,' Ellis agreed, 'though I did have some correspondence with a rabbi who was pleased that there were still people like us around.'

Yet, the debate isn't simply between flat- and spherical-earthers. I learned from Ellis that there are people who think we're living on the *inside* of the earth and that there's an inside sun. Then there's the man who claims that the entire cosmos is shaped like an egg. And we mustn't forget the gentleman who declared that the earth was hollow, consisting of a number of concentric spheres, one within the other.

None of this, though, has the solid, empirical evidence of the flat theory. Ellis will happily tell you of a nineteenth-century experiment with theodolites, carried out on the Bedford ship canal. No evidence of curvature was found over 20 miles. 'The earth,' declared Ellis, 'is flatter than you think.'

CONTACT
See entry on Ellis Hillman in *Who's Who*.

The Floatation Tank Association

If, in the darkness, I lift my arm, I feel the drips of water upon my naked chest. Sensation. This is a limited world. Understatement. It makes the works of Samuel Beckett seem like thrillers. Even the chatter of the mind starts to go. Nothing to see; smell and taste not options; the ears plugged. Though sometimes, like a corpse in a river, I drift to one side, and then my shoulder may knock the wall of the cubicle.

Twice in my life I have entered a sensory-deprivation tank, or floatation tank, as these enclosed chambers are nowadays more often called. The body floats in water containing three-quarters of a ton of Epsom salts; it is as buoyant as the Dead Sea.

With the first float, I remember, music played to let me know my time was up. In spite of the plugs in my ears, in spite of the blandness of the composition, the melody was a tidal wave. I was swept along, and up, yes up; I had the impression of being carried aloft by sound. *I was flying.* I presume that my senses had been so starved during the previous hour that even 'Three Blind Mice' would have sounded magical. After I had dried myself, and walked on to the street, the colours of posters on the billboards were amplified.

This second float, I merely relaxed. At times, my mind just wasn't there. I wasn't arguing with myself, or with imaginary others; there were no problems, there was nothing to ponder, there was nothing *with which* to ponder. Of course, you cannot perceive your own mind's absence, but when it comes back, you know it's been away.

On this second time, the tank belonged to Sarah Dening, who runs the Floatation Tank Association. The association can offer advice on floating, including the whereabouts of the nearest tank. She explained to me that, in a tank, one's brain is somewhere between awake and asleep. 'A lot of people poke fun at the tanks,' she said. 'If I mention that they're a wonderful way to relax, someone will say that it's cheaper to go down the pub for a gin and tonic. Or even to fill your bath with salt.'

Her message is that people should try out the experience. Tanks have varied uses: songwriters find inspiration for tunes when floating; some people use them to learn a language. (Play French in total darkness, with no other distractions, and your thoughts will turn to *pensées*.) And people under tension find tanks especially beneficial. 'There's always an upsurge in demand from students when the exam season starts,' she said.

And no, she told me, if you spend a long period in Epsom salts you don't get crinkly fingers.

CONTACT
Sarah Dening
The Floatation Tank Association
3a Elms Close
London SW4 8QE
Tel: 071 350 1001

Flounder Tramping

There are two containers into which you can pack all the fishing equipment you'll need: they are called your left and your right shoes. For in the form of angling known as flounder tramping, a fisherman has no rod, no line, no net – maybe as an optional extra, he might employ fishnet stockings. Flounder tramping is fishing with the feet. To understand what it involves, I tweezered out my toejam – should I have left it in as bait? – and went north of the border, to the one-shop, one-pub village of Palnackie, where every summer the world flounder-tramping championships take place.

We shall never know the name of that first Scotsman who waded across a river and realized that he'd trodden on something – his breakfast. Legend has it that Robert Burns himself had fisherman's feet in his socks as well as metrical feet in his verse; and there are reports of Scottish emigrants carrying on the tradition in Nova Scotia. None the less, it is only in Palnackie in modern times that tramping has become a competitive sport. It all began twenty years ago, in a pub of a neighbouring village. A small group of trampers had a wager amongst themselves for a bottle of whisky; the prize would go to whomsoever caught the largest flounder in the River Urr. Sam Paterson, a Palnackie man, won the bottle and was inspired to start the world championships. After all, he reasoned, other villages had their fêtes and their galas, but Palnackie had nothing – except a tradition in the last century of smuggling brandy and tobacco.

Now, the mudflats of the Urr are ideal for tramping. The flounder, a flatfish somewhat like a plaice, leaves the Solway Firth for the Urr's shallow estuary, and when the tide goes out it lies on the bottom and buries itself in the mud. There, as it waits for the tide's return, it is vulnerable . . .

On the day of the championships, 200 of us waded in waist-high, even chest-high. We foraged with our naked toes. The correct technique is to walk slowly until you detect a wriggling; then, if you can, try to get a good, sound foothold on the middle of the fish. Under the rules, it is permissible to use a three-pronged spear called a leister to bring the fish to the surface, but this is frowned upon by purists. The exponent of pure tramping keeps a firm hold with the sole until the fish stays still, then reaches down into the water, feels for the head, and hooks a thumb under the gills. The fish is brought to the surface and dropped in a bag. And it must be alive at the weigh-in: dead, it doesn't count. This restriction dates back to the early 1980s, when there were suspicions of cheating; rumours that a prize-winning flounder had been caught not in the river but on a fishmonger's slab.

For me, a first-time tramper, the Urr was not a pleasant place. Every so often, someone would jump half-way out of the water and cry, 'Bloody crabs!' thereby putting you in fear for your toes. And the water is impenetrably murky. Your feet often brush against *something*, but what? Is it a strand of seaweed, or – ugh! – the fin of fish? Imagine being stroked in the dark. The instinct is to lift the foot as fast as an Olympic hurdler.

So, it was hardly surprising I caught nothing. In the end, the new world champion was a Dalbeattie man, John Robertson, who collected the £150 first prize for a fish weighing 2lb 7oz. And one woman speared her own foot!

CONTACT
The Glenisle Inn
Tel: 0556 60284

Flower Communication

A rose stands in a vase and I am watching it. I half close my eyes and strain; I open my ears and listen. Still no signal, though I have waited these fifteen minutes or more. 'Rose,' I am on the point of telling it, 'since you are the colour of lips, will you not speak, just this once? Give me your message, give me your meaning. I know you are able . . .' But the petals stay coy, and cover themselves.

Fifteen minutes! Seized by a hooligan spirit, I contemplate tearing the flower and plucking at its petals and pulling at the head till it's gone – but no. I stop and reflect. What is the meaning of a rose? Since I have no idea, a rose is like a word I have read whose definition I do not know. Suddenly, in my imagination, I go tumbling back to the past, to my schooldays.

There I am, in class, reading a passage from D H Lawrence, and there are words, mainly to do with flowers. What is saxifrage? What is an auricula? I have inklings, vague conceptions – of greenery, of petals, of buds – but I am not really sure. And I have entered this world, created this place, simply by staring at a rose.

Which is exactly what Ruth Rankin – an expert in flower communication – would expect. Ruth defines flower communication as 'a method of accessing energies or "essences" in flowers'; and in her workshops and one-to-one sessions she explores the effect that flowers have upon moods, emotions and creativity. 'A favourite of mine is pansies,' she told me. 'If you look at them, they're like little faces. Pansies are about facing the world and being open. They're to do with self-esteem. But every flower has its own signature, its own properties.'

Ruth believes her purpose in life is to act as a communications link between nature and human nature – a bold statement, and I wondered whether her fascination with things floral had begun early. 'When I was growing up,' she said, 'I loved to make daisy chains. I can remember getting very upset when the grass was cut. People said it was just grass – but the mower cut the poor daisies' heads off. And to me, they were like my little friends.' To this day, Ruth sees daisies as being about recognizing the value of small things in our lives. 'Every little thing can be a teacher for us on our life-path,' she told me.

Daffodils for joy, Easter lilies for removing guilt, field poppies for discovering strength within – there are many moods that Ruth finds flowers engender. 'I can also attune myself to the flower simply by holding the seeds,' she said. The flower doesn't even have to be real – a photo or a painting will do. Indeed, a plastic flower can have potency. My own rose, which created such peculiar sensations at the beginning of this piece, started life not in the ground but in an injection mould.

After she had told me about the sense of grace that can be derived from looking at *Narine bodenii*, Ruth talked about the most important aspect of her work: its practicality. While some gurus might advocate a trip to a mountain or six years in an Indian monastery as ways to spiritual insight, Ruth believes that a windowbox can have the same effect. 'We can look at a flower,' she told me, 'and feel totally fulfilled. Even in the middle of the city.'

I left her house, hit the streets, and found myself staring at the grass that grows in the cracks of the pavement ...

CONTACT
Ruth Rankin
20 Woodstock Grove
London W12 8LE
Tel: 081 740 4764

The Flying Trapeze

These words exist because my writer's block now doesn't. And just as a mind and a pen can be numb and frozen to the spot, so sheer blind fear pushed nails through my feet – that day I stood, and couldn't move, on the sacrifice platform of the flying trapeze. I had no faith to fly.

Under the guidance of Circus Space's trapeze tutor, Jonathan Graham, I had every reason to feel safe. I wore a harness that would hold me up like a marionette on strings to break any fall; there were padded mats down below; and the launch platform wasn't very high – no more than 4 yards at the most. Why, I had even had one successful swing: I had simply climbed the ladder, put one hand on the bar, then the other hand, and stepped down, becoming the bob of a human pendulum. I heard someone say, 'That was pretty good for the first time.'

Ignorance can create that sort of skill. You just do things. They're fresh and there's nothing in your head to make them go wrong. When you try again, you start thinking, weighing things up, and that's when you're in trouble.

I climbed the ladder a second time. I reached out again, took the bar, put my second hand on – and my feet froze. My head was full of panic and disaster. I could not move. Four yards? It was sixteen! 'Think of anything else,' Jonathan called up from below. 'What you were doing last week, what you had for dinner, anything at all. And just step forward.'

I couldn't. What good was the harness and its puppet-strings? I wanted to unbuckle, climb down and go home. I shouldn't have come.

There are always two other people on the platform. They hold the bar for the acrobat's launch; they try to keep you talking to take away the fear. One of them, a girl, whispered as sincerely as she could, 'You've got a lot of courage.' And so . . .

I should explain that in an unsuccessful launch the trapeze artiste does not swing in an arc. Often, the novice will end up being dragged across the floor still attached to his puppet-lines. But in my case, that wasn't the only humiliation. For the friction of my clothes against the mat pulled down first my trousers, then my underpants. I shall perhaps have to discontinue my puppet metaphor, because puppets are not usually anatomically correct.

Speaking to Jonathan, I learned that the fear never quite goes, no matter how great the artiste's experience. He told me also that the top acts are very protective about the techniques of their profession and are unwilling to pass them on to new-comers. He did let me in on one trade secret, though: because of the tension imposed upon the stomach muscles during the swing, trapeze artistes often break wind in the middle of their acts. One's heart goes out to the catcher.

I climbed the ladder, was afraid and crashed, was afraid and crashed, was . . . But eventually, believing in myself, I had a successful swing. After all that failure, this was one of the great experiences. Myself, a Robert the Bruce spider . . .

You may not believe me about the writer's block, but then, everything's a matter of faith.

CONTACT
The Circus Space
United House
39–41 North Road
London N7 9DP
Tel: 071 700 0868

The Frontier Research Network

One name keeps on coming to me: Baron Frankenstein. I am not accusing anyone of robbing cemeteries and waiting for lightning storms, but there comes a point, as in Mary Shelley's book, where science seems to merge with dabbling in the occult, so unorthodox are the investigations. This appears to be the case with the so-called 'borderland science' of the Frontier Research Network.

'Why was I drawn to the borderland stuff?' Martin Wacey, the group's organizer, stood up and pondered my question. We had been discussing matters such as the spontaneous generation of life and the ethereal energy sources that people may be able to tap into. 'I wanted to get to the bottom of things,' he said. 'I was dissatisfied with everything else.' He passed me a few issues of an American publication, *The Journal of Borderland Research*.

The very names of the topics were evocative: electricity and the evolving soul; the cosmic pulse of life; the photography of the invisible; the psychic life of micro-organisms. I found an extraordinary condemnation of hydroelectric power. 'Clamp one of your arteries and see how your health proceeds,' said the article, 'for such is the reality of damming rivers.' Another contributor held a view I had never heard expressed in my science class at school. 'It is my belief,' I read, 'that substances are not built out of atoms and molecules but rather that atoms and molecules are the result of the breakdown and decay of substance.'

Though not a scientist himself, Martin described a research area which interested him: a combination of chemistry and astrology – the effect of planetary alignment on chemical reactions. It seems that if you do a certain experiment with gold chloride or silver nitrate before, during and after a solar eclipse, the results differ: before, specks of precious metal crystallize on a filter paper; then, during the eclipse, there is nothing; afterwards they come back. 'Something unusual is going on here,' he said. 'Borderland science is about making this sort of discovery.'

I had actually first seen Martin when he was sitting at a bookstall, trying to sell a range of material, including a guide to perpetual-motion machines for the would-be experimenter. As you might expect, the quest for 'free energy' is one of the main areas of borderland research. He showed me a Xeroxed photograph of a device with two cylinders and a disc in the centre. It purports to be the first fully functioning *perpetuum mobile* in the world. Constructed in the community of Methernitha, in the Swiss village of Linden, the machine can supposedly generate a current of 220 volts out of thin air. Does this mean that a new golden age of free energy is about to be ushered in for mankind? Can the electricity companies stop sending out bills? Can you leave your lights on all night and not worry? Will torch batteries never run out?

Er, well, there is a problem. The community that owns the device is run on strict Communist principles with no private property, but for people so used to sharing, they are remarkably unwilling to share their discoveries with the rest of us. Mankind isn't ready to receive such knowledge, they say. 'If you cannot accept this point of view,' they proclaim in a letter to the world, 'please discover a free energy device by yourself.' So, you know who to contact to start your programme of research.

CONTACT
Frontier Research Distributors
PO Box 3144
London E17 8TA
Tel: 081 521 8733

The George Formby Society

Standing on the platform at Blackpool, waiting for the late train to Euston, the one thing that wasn't going to depart was the memory of my first ukulele lesson.

It's very easy to get hooked on the uke and its plink, plinkety-plunk. Sure, the fretboard was no longer in my hand, but mentally my fingers were still forming chord shapes. Rather like amputees who want to scratch the empty air where a limb once grew ... But such comparisons are too morbid for the song I'd learned, 'When I'm Cleaning Windows'.

> Ladies' nighties I have spied,
> I've often seen what goes inside,
> When I'm cleaning windows ...

Fifty years on, it's still worth a chuckle, though it does sound a little odd when you hear it performed by a boy as young as eight. You see, there is no age discrimination in the George Formby Society. I had attended their convention in the Winter Gardens, Blackpool, covering it for *City Limits*. I had never seen so many ukuleles in my life.

In the 1990s, it's hard to realize how a big a star George Formby once was. During the Second World War, he was Britain's highest-paid entertainer, earning £100,000 a year even in those times. His fame stretched as far as the Soviet Union, where in 1943 he was awarded the Order of Lenin – apparently for a morale-boosting film scene which showed him socking Hitler on the jaw. Now, thirty years after his death, the 600 members of the worldwide George Formby Society continue to sing his songs and keep his memory alive. But why? What is Formby's appeal?

'He was an extraordinary ordinary man,' the society's president, John Croft, told me. 'He'd do things like going to the chip shop in his Rolls-Royce – that's if his wife, Beryl, let him have thruppence for some chips.'

A number of the members told me of the power of Formby's charisma, and from the posters and photographs on display at the Winter Gardens, it was easy to see what they meant. It's in the face. The mouth, the buck teeth, the saucy wink – you can't take your eyes off Formby, even if you want to. He may have looked like a cross between Goofy and Olive Oyl, but he had the stamp of a star.

At the opening of the convention, Formby's eighty-four-year-old sister, Louisa, was introduced to the members.

'What do you think, Lou?' asked the MC.

'Turned out nice again,' she answered.

We all settled down for a concert as the members came up one by one to perform ukulele classics like, 'When I Come Up on the Football Pools' and 'Chinese Laundry Blues' ('Oh, Mr Wu . . .').

But as I glanced at the people in the audience, I saw one face so famous I couldn't believe it was really him. My thought was: It's a look-alike. Then it was confirmed. 'Yes,' I was told, 'that is George Harrison. He's a fully paid-up member of the society.'

I approached the former Beatle and told him that I was writing an article about the convention for *City Limits*.

'I thought you didn't quite fit in,' he said.

I asked George why he liked George Formby. 'Anyone who's picked up a ukulele knows that it's got a very happy sound,' he said. 'It's hard to play it without laughing. With all this war and killing that's going on, the ukulele offers some light relief in a world obsessed with madness.'

Any reader with a copy of *Sgt Pepper* to hand is invited to play it now – particularly Harrison's sitar-laden track 'Within You, Without You' – and speculate on what might have been . . .

CONTACT
Stan Evans
Tel: 0925 727102

(Ancestral) Ghanaian Drumming

We were about an hour and three-quarters into the appointment, and my taxi would hopefully not be long, when Godfrey's wife came by the room. 'Have you told him about the trances?' she said. And walked out.

It was as though she had put a heaped teaspoon of Andrews' Liver Salts into the glass of our conversation. 'The drums,' said Godfrey, 'can take you away. People go into trances when they're listening. The rhythm goes on and on and on and people become possessed. They don't know where they are and they don't know what's happening.' He started playing a rhythm – de-do-do-de-do – repeating it over and over again.

Godfrey Mensah is probably the only person in Britain who can teach you the techniques of ancestral Ghanaian drumming. It was the combination of those three words – especially that mysteriously simmering 'ancestral' – that made me think I should meet this man. Unfortunately, when I arrived at his home in Stroud, he confessed that he didn't know why traditional Ghanaian drumming was called 'ancestral' and that it was really just decoration. 'Anything invented some time ago could be "ancestral",' he said. 'You could have an "ancestral" fridge or an "ancestral" radio. But some people like the word "ancestral" and they go, "Oh, wow!"'

So it was plain drumming, then. Not a particular interest of mine, no matter what tradition it was from. I listened politely as Godfrey, who was born in Togo but educated in Ghana, showed off his music. He positioned the drum – like a bongo, but made out of a log and covered with antelope skin – between his thighs and began to play. Twenty years of experience beat out rhythmical patterns so quickly that, even when Godfrey stopped his hummingbird hands and did a single tap, it was so fast it was as though his fingers had never moved. 'In winter, when it's cold,' he said, 'playing hurts like hell.' Rather half-heartedly, I took the drum and had a go, but my notes sounded dull. I couldn't cup my palm in the right way and there was no resonance. 'It can take years to learn,' he said. 'People think they can play in one day – and at the end of the day they go home disappointed.'

He had summed up my mood. And then, with a quarter of an hour to go, his wife came in and suddenly I knew that my decision to see Godfrey had been vindicated.

'In Ghana, we say that a person is possessed by a ghost,' said Godfrey. 'In the trance they start seeing things. They start predicting that things are going to happen. They can tell if a person is going to be ill – maybe because he's done something wrong, or maybe because he's been poisoned by someone.' He spoke about how the drumming of the fetish priests can go on for days, with the various members of the Ghanaian clergy working in shifts to keep up the rhythm. 'If you've got maybe fifty people listening, then ten would be in a trance.'

He said that when he teaches, he warns his students. 'You've got to be careful when you play. You can hypnotize yourself. I tell people not to get carried away by the rhythm.' If he ever felt it was happening to him, he would stop immediately before he was taken over.

It's funny. A strange endless loop, where you drum yourself into an oblivion and then cannot stop drumming, where you cannot feel the soreness though your fingertips are bleeding, and where your only chance is a muscle-spasm that will break the rhythm. Or an antelope skin that bursts. Or the call of the taxi that has come to take you home!

CONTACT
Godfrey Mensah
Obi-Nka-Obi
Stark Hill
Edge
Stroud
Glos GL6 6NR
Tel: 0452 812983

Ghostbusting!

The sound was soft, but real – a drawn-out groan, repeated every so often, like the creaking of a ship's timbers. The gooseflesh began bubbling along my arms and legs. The noise was coming from the tunnel. We had all been warned. What else can one expect when hunting the walking dead?

It was 3.00 am. at Fort Amherst in Kent. Hours earlier, I had arrived with thirteen members of the Association for the Scientific Study of Anomalous Phenomena, or ASSAP, a group of paranormal investigators who hold all-night vigils in haunted locations.

Only weeks before, an ambulance had been called to the fort because a man in his twenties had fainted, believing he'd seen a ghost. On the night of the stake-out, one of the fort's managers, Richard Wozencroft, told us that he himself had had no unusual experiences, but . . .

He mentioned that in one part of the fort, an old mezzanine floor had been removed and visitors had reported hearing footsteps above them, in midair, as if feet were still walking upon the boards. 'Some of my staff refuse to go into the tunnels at night,' he said, the moon shining as he led us into those very passageways.

The word 'warren' is inadequate for Fort Amherst. There always seems to be another turning. Hewn from the chalk by Napoleonic prisoners of war, the tunnel walls have weathered over the years into a joyless grey-green. The atmosphere at Amherst belongs to Gothic literature: fingers of cold air stroke your cheek; footsteps echo; you cast long shadows. There are many alcoves – I did not not allow my eyes to dwell too long upon their depths.

We split into groups and stationed ourselves in different parts of the fort. Monitoring equipment was set up – video cameras and temperature sensors – but once that was done we simply had to wait. To pass the time, we chatted about the paranormal. In the environment of Amherst, it was easy for ASSAP members to recount experiences that sent a tingling up and down my spine. David Thomas, a long-standing ASSAP member, said that he first became interested in ghosts when he was thirteen. He was living in a council house with his parents at the time, and was about to climb the stairs when he was aware of a *presence* behind him. He turned – to see a man in top hat and tails. The young David ran screaming up the stairs. The man vanished. Since then, David claims to have had 'glimpses of this, glimpses of that'. When I pressed him for details, he mentioned the family's cat. 'After the cat died, we went to a new house,' he said. 'Then one year we went on holiday, and when we came back the neighbours said that it was cruel of us to leave a cat behind. We wondered what cat they meant.' The neighbours described the deceased pet. They had seen it inside the house, looking out of the window.

Other investigators told of occurrences at previous all-night vigils. Strange bangs; a hint of perfume, as if a spectral woman was walking around; the time a door of a castle rattled; or when an investigator, listening through headphones, heard a low voice say 'Hellooooo.'

Hours passed and, after many changes of station, I found myself in an annexe which was a mock-up of a Second World War ARP headquarters. There were two of us on look-out duties here – as well as the wax effigies in battledress, which every now and then I checked to see hadn't moved. Beyond was an open doorway leading to the tunnels. Richard Wozencroft had told us that, a few months earlier, an electrician had been working in this annexe when he was scared out of his life. While on a rewiring job, he was barged aside by *something*. He caught a glimpse of a black shape – it went through the doorway and into the tunnels, where it disappeared. The electrician ran out and refused to finish the work. In this very place, at 3.00 am, my colleague said, 'What's that noise?'

It was the groaning I have mentioned. I went cold. He said he would investigate and I didn't stop him. I didn't join him either.

He returned after a few seconds. 'It's OK,' he told me. 'It's one of the ASSAP members. He's fallen asleep in a chair and is snoring his head off.'

CONTACT
Dr Hugh Pincott
ASSAP
20 Paul Street
Frome
Somerset BA11 1DX
Tel: 0373 451777

The Gird 'n' Cleek Championships

I had better begin with a translation. 'Gird' is the Scots words for hoop, the 'n' you will know from rock 'n' roll, and 'cleek', another Scots word, turns the whole expression into something you might call 'rod 'n' roll' – because in the sport of gird 'n' cleek you have to roll a hoop which is attached to a rod while racing around a running track. In the words of the rhyme:

> We'll have a go wi' gird 'n' cleek,
> They say it's easy when it yer peak.

Which means, I suppose, it's difficult when you aren't. Still, as always, I'll have a go. I went to the village of Parton in south-west Scotland, where every summer the world gird 'n' cleek championships take place.

The championships are the brainchild of a local farmer, Mungo Bryson, who some years ago found a rusting gird 'n' cleek in a scrapyard. Reminded of hot-blooded childhood in the streets with his pals, thoughts began to congeal. What about an annual event? Something in which everyone could participate. And something that was a total contrast with the commercialization of the Olympic Games – the first, second and third in his event would not win gold, silver and bronze. Instead, there would be a haggis for first, a clootie dumpling (plum pudding in a cloth) for second and a Scotch mutton pie for third. Thus the event became a reality – though there was one year when a competitor's cairn terrier awarded himself that third prize.

As I stood on Mungo's field at Parton, I heard many people say, 'I haven't played with one of those since I was a kid.' One man recalled that when his mother asked him to run messages, he would cry unless allowed to take his precious circle and rod. 'If you didn't have a gird 'n' cleek,' he said, 'nobody wanted to know you.'

I started to practise. The gird itself is about 2 foot 6 across, made of iron, and the cleek is attached to it by a loop – as if the gird is threaded through the eye of an enormous needle. You can, of course, find girds with separate cleeks, but the attachment of the two means that running requires more skill, for the cleek can interfere with the roll of the gird, acting as a brake and causing it to topple over. But the attachment *does* make for accurate steering. 'I expect one day they'll hold a slalom,' said an onlooker.

I practised till my palms turned orange-brown from the cleek's rust. People gave me hints – 'Hold the cleek low down on the gird' – but the best I could do was a few steps before the gird wobbled and fell. It made images of itself; it looked briefly like the coils of a spring and then like a coin that's nearly settled.

It took me an hour to get the knack. A gird in spin is a wonderful noise: it's like a metalworker's lathe, or how a bee would sound were its wings made of high-grade steel. I was ready for the race.

In my heat were fit men. The starter got us away, and immediately I botched my opening strides. The cleek braked the gird, or vice versa – I don't know what happened. I started again and this time managed to get the gird going. For about two-thirds of the race – down the straights and round the corners – I was running and rolling. Until I hit a patch of bumpy ground.

My rhythm destroyed, I finished last, but I didn't feel I'd disgraced myself. No one could deny I knew how to cleek my gird. I sat back on the grass and watched the rest of the heats and eventually the final. The winner, in a close contest, was young Mark Adams. I asked the new world champion what he would be doing with his haggis prize. 'I'll probably let my dad eat it,' he said.

CONTACT
Mungo Bryson
Tel: 06447 282

Glassblowing

I plunged the metal rod into the furnace's mouth and gathered glass as though it were a fondue. Food is not a bad comparison, for when you take the rod out of the furnace, there is a delicious red-glowing toffee-apple-sized glob. 'You feel as if you can lick it and eat it,' said my tutor. For a joke he chomped on the air. I was with Peter Layton, founder of the London Glassblowing Workshop – one of the few places in the UK offering beginners the chance to blow.

'Oh, we often drop what we've made,' he said. 'Our biggest ever bowl crashed on to the floor. And it's a bit like the one that got away – the one you drop is always the best thing you've ever done.'

I hoped that my poor little pieces would survive – my Aladdin's-lamp-shaped bowl, my paperweight with a protuberance. As I felt the furnace's blast on my cheeks, I knew I had the privilege of working with one of glass-art's masters, for Peter's work is sold internationally and is even renowned in Czechoslovakia, the greatest glass-making country in the world. 'In the early 1970s,' Peter said, 'the London Glassblowing Workshop helped to create a market in Britain, when there wasn't one. At one time, shops simply weren't interested, and we were fobbed off with excuses like, "You need special lights to display glass."'

I watched as he tweaked the molten material with tongs; shaped it with moist papers and twirled it on the blowing rod like a majorette's baton. Had he never injured himself? Peter was anxious that I shouldn't dwell on accidents, for when there is a workshop full of artists, you find such coordination: the artists move in and out of each other, not hurried, not rushed, like a dance, a ballet. 'But very early in my career,' he said, 'I poured molten glass all over the back of my hand. Actually, the back of my hand came off. But I didn't feel any pain at the time. I only knew that I'd had an accident when I smelt my own flesh burning.'

CONTACT
The London Glassblowing Workshop
Hope (Sufferance) Wharf
109 Rotherhithe Street
London SE16 4NF
Tel: 071 237 0394
or
The Craft Council
44a Pentonville Road
London N1 9BY
Tel: 071 278 7700

Goldpanning

You had to watch out for the sheep droppings, but I guess it was pretty much like the Klondike.

North Wales was where I was. Where in North Wales? Best to keep that to myself. Let's just say I was by a stream, rinsing out a dirty pan, washing some filthy lucre. Have your eyes never strayed to geology maps showing deposits of metal in Wales? It was a day out and I was looking for gold.

In theory, it's quite simple. Take a pan, put in a fistful of dirt, then go to the stream. Fill the pan with water and start jiggling it. The water will spill out, carrying away the lighter particles of soil. Gold, being heavier, should sink to the bottom. Keep on washing off the soil until only the gold remains.

That's the theory. In reality, there is a knack to shaking the pan. Too fast, and you'll lose gold as well as dirt; too slow, and you'll never make it pay. Another problem is that you may not recognize gold when you see it. As my companion for the day, Gerard Gibourg, told me, 'I have so often watched beginners throw away panfuls of sediment, not realizing that that's where the gold is.' Let me emphasize too the size of the precious flakes: smaller than the full stop you're now going to see.

Yet if you're persistent, gold you will find. Gerard had already shown me an ingot made from flakes collected over the previous few months. The ingot was the size of an ashtray. It could cap an elephant's tooth.

For sure, you have to know where to look – and that could take years of experience. You have to recognize the soil colours that suggest higher concentrations of gold; you have to understand how rainfall will flow over the terrain, shifting the location of paydirt. And once you've struck gold, you will naturally be wary about sharing the secret. In one spot, Gerard and I encountered another prospector and there was immediate animosity from this man. 'You're not welcome here,' he said.

Gerard's own passion is less greedy. Though he does admit that sometimes he hoovers under rocks to get the dirt up faster. 'I do it for the excitement, for the ambience, to be in touch with nature,' he told me, as he mentioned this novel use for a car vacuum cleaner. 'I don't do it to become rich.'

Certainly, only a man with infinite time would believe that Wales is the path to fabulous wealth. True, every speck you find can be added to your hoard, but you'll have to go through an awful lot of muck before you see that mickle makes a muckle. The ingot Gerard showed me was worth thousands of pounds, but if you were to take into account his labour, the economic return isn't obvious. What keeps a prospector going is the hope of a big strike, and Gerard kept *me* guessing as to whether, for him, that had already happened. 'One day I'll make an announcement,' he said, smiling. Teasing? He looked up at the hills and told me he just knew in his bones that one day there would be a gold rush in Wales.

In the meantime, I had to content myself with glowing flyspecks. What am I saying? I wasn't that blasé when I was down by the stream. I defy anyone to be indifferent to gold, even small amounts of it. Good as gold, golden rule, golden handshake, all that glisters – it's an ore in our language as much as in our land, and no one can forget its cultural significance. Tiny though they were, the grains in my pan were the genuine stuff of wedding rings and Bank of England reserves. I could scarcely believe my luck.

When Gerard and I had finished for the day, we went for a drink. After a long session of panning, your eyes become so attuned to staring at sediment and small matter that you look at everything in a different way. Even the dregs of a glass of beer

116

have a new fascination, believe me. That's how gold fever gets you.

CONTACT
Michael Gossage
The Goldpanners' Association
12 Pikepurse Lane
Richmond
North Yorks DL10 4PS
Tel: 0748 822515

Graeco-Roman Wrestling

My shoulders were pinned to the mat. My opponent's sweat dripped from his chin to mine – an unpleasant but in this case soothing balm. Because a few seconds earlier, in his enthusiasm to escape my hold, his head had swung up, crashed into my chin and shut my jaws like he was slamming a door – the entire lower half of my face was still recovering. But I had no one to blame. I knew that attending a class in Graeco-Roman wrestling was hardly going to be a pillow-fight.

I ought to say that I do not really understand what is meant by Graeco-Roman wrestling. The instructor, George Zorica-Lyuboevich, had tried to explain the difference between this classical form of the sport and the free-style form, but my neck was under his armpit at the time and I didn't take much of the information in. However, I realized that this was a highly technical game of equilibrium, all to do with keeping your own balance while trying to overbalance someone else; and hopefully you leave the gym with as many vertebrae as you had when you entered.

Anyway, George paired me with a man who was roughly my size, and then it was a question of learning from experience. After a little pushing, I was breaking into a sweat, which was one of the main themes of the class. 'Just let me wipe my palms,' I said, and I rubbed them on my top. I was trying to create the impression that I wouldn't be able to grip with that much moisture; in reality, I was seizing a few moments' breathing-space. But then we got together again.

Suddenly, his head ducked under my elbow and all I can

117

remember is that my joints were sticking out. Our bodies were just a pattern of triangles formed by his limbs and mine. And then I was down. Where should my feet have been? This wasn't a sport of strength – it was about physics, knowing how one body can lever another.

Looking back, I can remember being thrown over his shoulder. I can also remember being on all fours, behind him, when a flick of his hips sent me spinning and crashing to the mat. And I can remember cooling down in the bar afterwards – discussing the passage in Genesis where Jacob wrestles with God. Oh, and I can remember raising my arm the next day, to look in the mirror: there was a bruise below the armpit which was just like a thrush's breast.

CONTACT
The British Amateur Wrestling Association
The Wrestling Academy
41 Great Clowes Street
Salford
Manchester M7 9RQ
Tel: 061 832 9209

Hedgelaying

Downwind of a cowshed and crossing a field as muddy as the Somme, I was already wondering what in heaven's name I had signed up for. In an abstract sense, I knew. It was a training day in hedgelaying, held in East Grinstead, organized by the South of England Hedgelaying Society.

Hedgelaying . . . what is that, exactly?

By then, it was too late to ask – too late for cold feet, when the mud was seeping through the very eyelets of my boots. So, with the party of forty, I walked towards the target: the hedge. Twelve feet high, hundreds of yards long, it bristled round the field like an old man's whiskers, and now we were putting our razors to the strop.

Like the other beginners present, I was immediately assigned to a tutor. 'We have to get rid of the rubbish first,' he said. By the sound of it, the axes and the power saws were in full agreement. Picking up a billhook, I selected the most offensive-looking trunk I could find. The thickness of a man's forearm, it was discoloured tombstone-green with time and lichen. What's more, it had spikes. I started hacking, and I hacked till my palm ached.

By the time I was through, some fires had been lit. It was only when I was proudly dragging the tree to the flames that a man came forward. 'That's blackthorn,' he said, pointing to the trunk. 'That's part of the hedge. It's the brambles you needed to get rid of.' Unlike George Washington, I might have told a lie. But it's a bit unconvincing when holding an edged tool in your hand.

My tutor took me aside and explained that hedgelaying begins by expelling its serpent from Eden – or, by getting rid of the brambles. He made the justification quite clear: if it's not done, the hedge will have the life choked out of it. He then checked that I knew what brambles looked like.

As I endeavoured to put all his teachings into practice, I realized one simple thing: as a leisure-time pursuit, bramble removal is not for everyone. It means going deep inside the hedge, amongst the branches – trying to avoid having an eye poked out – and even when a stem is severed, it still has to be pulled free. Since the brambles have twisted themselves in and out of the hedge, this is like a tug-of-war match using a length of barbed wire. (*If only* I'd brought thicker gloves.)

Time passed, my billhook slowed, my interest waned. Why

had forty-odd people given up their Saturday? I did question a number of attendees, but the answers were invariably vague.

'It's just satisfaction,' said one.

'I like anything practical,' said another.

'If you don't like hedgelaying, you shouldn't do it,' said a third.

After hours of brambles, we moved on to the process called pleaching. This means that wood is chopped from the side of every tree. The first cut starts about 18 inches from the ground and many axeblows later, there is only a *hangnail* of wood connecting the upper trunk to the roots. It seemed impossible to me that the tree could live, but I was assured that a laid hedge could last for fifty years. Laid, because what happens next is that the tree is bent over to its side – which is done very easily because so much of its wood has gone.

Tree after tree, we went through this sequence of cutting and laying, until a series of sloping parallel lines, never seen in nature, was made from the trunks. It was like taking an enormous plastic comb and applying pressure so that the teeth all slant one way.

After several more hours, it was time to interweave stakes among the branches, and thin, whippy stems, called hethers, were placed crosswise to bind the structure together. What was left was an unusual form of fence – a *living* fence. As I stood back and looked, it seemed to me that I'd been involved in grand-scale occupational therapy. There was basketweave around an entire field. Finally, hedgelaying was defined.

I was tired and filthy and cold. I still felt unsure as to why someone would want to become a weekend hedgelayer. Some experts even tackle each other in competitions, when every twig has to be in place and every cut clean. Now, I know it's nice to preserve traditional crafts; perhaps also it's morally just to defend the countryside against the encroachment of wire fences; and it's true too that a laid hedge can provide a habitat for smaller birds like wrens and long-tailed tits. Even so, the next time I cut a hedge, I hope it'll be privet; and what's more, I think I'll use a Black and Decker trimmer.

CONTACT
John Blake
The South of England Hedgelaying Society
53 Finches Gardens
Lindfield
Haywards Heath
West Sussex
RH16 2PB
Tel: 0444 483999
or
The National Hedgelaying Society
c/o The YFC Centre
National Agricultural Centre
Stoneleigh Park
Kenilworth
Warwicks
CV8 2LG
Tel: 0203 696544

Hot SPICE 1: Fire-eating

The Special Programme of Initiative, Challenge, and Excitement (SPICE) is a multi-activity leisure club, with many regional branches. The emphasis is on adventure sports like canoeing, gliding and ballooning – activities which do not quite fall within the scope of this book. However, SPICE organizes a host of events all year round, and fire is a feature of the SPICE calendar. I am therefore including three 'Hot' SPICE activities: fire-eating, fire-walking and the human torch. Obviously, these involve a degree of risk – and under no circumstances should they be attempted without the expert supervision provided by SPICE.

They turn a visit to the local tandoori into a showdown. At stake is their pride, their 'curry machismo' – that swagger, that chip (or chapati) on the shoulder, that ever-present boast of 'I can swallow hotter than you, pal.'

Hot-curry fiends are bores who deserve a come-uppance, but how do you trump them if, like me, you're a throat-wimp and you struggle to down an extra-mild korma? The answer is easy. You become a member of SPICE, for in this club they eat the real hot stuff: fire. I joined them for a meal.

Fifteen of us gathered in the King George V Dock, home to London's jet-ski set. As the bikers of the water went by, we encountered Bob Eager – known as 'Daft Bob, the Skallywag and Jester' – who has been a professional fire-eater for twenty-two years. During that time, he has busked in Marrakesh, shared a dressing room with Madonna when they appeared on Jools Holland's *The Tube* and taught over 600 SPICE members the secrets of his art.

Bob took us through a series of exercises, all part of the build-up. He made us jump blindfold from a stepladder, to improve confidence; he made us shout the word 'buzz' the instant he pointed, to improve reactions; he made us roll over each other, men and women together, to improve God knows what, but it was kind of fun all the same.

Next, we had to practise putting an unlit 'firebrand' into the mouth, for without dummy runs, he told us, we would miss the target. As I didn't fancy a poke in the eye with a burning stick, I had no intention of shirking on the training. Then all we had to do was repeat the action with the firebrand alight ...

Well, there is more to it than that, but just in case there is someone out there who is stupid enough to try it without expert supervision, I'm not going to reveal all the secrets. I will merely say I did it. I stuck a blazing firebrand right into my mouth. True, I had qualms – millions of years of genetic programming tell you it's not a very good idea to chew on naked flames. But once you've overcome that fear, you get to like it – the ultimate acquired taste.

As to how to become a flamethrower, Bob introduced this part of the workshop by indulging in his favourite pastime: insulting the French. 'French so-called fire-eaters can't blow a flame to save their lives,' he said. 'And even if they do, it smells of garlic.' Could any Frenchman, he asked, ever blow a 20-foot flame over the front twelve rows of a theatre audience? Bob can. And he was going to show us how.

Basic technique for flamethrowing involves taking a swig of a certain highly flammable liquid and spitting it out at your firebrand. Woooooooffff. Send for Red Adair. The danger is that the wind will change direction and blow a fireball back into your face. This happened to one SPICE member. Fortunately, there was rescue without a moment's delay: out went the flames in his hair, smothered with a wet towel. Bob's reaction-training – the seemingly pointless saying of the word 'buzz' – had paid off.

As the day came to an end, I was faced with a problem: my breath smelt like I was the worst wino in town. It's inevitable that you'll swallow some of the 'highly flammable liquid', but I seemed to have had more than my fair share. It had another side-effect too. Next morning, I had to phone my boss. 'I'm sorry,' I said, 'but I can't come in. I've got diarrhoea from learning fire-eating ...'

Hot SPICE 2: Fire-walking

One of the single most astonishing news images of the 1960s was the photograph of a South Vietnamese monk burning himself as a protest against the Saigon regime. The picture's power to amaze derives from the passivity of the monk: there he sits, calmly, in the lotus position, while flames engulf half his body.

That photograph may represent supreme mental control, one man's spiritual conquest of pain, but the outcome was never in doubt: people burn.

But do they always? Because there is a phenomenon which seems to contradict all evidence of human vulnerability to heat. I refer to fire-walking, or striding barefoot over red-hot coals. Recently, I removed shoes and socks to give this feat of the feet a try.

Let me say first that there are no tricks. No chemicals are applied to the skin and you need neither hypnosis nor thick, callused soles. But one factor looms large in the fire-walker's craft: self-belief. You have to be absolutely convinced that the coals can be crossed without pain or harm. The fire-walking class I attended was really about making people think they could do it. As a preparation, inspirational music was played (like the *Chariots of Fire* theme and Bonnie Tyler's 'Holding Out for a Hero') and then there were several instructions we had to follow.

We had to imagine that we had already completed the fire-walk, that we had already conquered the impossible. We had to feel the elation of that experience and come up with some gesture, personal to ourselves, that expressed it – my gesture was to punch the air and shout 'Yes!' We were told that, when we were standing at the threshold of the coals, we should repeat that gesture over and over again until we felt ready to walk. And when it came to walking, we should look up and say, 'cool moss, cool moss,' as we strode. One member of the class was from Saudi Arabia, and he repeated the words in Arabic.

The full psychological training takes several hours. It starts in the afternoon, when you see the brazier where the coal is being prepared. Then you feel the heat on your face and you think: Oh my God, what have I let myself in for? But by the early evening, the fear has vanished. Your posture says it all: you strut, you put your hands on your hips, you *know* you are going to walk on fire.

So, the entire class went to the car-park, where we faced a 4-metre bed of glowing coals. Quite simply, one by one, we walked across.

What did I feel? I can honestly say: nothing. I had no sensation of heat whatsoever, and these were coals at 900° centigrade. All I can recall is the crunchiness of the bed underfoot. There was no pain and I was totally unscathed. I couldn't understand it, but I'd done it. 'Yes!'

Subsequently, I *have* heard attempts to explain fire-walking scientifically. It's supposed to be possible because of the low speed of transference of heat from the coals to the body. But there is a problem with this, which makes me think it's not the full explanation. At the workshop, a radio journalist came along to interview us for a feature and she decided to walk on the coals herself. If the scientists have got it right, she should have done it easily. But she, unlike the rest of us, had not gone through several hours of mental preparation, and she was the only person there who complained about burning her feet.

Hot SPICE 3: The Human Torch

I had received by mail a notice of the precautions I should take: specifically, that under no circumstances should I wear any clothing made of artificial fibres. Although the clothes would be covered by outer garments and wouldn't be burnt, such would be the heat surrounding the body that nylon and polyester might melt. So, before setting out, I double-checked the label in my

124

underpants. Well, you've got to be careful if you're going to set fire to yourself.

Five of us, four men and a woman, met in the grounds of the Chatterley Whitfield Mining Museum near Stoke-on-Trent. The intention was for each of us to simulate the stunt performed in hundreds of action movies. You'll know the scene: there's a car crash, or an explosion, and a man staggers out of the wreckage with flames dancing all around his body. The man in charge of the 'Burning Desire' workshop was himself a stuntman, Mark Angel, who has gone up in flames many times. 'Trust me,' he said.

Obviously, we had to wear protective suits. I am under oath to keep the secret of precisely what the protection is, because Mark doesn't want anyone to turn themselves into Baked Alaska without the help of an excellent chef (ie Mark). But when that protection is on, a genuine gasolene fire is started on your back and the flames lick you with a thousand tongues. We did it in the evening for a better effect, and when burning people go for a walk it looks satanic – the damned on a stroll out of hell. Other shapes suggest themselves: gigantic butterfly wings of fire, flapping in the night air; or flame-prickles, like a dead holly leaf, coinciding with a person's trunk.

But the experience of being, rather than watching, a human torch is not what you would expect. Inside the protective suit, you do feel *some* heat – as if you were standing too close to an electric fire – but that is only towards the end of the forty-second burn. The main sensation is actually that of being cold and damp, because as an added safety measure the protective suit is made sopping wet. Also, the suit's headgear allows little side-vision and so you have no appreciation of the flames around your body. What I especially remember is not being on fire but the strike of jets of water hitting my head, as Mark and his assistant tried to stop the flames from encroaching too much.

So there was something of a divergence between my outer image and my inner reality. I may have looked like the guy on 5 November, but really I felt like I was sprawling on a wet fish counter.

CONTACT
SPICE
89 College Piece
Mortimer
Reading
Berks RG7 3XH
Tel: 0734 333531

125

or
Dave Waterhouse
Adventure for Life
Hill Top House
Oakhanger
Nr Crewe
Cheshire CW1 1UZ
Tel: 0270 878102
Fax: 0270 872544

Dave is a former SPICE coordinator who is now running Adventure for Life, an organization which offers opportunities for many adventurous activities, including those with fire, while raising money for charity.

Hypnotic Regression

Only *aficionados* of Batman trivia would have heard of Professor Carter Nichols, but during the 1940s and 1950s DC Comics ran a series of adventures featuring Nichols, a Gotham City scientist, who had developed a technique of time travel based upon the exploration of the mysteries of the subconscious mind. In the comics, Bruce (Batman) Wayne remained slumped in a chair during deep hypnosis, but upon awakening he reported that he had been both physically and mentally present at the time of the Caesars, Marco Polo or the Hanging Gardens of Babylon. One thing I share with Batman is that I too have undergone the Carter Nichols experience. For recently I visited a hypnotist, Jack Hardy, who specializes in sending subjects back to the past. Placed in a trance and returned to a time prior to the womb, I explored three 'previous lives'. All details were tape-recorded.

In 1847 I was a twenty-year-old woman of leisure called Miranda Rawnings. My father, who was part of a British trade mission, spent two years in Russia. I accompanied him, and in Moscow I met my future husband – a British army officer called Ronald Blackstone. Soon after our marriage, I grew to despise Ronald. Showing too cruel a devotion to the arts of war, he would unnecessarily clean a bayonet in front of me, flaunting the keenness of its edge. I shed no tears when he died in a munitions explosion.

In 687 BC, I was a hunter of rabbits and birds. My name was Prow and my hunting-ground was in south-eastern Europe, perhaps in the region of modern-day Albania. Socially, I was an outcast – my leg was deformed and I lived in a meagre hut by a river with my wife, Borgo. I died when climatic conditions worsened. My last words were, 'I'm hungry . . . and cold.'

In seventeenth-century Germany I was a quack doctor called Johannes Korman. With my pestle and mortar I created medicines using ingredients such as ground bones, clay, flower extracts and wood. Sometimes I cured the sick, but on one occasion my potions led to the death of a patient. I was nearly lynched by a mob. They wanted to drown me – I can still recall my wife's screams as they dragged me to the river – but I pleaded with them, quoting my past successes as a man of medicine. Eventually, they let me go.

Towards the end of my life as Johannes, I started experimenting on myself. Once, when suffering from a head cold, I saw a rat swimming and this led me to think about the curative liquids which might be extracted from its organs. After all, rodents survive in the dankest and most inhospitable of environments – if only human beings had the resilience of rats. I picked up a branch, struck the creature, killed it, flayed it and chewed a piece of its skin. Soon afterwards I succumbed to a fatal fever . . .

Each of these lives was full, vivid and consistent. My accounts could have been autobiographical. So were these examples of reincarnation? Did I, in a sense, travel in time?

As Miranda, I had given my address as 17 Mossley Square, London. This led me to search street directories and census records for the early nineteenth century, but I found no Mossley Square. The closest street name, Mosley Gardens, had no resident called Rawnings.

But even if all three lives were constructed by my subconscious, the experience of hypnotic regression was still rich and rewarding. And perplexing. Why should I adopt these particular identities? How many others are locked away inside me?

Forget comic books. The Carter Nichols experience raises many profound questions about oneself and one's psyche.

CONTACT
Jack Hardy
Tel: 081 688 2211/0641

Indian Head Massage

Next time I am at a fruit stall, I shall finger the melons and think of *The Day of the Jackal*. Remember that scene where a melon is the target in the assassin's rifle sight? Fruit makes a fine stand-in for the head of a head of state, and a guy needs to practise his craft – as I do. Because a few days before writing these words, a blind man with ultra-sensitive hands gave me a certificate for a newly acquired skill. It makes me as concerned about heads as the Jackal, though I will be somewhat gentler than he. I will buy my melon only to touch it, to practise the technique known as Indian head massage.

In his flat, Narendra Mehta, a physical therapist and osteopath who has been sightless since he was a baby, took fifteen of us through a weekend's syllabus of touching, stroking and kneading every inch of each other's noddles – all part of a thousand-year Indian tradition.

At its gentlest, head massage can be a simple laying on of hands – think of the 'See no evil, speak no evil, hear no evil' monkeys and you will have a rough idea of where to touch someone's face. Other times, the going gets more energetic, with the scalp, shoulders, neck or skull receiving 'brain shaking', 'piano playing' or the dreaded 'windscreen wiper', which destroys all known hairstyles.

Narendra believes that regular head massage yields many benefits, ranging from the promotion of hair growth to the relief of headaches and the elimination of muscular tension. Yet as it requires no undressing other than the removal of a hat, it cannot be associated with the activities of massage parlours. (Other forms of massage may require a pomegranate for practice, full of seediness; head massage just needs a melon.)

'Learning head massage will help your friends . . . and those who will become your friends,' says Narendra. For the tranquillity inside a well-rubbed head has to be experienced to be believed. I have heard that in a state of relaxation a brain emits alpha rhythms, which can be detected on an electro-encephalograph machine; a woman on the course became so relaxed under head massage that her brain went to the other end of the alphabet and produced the zzzzz of a full-blown snore.

As fingertips roamed over my own face, I can remember thinking, 'If death came now, it wouldn't be so bad . . .' With eyes closed, such thoughts of black bliss are interrupted only by the sudden recollection of head massage's single drawback: the snowstorm of dandruff which the technique rakes out of your scalp and deposits on your shoulders for all to see.

CONTACT
Narendra Mehta
136 Holloway Road
London N7 8DD
Tel: 071 609 3590

The Inn Sign Society

It was like a psychiatrist's word-association test.

'OK,' I said, 'what about really unusual animals?'

'There's the Gnu Inn,' he said.

'All right.' I paused. It would be too easy to suggest the Second World War. 'The Falklands War?'

'Major-General Jeremy Moore is on a sign.'

Hmmm. 'Inventors?'

'Well, you've got the Jet and Whittle.'

'Pop stars?' With the possible exceptions of Elvis and the Beatles, I doubted that there would be any at all.

'Who's that chap who died of Aids?' he said.

'You mean Freddie Mercury?' 'Yes. He's on the Queen's Head in Sussex.'

'Um ... OK, cartoon characters?'

'Well, there's the Cartoonist, which changes its sign every year, and will have a picture like Giles's Grandma.'

'I suppose the 1966 World Cup victory is celebrated?'

'Moore's on a sign, Ramsey's on a sign ...'

To acquire this level of knowledge about pub signs you have to work at it, and that is what Jimmy Young has done. He is credited by *The Guinness Book of Records* as the world-record pub-crawler, having been to 23,980 drinking establishments, about one-third of the UK's total. In his prime, he would visit forty pubs a day, 280 pubs a week, simply following the sequence of going in, having a glass of wine and going out again.

'I've always been drinking, ever since I was fifteen,' said seventy-five-year-old Jimmy, as we downed a pint in his local, a riverside hostelry called the Double Locks, in Exeter. 'And when I went on a Rugby trip or a hockey trip with the school team, we'd stop at some pub or other, and I'd wonder, why is that called that?' Many years later, in 1988, Jimmy founded the Inn Sign Society. It now boasts 350 enthusiasts who, like himself, 'collect' visits to pubs – not necessarily because of an unquenchable thirst, but so as to see the sign outside and to understand the reason for the pub's name.

Jimmy passed me a copy of the society's journal, *At the Sign of . . .*, which functions as a travel guide for the sign-spotter and also gives explanations for unusual names. I discovered that in Jersey is Jeffrey's Leap, which is named after a felon called Jeffrey, who was sentenced to be executed by being thrown from the cliffs at Gorey. (The tide was in and he survived, but as well as being a felon, he was a fool – because he decided to jump again, by which time the tide was in and he landed on the rocks.) However, at Islington in London you can find a celebration of a life which was certainly not cut short. I refer to Old Parr's Head, which takes its name from a certain Thomas Parr, who is said to have been born in 1483 and died in 1635, aged 152. He also married at eighty, and again at 120, and fathered an illegitimate child at 102. And whilst on the subject of extra-marital dalliances, we might mention the Fanny Grey in Salterforth, Lancashire, which is named for a farmer who would tell his wife that he was off to see the grey mare, though this was merely an excuse to have an assignation with the mare's owner, whose name was Fanny. Which perhaps leads to consideration of the Naked Man, in Settle, North Yorkshire, a pub which has now closed, but a stone carving of its sign can still be seen on a nearby café. The date 1663 is strategically placed.

And so it goes on: the Elastic in Coventry, in an area where many small family businesses were operated from home, using elastic made at a large factory nearby; the Deacon's Alms in Salisbury – no, that is not a spelling mistake; the Contented Sole in the fishing village of Eyemouth, Northumberland; and the Bus Stop in Liverpool, with a sign featuring Marilyn Monroe. The Inn Sign Society hopes to record for posterity every pub sign in existence, together with the true explanation for its name. The one thing Jimmy cannot stand are names like Frank's and Henry's, which have no cultural or historical significance, being named after the landlord.

'Pub signs are full of history,' he said. 'You've probably got every king since Canute on a sign somewhere in the country.' He went on to explain how common names like the Rising Sun and the Half Moon go back to the crusades, while the commonest of all, the Red Lion, dates from the time of James I, who wanted public buildings to display the rampant lion of Scotland. 'Children should learn about pub signs in school,' he said.

At some point in the conversation, I wondered whether any signs had ever undermined a pub by causing offence to customers. Jimmy mentioned the Silks, near the Bristol law courts, which shows a woman dressed as a barrister, flashing silk stockings. Also controversial is the Nag's Head in St Leonards-on-Sea, which shows a woman in a bridle. The most controversial sign he could recall, though, appeared thirty years ago on a pub called the Bull; Jimmy could not remember the pub's location, but he did know that the locals objected to the sign's prominent portrayal of the animal's testicles. 'The artist was called back to moderate them,' he said.

CONTACT
The Inn Sign Society
2 Mill House
Mill Lane
Countess Wear
Exeter
Devon EX2 6LL
Tel: 0392 70728

Instant Jazz

'So what do you know about jazz?'

'Nothing,' I said, a hint of smugness in my voice.

It was the wording of the small ad that had led me to the music room. 'No experience necessary,' it said. OK, I thought, my CV fits the bill. 'Only enthusiasm required.' Hmmm. A bit of a problem there. You see, jazz has never been my turn-on. It's a music that's always struck me as pointless, passionless, a bit of a bore – didn't John Lennon, or maybe it was someone else, call it musical masturbation? Then I began to wonder: just what *could* a jazz teacher do with a total novice? Thoughts of *Pygmalion* entered my head. Hmmm. I dialled the number and Peter Muir accepted the challenge. In the space of one afternoon he would attempt to turn me into a jazz performer.

The first task was to define jazz – after all, I knew nothing. Peter decided to explain by comparing it to other forms of music. 'In classical music, 98 per cent of what you produce is fixed,' he said, as he went to the piano. He took out a piece of sheet music and began playing a Beethoven sonata. 'But in jazz,' he said, turning round on the stool, 'maybe only 10 per cent is fixed. Or to put it another way . . .' He struck up a jazz version of 'Eleanor Rigby'. It was blurred, it was jagged, it was thin, it was fat, it was the hall of mirrors version of the original. 'Jazz is about being slightly naughty,' he said. 'It's not about playing *on* the notes, it's about getting in between the *cracks* of the notes.' He remarked that classical musicians fear their mistakes, but in jazz some of the best music actually comes from mistakes.

OK, I had the theory sussed. But I needed some specifics. So Peter, who can play in every style, decided to take me on a musical odyssey of the twentieth century. He gave me a ten-minute piano history of jazz, from blues to ragtime, from be-bop to cool, from jazz rock to beyond. Pretty damn soon, I got to know my Fats Waller from my Thelonious Monk. Along the way, Peter fleshed out the music with biographical details of the leading names.

'Many performers die young,' he said.

'Do you fear an early death?' I asked.

'I try to keep my life very together,' he said.

It was time for me to perform. Since my knowledge of piano doesn't extend too far beyond the insight that middle C lies pretty close to the lock, Peter thought I should stick to vocal improvisation. As he played the blues, I began to sing whatever came to mind.

> Oh, I woke up this morning, feeling ill,
> Doctor said, 'Son, you've got to take a pill . . .'

Not bad, I thought. I felt more than ready to attempt a jazz classic. So Peter sang the basic tune of 'Summertime' and then turned the spotlight on me.

'Summertime,' I sang, in my smokiest voice, 'and the livin' is easy . . .' God, I liked my sustains on some of those notes. Next line, then. 'Fish are jumpin' and the cotton is –' I was going to do something really stylish now. I kind of skidded vocally, really swerved, as I hit the word 'high . . .'

Of course, it was a travesty. Peter, using his skills as a

teacher, worked on me, explaining that jazz is about achieving a sense of honesty, of sincerity. I had been singing with masks on, copying showbizzy tricks that I had learned from listening to too much rock music. But by the time we came to the end of the session Peter had wrought a transformation. I was able to sing 'So hush, little baby, don't you cry ...' as if I, me, this little individual here, was singing it, not some bad impersonator of Bryan Ferry. The masks were off. We may have had only one afternoon together, but I had discovered the meaning of jazz.

CONTACT
Peter Muir
49b London Road
Forest Hill
London SE23 3TY
Tel: 081 291 3829

Italic Handwriting

This sentence is written in italic handwriting.

Well, obviously it isn't. To see a paradox resolved, you must re-write the words after contacting the group that promotes the style. But when the secretary of the Society for Italic Handwriting, Janet Pamment, told me that anyone could learn italic, I held up my notepad. 'Even someone who writes like this?' I sometimes find it difficult to read my own notes after an interview.

Janet screwed up her eyes. She had to think carefully about the answer, but then she said, 'Yes.' We started at 'a'.

Italic handwriting – if my notes do not deceive me – is a style which dates back to the 1500s, when it was developed by scribes who needed to write with speed and clarity in conducting the business of the Pope. It was also the hand of Elizabeth I. Sometimes it is said that the key to italic is the elliptical 'o', which sets the tone for the whole alphabet; but every letter has its rules, and in a manual that Janet showed me there were arrows to indicate the proper sweeps of the pen – a little like ballroom-dance training, but with positioning for a nib, not feet.

To inspire me, Janet brought forth some 'before' and 'after' examples of her students' handwriting: from jerky and disjointed peaks and troughs to the beautiful tide of italic. 'It changes people,' she said. 'There are people I teach who say they feel wishy-washy and ordinary, and then, when they find they can do italic, it gives them amazing self-confidence.' Which leads to a reappraisal of graphology: perhaps it is not personality that determines handwriting, but the other way around.

Janet reminisced about how, when she was a little girl, she was taught italic by an uncle. 'I can remember the day he came to give me a lesson,' she said. 'Long after he'd left, I was still doing the letters. In a way, it changed my life.'

If you think that sounds too grand, then consider this: whenever Janet has written a letter applying for a job, she has *always* been invited to an interview.

So can I now resolve the opening paradox myself? Have I done enough practice? Let me merely say, 'My handwriting used to look like this,' but now 'It looks like this.'

CONTACT
The Society for Italic Handwriting
Timbertrack
53 Sea Avenue
Rustington
West Sussex BN16 2DN

The Janet Ellis Fans

It is not simply that he records her every television appearance, though naturally he does that. No, what makes Nicholas Hall such a special fan is that when he goes to work, he leaves the VCR running, just *in case* Janet Ellis should appear. You see, Nicholas Hall stands at the core of a small but very dedicated group of fans: he edits the specialist publication, *The Janet Ellis Fanzine*, aimed at those who follow the career of the former *Blue Peter* presenter.

You may be thinking that nobody would read a magazine about such a – with due respect – minor celebrity as Janet Ellis. You're probably wondering how this magazine can exist, because what on earth is there to say about her? It's not as if Janet is Madonna or Monroe or even Sam Fox. She's never had a hit record, never appeared in a movie, never done a cheesecake photograph – though since leaving *Blue Peter* she has featured prominently in a Daz advert. She doesn't do *anything*, you would think, that fans could latch on to. But that is wrong. To prove the point, Nicholas showed me a file of correspondence, several inches thick, from fellow Janet enthusiasts. My eyes were opened as soon as I started reading.

There were letters which analysed her minutest mannerisms: 'She has a very characteristic way of drawing her lower lip into her mouth, extending her chin slightly and nodding to denote agreement.' There were letters testifying to her inspirational qualities: 'There is something about sitting back and concentrating on Janet Ellis. Just a picture of her is more than ample reason for all other matters to vanish and make you feel good enough to tackle anything.' And there were letters which talked of her 'supernatural sex appeal' and 'her radioactive attraction'. Sometimes, there was just worship: 'I love everything about her: the flare of her nostrils, the curve of her bottom, even the delicate arch of her instep . . .'

Nicholas's own enthusiasm is unique, because it did not begin with *Blue Peter*. He first spotted Janet five years before she had any involvement with sticky-back plastic and bring and buy sales, when she was playing a bit-part in a 1978 episode of *The Sweeney*. When I visited Nicholas at his home in Poole, Dorset, he showed me the very clip that changed his life. It cannot last longer than a minute, but that was enough for him to be smitten. All those years ago, he waited till the credits came up to see the name: Janet Ellis. 'I honestly thought she was the most attractive woman I'd seen on TV,' he said. He told me that his ultimate ambition is to own a tape of Janet's stint on the toddlers' programme *Jigsaw*. 'I'd pay £50 for a tape of old *Jigsaw* material.'

The fanzine itself squeezes an impossible amount out of the Ellis phenomenon. Apart from a Janet-related crossword – where you might be asked the colour of the T-shirt she wore in that episode of *The Sweeney* – and articles on such subjects as Janet's problems with asthma, or the exclusive announcement of her latest pregnancy, particular attention is given to the clothes she wears. There is a top ten of her outfits (no. 8: grey jacket, black top, short black skirt, worn in the series *Parenting*, 'Multiple Births' episode), and in one case a review of Janet's appearance in a nuclear power video, so we can read an account of the likelihood of Armageddon juxtaposed with details of her clothing. ('Could a Chernobyl-type accident happen in Britain?' she asks. She wears a black jacket, black top and white trousers. 'Do leaks from nuclear power stations cause leukaemia?' She wears black trousers, purple sweater and red scarf.)

Best of all are the readers' recollections of their heroine's appearances. Says one reader, recalling an episode of *Blue Peter*: 'Who can forget the spectacle of Janet in T-shirt and shorts crawling on her belly across the mud-flats of the River Exe as part of an endurance test. "It was quite fun actually, once you were good and dirty," she assures viewers afterwards. Wotta gal!' Another fan reminisces about the episode in which Peter Duncan plays the inventor of a lemon-tea footbath and Janet is in a creamy-pink Edwardian dress: 'From beneath her long dress she places one petite and naked foot into the bowlful of cold tea. For months after that particular edition of *Blue Peter* I dreamed of holding Janet's little foot in my hand and kissing those tantalizing toes over and over.'

Like other minority groups, Janet fans have to face society's lack of understanding, perhaps having to hide their recordings of *Blue Peter* in the middle of the tape, so that no one finds them; or, in the case of a shipyard worker, getting teased for rushing home on Mondays and Thursdays.

The real question is, why do thirty-odd people regularly subscribe, with an additional 120 or so expressing occasional interest? Nicholas believes that Janet has a special 'natural' quality. 'You can imagine her coming into your home, patting the dog and sitting down,' he told me. None the less, almost all the subscribers are men. What they seem to like is the way that Janet Ellis manages to be sexy within the supposedly demure world of children's television. Even within the constraints imposed by a wholesome show like *Blue Peter*, she was prepared to wear short skirts, plunging necklines and tight T-shirts. She would show a lot of cleavage while tap-dancing and often she put on a low-cut bathing suit for some escapade involving water. Perhaps significantly, she is known as the *Blue Peter* girl who had a child out of wedlock – which led some Conservative MPs to demand that she be sacked from the show for setting a bad example.

Whatever the secret of Janet's appeal, Nicholas believes he will be a fan for life. He does not intend to get married and at the age of thirty, having been a Janet fan for fourteen years, he says that he is quite happy being single. He and Janet exchange Christmas cards, he sends her the first copy of every issue of the magazine – she owns up to being flattered by all the attention – and once a year, at the motorshow, he has the ultimate thrill of meeting his idol face to face.

I asked him what that was like the first time. 'When I saw her,' he said, 'it was like she had an aura. She smiled directly at me and my mouth went dry. I had to walk away to compose myself.'

CONTACT
Nicholas Hall
12 Alderney Avenue
Parkstone
Poole
Dorset BH12 4LG
Tel: 0202 722798

The Japanese Tea Ceremony

Imagine that the instructions for self-assembly furniture were written by a master of the Japanese tea ceremony. The plans for an MFI chest of drawers, say, might include footnotes, in the haiku verse form, on the sincere state of mind to adopt when slotting plywood panels into grooves. There would be advice too on the most aesthetically pleasing method of applying a spanner to a nut. Even the act of removing unassembled bits and pieces from their boxes would have choreographed rules for torso movements, hand positions and posture.

It is the combination of the everyday and the artistic that is the essence of the Japanese tea ceremony, as I discovered at the home of Michael Birch. He is the only man in Britain who teaches *chado*, the Way of Tea; his business cards read 'Tea Master'.

Let me describe the tea-room. Tea takes place on a *tatami* mat, a floor covering made from rice stalks. The four walls are as follows: behind are simple bricks; to the right, a painted wall scroll, showing Japanese characters; to the left, a yellow screen and lanterns; to the front, a full-length window, looking on to a garden of moss and paving stones.

Next let me describe the seating arrangements. Guests sit on stools raised just a few inches from the floor, stools so low that one effectively kneels. As a concession to novices, it is permissible to sit cross-legged on the mat. This is improper but necessary, since it takes many months for the muscles in the legs to become accustomed to the pain of sitting on the stools.

And let me describe the experience. When one first tries to learn the tea ceremony, its complexity is overwhelming. Every action is codified. There are rules for the placing of feet when carrying utensils into the room, just as there are rules for the conversation between host and guest.

As a specific example of one tiny part of the ceremony, for my first lesson I had to memorize the twenty-one separate movements involved in wiping a piece of lacquerware with a *fukusa*, a silken cloth. Although 'memorized' is the wrong word: every action should be invested with a special quality of attention, the mindfulness which lies at the heart of Buddhist philosophy.

The tea, which is green, cannot be sipped until the bowl has been turned two quarter-turns clockwise in the palm of the hand. Strangely enough, bowls need not be perfect. There is thought to be a deeper beauty in the blemished than in the unblemished; the pottery is particularly admired if it has been repaired. One haiku expresses the beauty of imperfection thus: 'The moon is not pleasing unless partly obscured by cloud.'

Historically, the tea ceremony evolved as a blend of Buddhism

140

and etiquette, reflecting its beginnings in monasteries and its later arrival at the emperor's court. Michael, who discovered the ceremony twenty years ago during a trip to the East, believes that there is nothing else to compare with it in the world. 'The simplicity and beauty of the tea-room and the atmosphere you have created are all focused for the purpose of making tea,' he said. 'It is a total unity. You imbibe the atmosphere and everything else.'

But do not expect to learn the complexities of the ceremony straight away. Patience is required. One of Michael's pupils has been taking lessons for ten years, and she is *not* a slow learner.

CONTACT
Michael Birch
4 Langton Way
London SE3 7TL
Tel: 081 853 2595

The Jigsaw Puzzle Library

'When there are three or more missing pieces.'

I had asked Pearl Crompton when it was time to retire a jigsaw puzzle. 'Or,' she continued, 'when there are blobs of coffee in the sky. It always seems to be the sky.'

In the 1930s, there were many jigsaw puzzle libraries in Britain. Now there is only one. Pearl, the librarian, administrator and maker of replacements for pieces eaten by dogs or sucked into vacuum cleaners, showed me the room full of shelves. There were thousands of puzzles, all in their individual boxes and all graded in difficulty from one to nine.

'What's the criterion for difficulty?' I asked.

'How long it takes me to do them,' she replied.

Pearl opened a box and allowed pieces to slip through her fingers like the coarsest sand imaginable. She explained how a difficult jigsaw will be cut in such a way as to make it harder to solve. 'The cutter of good puzzles will look long at the picture, and think well before he goes to the fretsaw to make the first cut,' she said. So, although you may have heard the advice 'do the border first', beware: a straight edge on a piece may lead you astray, with no guarantee that it belongs to the border at all. Or, a significant feature of the design, such as an entire animal or flower, will be completely removed from its background, and cut into segments. Where should they be placed? You have no clues. Cutting a jigsaw puzzle and committing the perfect crime have much in common. The difficulty is reinforced by the policy of the jigsaw library, for none of the puzzles has pictures as guides. 'I would never give up on a puzzle,' said Pearl. 'But one member does four puzzles a week and doesn't finish any of them.'

Which is a good straight edge within this article; time to go on to the second bit.

I decided to borrow a puzzle of medium difficulty – level five – called 'Metamorphosis'. I poured 500 pieces of irregularly shaped plywood on to the table in my living room.

Two weeks later it was still not finished. A few areas had crystallized. I knew the puzzle was something to do with tadpoles and frogs – I had completed the odd leg here, the odd bit of spawn there – but that was all. Don't think I had been lazy. Far from it. The damn puzzle was soaking up free time by capillary action, sucking up idleness like a sponge. (While that kettle is boiling, I'll just ... Before I go to the lavatory, I'll just ... I'm a bit bored with writing, I'll just ...)

You start to be convinced that there are pieces missing. There are desperate moments when you grab a piece, go through every other one in the pile and still can't find the fit. Then a friend drops by and says you'd do it a lot faster if the picture was of a naked woman. All this for an exercise of stupendous utter pointlessness. Suddenly you look at yourself, you, a man with free choice, and, crying that life is too short for jigsaws, you sweep the pieces back into the box.

A sense of terrible malaise can be cast over a room by an incomplete jigsaw.

CONTACT
Pearl Crompton
The British Jigsaw Puzzle Library
8 Heath Terrace
Leamington Spa
Warwicks CV32 5LY
Tel: 0926 311874

Mrs Crompton brought to my attention a society of jigsaw puzzle enthusiasts, the Benevolent Confraternity of Dissectologists, who not only do puzzles ('There is no better way of producing an enjoyable evening than sharing a jigsaw with a few friends') but also research into jigsaw puzzle history.

CONTACT
The Reverend T M Tyler
The Benevolent Confraternity of Dissectologists
32 The Limes
Rushmere St Andrew
Ipswich
Suffolk IP5 7EA

The Jolson Society

Though I shall be talking of two men, it seems to me it's really four, each man being also someone else too, a different personality.

The first and the second in the quartet are Al Jolson. Jolson, the so-called 'Greatest Entertainer in the World'; Jolson, the highest-paid performer in history. I do not mean to imply that he simply had two faces – one made up for when he worked and one raw for when he lived. No, with Jolson it went much, much deeper. At times the stage star became a quite different human being even to himself. 'You should hear Al Jolson sing that song,' he'd say, only to be told, 'But you are Al Jolson.' For Jolson was a man fundamentally ill at ease, only at home in front of an audience; and though he featured in the first successful talking picture, off-stage this same man was so nervous he was often too afraid to speak.

Also dual is Terry Quigley. Under normal circumstances he too can be shy and retiring. But get him on to the subject of Jolson and a change takes place. Terry becomes a lion. 'I marched up to the counter at the American Embassy,' he said to me, in his broad Leeds accent, 'and I told them, "I'm not moving till I get what I fucking want." I said they'd have to call the police if necessary. Because until I got that letter, I wasn't going to budge.' After Terry's one-man sit-in of six hours, America gave way. He had his letter – a note confirming that Al Jolson had played a wartime show to US troops in Scotland. 'I did it,' Terry told me, 'for Jolson.'

There is little doubt that Terry Quigley, the president of the British Jolson Society, is the greatest Al Jolson enthusiast alive. Certainly, he owns the world's largest collection of Jolson memorabilia. When I visited him in Yorkshire, he showed me his Jolson room, containing the 500 mint LPs, the 10,000 photographs, the countless cans of film. 'I spent ten years tracking down this out-take,' he told me. And overall, Terry's obsession has lasted for more then *forty* years, ever since his mother took him, as a schoolboy, to the local cinema to see *The Jolson Story*. He has subsequently seen that film 300 times. 'And I have to say,' he added somewhat ruefully, 'that's not a record in the Jolson Society.'

Of course, the whole idea of a 2,000-strong appreciation society for an act as racially dubious as Jolson's will be distasteful to many a person. Amongst the members are those who go as far as imitating Jolson – there are seventeen professional Jolson impersonators in Yorkshire alone, all of whom are members of Terry's society – though Terry does not approve of their blacking up. 'It's a thing of the past,' he told me. 'It's offensive to black people and I don't think it should be done today.' He pointed out that Jolson himself only blacked up because he was too nervous to appear on stage as a white man. 'And if you listen to the records and hear that lovely, deep, mellow voice, you can't see the colour.'

As we sat listening to tapes of 'Toot Toot Tootsie' and 'April Showers', the full impact of the voice began to strike me. Like it or not, that voice is comparable to nothing else in popular music – comical, overdone, razzmatazzy, rounded. I am no fan of Jolson's, but the voice is so much a one-off that it becomes almost of scientific interest: you feel you want to anatomize the vocal cords – using surgeon's knives, perhaps – to find out how it works.

But to those who love him as Terry does, who listen to him five hours a day as Terry does, who have stayed in the hotel room where he died, who collect copies of the death certificate, who indeed amass everything possible related to one Mr A Jolson, artiste, that sound is precious in its every murmur, just as gold is weighed by the grain. 'There's a new Jolson CD out soon,' Terry told me, 'and apparently it has a version of "Mammy" that differs by one word from the original. I am prepared to pay £10.99 for that one word.'

Al Jolson was born of two wombs: his mother's and the stage.

144

Likewise doubly born was Terry Quigley, finding a second life in the singer's voice. Though they never met, I left Yorkshire feeling that, whether they were two men or four, here was one of destiny's teams. No longer does Jolson deserve to be a star on his own. For Castor and Pollux read Jolson and Quigley: the ultimate performer and the ultimate audience.

CONTACT
Terry Quigley
President The British Jolson Society
82 Pollards Field
Ferrybridge
Knottingley
West Yorks
Tel: 0977 674393

The Jonathan King Fans

I had spent an afternoon listening to Jonathan King B-sides.

Surprise number two is that I enjoyed it. The records formed part of the collection of Richard Lysons, the man who edits *Streets Full of People*, a specialist publication aimed at Jonathan King fans. 'You've caught the King bug!' said Richard. He had heard my laughter; he realized that the stylus wasn't pricking at my ear and drawing blood.

For King's B-sides are so distinctive they are like thoughts from a subconscious mind – rarely surfacing, frequently embarrassing, yet offering a key to the man. Moreover, if they catch you in the right mood, they'll make you smile. A typical offering exploits a record-industry absurdity: a B-side earns its songwriter as much in royalties as the A-side, even though the B may never be heard, while the A is a massive hit. King takes this commercial rule to its logical conclusion. He records a cover version – which becomes a hit – and puts any old rubbish on the B-side, thereby earning songwriting royalties. You might call it money for old rap.

So I listened to 'In Praise of UK', in which King simply delivers a spoken eulogy to his own company – at the end, he has the gall to give the company's address! Then there is the B-side in which King reads out a list of the staff at B & C Records.

And the one in which he chats about the royalties controversy to Bob the engineer. With all this mention of the spoken word, I must take care not to create the impression that there is no music on King B-sides. After all, there is 'Lay It Down', in which a strummed acoustic guitar plays a simple chord sequence over and over again. And the instrumental version of 'In Praise of UK' – another chord sequence, released when there were complaints from the public about the original B-side of this name.

After a while, I began to see the appeal of King's work. Who else would have thought of recording 'Mr Tambourine Man' with an orchestra of fifteen tambourines? There are also King rarities: like the gold flexi-disc on which King made an election address when he stood for parliament in the 1978 Epsom by-election as a Royalist; and still on a political theme, there is 'We Can't Let Maggie Go', a cover of the old Honeybus song, issued by King at the time of Mrs Thatcher's resignation. I wondered whether King rarities are highly collectable?

'Hard to find, rather than collectable,' said Richard. 'I do go to record fairs. I'm not embarrassed to ask for Jonathan King stuff, but most people haven't got any.'

'Are there any Jonathan King bootlegs?' I asked.

'I wouldn't have thought so,' he said.

Richard's belief is that King is too clever to be written off. He sees him as an important influence on 1970s pop, producing disco music before anyone else was into it and pushing forward gifted bands like 10cc and Genesis. Even singles like 'Una Paloma Blanca' were innovative, anticipating cheap holidays abroad. And there is no denying that King's label, UK, was one of the most successful of the 1970s, with King churning out hits under pseudonyms like '100 Ton and a Feather' and 'The Piglets'. In the fanzine, there is a list of thirty aliases, including some I'd never heard of, like Hot Squirrels and Sean Hoff and the Headbands.

I could see that King has something. A style of his own – not exactly kitsch, but a knowing kitsch. 'King admits that some of his records are rubbish,' said Richard. 'But people have ignored his sense of humour. He loves music. He's got an ear for a hit. And the records are a manifestation of his personality – King the fan and King the businessman.'

But the sad truth is that just before I left, Richard asked whether I'd like a few more copies of his fanzine. Did I perhaps

know someone who'd like one? I thought for a moment, but had
to say no.

CONTACT
Richard Lysons,
31 Norton Road
Syke
Rochdale
Greater Manchester OL12 OBJ

Knot-tying

I asked Frank Harris how to tie a hangman's noose. He took a piece of string and in a few moments it would have made Pierrepoint proud: a tiny noose, just the right size to hang Action Man for war crimes. 'It's the one knot I never demonstrate to Scouts,' he said.

I said that I'd heard of a knot that could be used to tie up a horse but could be loosened in an instant to make a quick getaway. 'Ah yes,' he said, 'the Highwayman's Hitch.' So he re-enacted scenes from the life of Dick Turpin using the leg of his coffee table.

Frank is one of the founder-members of the International Guild of Knot-tyers, a group set up ten years ago with the aim of promoting the art, craft and science of knotting. Though its initial membership was just twenty-five, nowadays it has over 700 members scattered throughout the world, from Japan to the Shetland Islands. As you would suspect, many of the group are former Scouts or seamen, yet there are also mathematicians. To prove it, Frank handed me a spiral-bound treatise. Full of algebraic formulae, and written by a so-called 'Topological Knot Theorist', it was too advanced even for Frank. 'I'm a Turk's Head man myself,' he said. He asked whether I'd like to try one.

Now, a Turk's Head is one of the most versatile knots of all. Aside from its decorative uses, it is a practical knot, applied to everything from scarf woggles to canoeists' paddles. 'It stops water from rolling down the paddler's arm,' said Frank. Following his instructions, I festooned my fingers with string. Some loops were bridges (which I went over with the cord) and some were underpasses (which I went under).

When I had finished, when I had everything I needed to go canoeing apart from boat, paddle and water, it was a question of what next? Frank passed me the knotter's encyclopedia, *The Ashley Book of Knots*, containing 3,800 uses for string and rope: Butchers' Knots, Surgeons' Knots, the Double Oysterman Knot, the Three-legged Race Knot, the Alpine Butterfly Knot . . .

'How many of these have you tied?' I asked.

'All of them.'

'Do you remember how to do every one?'

'*Ashley* is like a cookery book with recipes,' he said. 'It's there if I need it.'

But just as the International Guild of Knot-tyers refer to

Ashley, so some people refer to them. In particular, the police. Frank told me about a dead body that was found in a theatre. The corpse was trussed up in ropes and death was caused by a fall from the balcony. It all pointed to murder, and to see whether the ropes had any clues, the Yard called in the Guild.

But the dead man was a scenery shifter, and the ropes were tied with scenery shifter's knots. People don't commit suicide only with a noose.

CONTACT
Nigel Harding
Secretary
The International Guild of Knot-tyers
3 Walnut Tree Meadows
Stonham Aspal
Stowmarket
Suffolk IP14 6DF

150

The *Land of the Giants* Appreciation Society

On the platform at Stoke-on-Trent railway station is a peculiar piece of stone – a statue of a human hand. Posed like the symbol of Ulster, it is remarkable because of the size: the fingers are the length of legs and the thumb as long as an arm. Seeing it for the first time, a passenger might say, 'How ugly', or 'How interesting', or 'I wonder what that means?' But as the train drew into the station, the sight of the statue woke me from my thoughts with a jolt. To think I saw it *then*, while I had been considering *that place*. For when it passed my window, I had been reflecting on a world where a hand of those dimensions would be common – and would not be made of stone. Imagine the plight of being gripped by such a hand, held like a doll, having your breath squeezed away by thumb and forefinger . . .

'Intelligence can still beat the giants,' said Jeannette Georgala, as I sat opposite her in a London pub. It was a few days before my train journey. 'Being a small person in that sort of world doesn't mean you're weak.' She thought that there was a moral to be learned: that little people in society *can* succeed, despite the odds. She added, 'I always support the underdog at sporting events.'

Jeannette is the founder of the *Land of the Giants* Appreciation Society, which honours the series originally shown on TV from 1967 to 1970, when Jeannette was a little girl. The *Land of the Giants* tells the story of a sub-orbital spaceliner, the *Spindrift*, which passes through a mysterious space-warp on a routine flight from Los Angeles to London. The ship crash-lands in a world which is very like earth, though not quite as technically advanced – it would compare to 1950s America. There is, though, what you might call an *enormous* difference between this place and earth. 'What do we tell the passengers?' says the ship's captain, when he sees a pussy cat as big as an elephant.

'People try to make fun of it,' said Jeannette. 'They say, "Why do you want to watch a children's show?" But when I'm watching *Land of the Giants*, I think I'm watching a ballet. There's such a fluidity to the action.'

Though one can find precursors to the show, including *Gulliver's Travels* and *Jack and the Beanstalk*, nothing else has so fully explored the theme. We are talking about a world where crossing the road means you need a leg-up to climb the kerb; where you might be captured by a butterfly collector; where a giant might lash you to a stake and throw hoopla rings over your head.

'It's still a dream of mine to own a genuine prop from the series,' said Jeannette, as she spoke about the society meeting when members brought along items they'd acquired from novelty shops, including a larger than life safety-pin and a pencil that was longer than a spear.

As chance would have it, the *Land of the Giants* is being repeated by Channel 4 at the time of writing this piece, so perhaps it doesn't seem unusual that there is a fan club. But remember that Jeannette kept the torch burning during the twenty-odd years the show was *off* the air. Even today, all those years after first seeing little people use ropes of cotton to climb the furniture, she confesses to spending around forty hours a week on *Land of the Giants*-related activities: compiling the fanzine, plotting the careers of the show's stars, establishing contact with other fans. 'I love the show so much I want to give something back to it,' she said.

As for me, if I reflect long and hard on the show, particularly when it's late at night and I'm tired, my mind starts playing tricks. Many of the people I have met call their hobbies a drug, but the *Land of the Giants* can *really* be like a consciousness-altering substance: think about it for a while and you start to stare at paperclips, coins, pens – whatever is at hand – and you begin to imagine a change in relative size.

I have looked at a screwdriver and wondered how many people it would take to lift it . . .

CONTACT
Giants Log
11 Kimbolton Court
Kimbolton Road
Bedford MK40 2PH

The Letter-box Study Group

There is a problem which might be called 'letter-box amnesia'. It's that experience of walking up the road to post a letter . . . and afterwards being unable to recall actually putting it in the box. 'You must have posted it,' you tell yourself. 'You *did*.' You hope.

The amnesia wouldn't happen if we took more notice of the boxes themselves. One group of people would *never* take a letter-box for granted: the 700 members of the Letter-box Study Group, whose aim is to accumulate and disseminate information on all aspects of letter-boxes. I went to meet founder-member Ron Hall, who has collected photographs of letter-boxes from all over the world – yellow boxes from France, blue 'trashcan' boxes from the USA and hundreds of red boxes from the UK. Like many within the group, he has carried out a complete survey of his home town, photographing every box on the streets of Leamington Spa. 'It's just one of those things,' he told me. 'I'm a born collector. The idea of having something to look for is important. I carry my camera everywhere, in case I see an interesting box.'

Letter-boxes are more interesting than might be supposed. Take the problem of snails. 'There was a case of a letter-box being removed from service because of that particular menace,' said Ron. He showed me an envelope which was intact but for a missing semicircular section along one edge, as if a tiny pastry-cutter had been applied directly to the paper: a snail's teeth had been at work. This led us to talk of the damage that another species, human beings, can cause to the mail, and Ron told me about the Scottish Elizabeth II box. When Queen Elizabeth was crowned, a new box was introduced throughout the UK bearing an EIIR cipher. This offended Scottish Nationalists, because the first Queen Elizabeth was never on the Caledonian throne. Scottish protesters bombed a box, so a special Scottish symbol was introduced showing no cipher, just a crown.

Although no letter-box enthusiast would ever bomb a box, members do have likes and dislikes. The most controversial design is the so-called 'Model K', a modern box which has a functional, twenty-first-century look. 'Lots of traditionalists hate the Model K,' said Ron, 'but I like it. It has a good-sized posting slot, which is well protected from the weather, and instead of having to insert numbers to indicate the next collection, it has a dial.' He handed me a miniature of the box, but I found myself on the side of the traditionalists. The little Model K reminded me of a pepper-pot you would find in a cheap café. Yet it was odd to have these sort of thoughts at all; never before had I held *opinions* about letter-boxes.

After a discussion on the history of the letter-box from 1852 to the present day – covering early Channel Island hexagonal pillars, as well as the fluted boxes of the Victorian era and curiosities such as the Rochdale box with a gas-lamp on top – it was time to go. As my taxi went through Leamington Spa, the letter-boxes we passed seemed somehow *fresh*: the red bolder, the boxes more prominent. I was noticing differences in shape ...

I *used* to suffer from letter-box amnesia.

CONTACT
Sally Jones
Secretary
The Letter-box Study Group
43 Miall Road
Hall Green
Birmingham B28 9BS

The Lewis Carroll Society

There is a special sort of fancy-dress party at which people dress exactly as they normally do, in their ordinary, everyday clothes. Nobody told me that I would be attending a party of this particular kind, and so it was that I turned up dressed from toe to head as the Mad Hatter, complete with a 10/6 label in my stovepipe hat, while everyone else was in suits and ties. Of course, the concept of an un-fancy-dress party would be of interest to the Hatter's creator, Lewis Carroll, for Carroll is the man who invented the un-birthday party, to be celebrated 364 times a year. And to celebrate all of this man's achievements, from his deductions in symbolic logic to his dabbles in surreal literature, a Lewis Carroll Society has been formed. The society's Christmas party was a kind of wonderland in its own right ...

And right from the start, I thought there was something, well, a little *curious* about the way in which Ellis Hillman, the president, introduced me to some of the members: 'Here's a geologist. And here's a geologist. And here's a theologian. It's all the same thing ...'

154

Eventually, I found myself chatting to Selwyn Goodacre, the society's chairman. 'I have about 1,500 copies of *Alice*, mostly in English,' he said. 'And I also have some of Carroll's mathematical works, such as *An Elementary Treatise on Determinants*.'

'Can you read it?' I asked.

'No,' he replied, 'not a word.'

Someone who probably could read the entire *Treatise* was Toby, a member who was trained as a mathematician and philosopher. He has the extraordinary habit of referring to obscure texts, which I had never heard of, and adding after the titles, 'which presumably you're familiar with'. He was also at pains to assure me that Queen Victoria was *not* the author of the *Alice* books. 'Two computer programmers in California,' he told me, 'analysed the style of Carroll and decided that it was exactly the same as that of Queen Victoria. But that's nonsense – look at the dates.' He told me that Alice was published in 1865 and Prince Albert died in 1861. 'The idea that a woman who was embarking on a forty-year mope could have written *Alice in Wonderland* is quite preposterous,' said Toby. I told him that I would I do my best to allay the fears of all my readers who were worried that Lewis Carroll was the former Queen of England.

The next person I met was Charles Lovett, chairman of the North American branch of the society. In his remarkable collection of Carrolliana is a pornographic novel called *Blue Alice*, featuring a girl 'with breasts as white as whipped cream'. I flicked through the pages and noted the following variation on Carroll's children's classic: 'Her ear throbbed and pulsed around the great thrusting thing that Horatio H. Dumpty was shoving into it . . .'

Deciding it was time to move on, I turned to Edward Wakeling, who has translated *Alice in Wonderland* into code. Edward also admits to owning a box of costumes (one hare, one hatter and two tweedles) and is particularly fascinated by Carroll's use of the number forty-two, which recurs throughout the collected works. 'Once you know about forty-two, I'm afraid it'll be with you for the rest of your life,' he said.

Passing amongst the members, I heard about the Dutch woman who had collected an album of *Alice* quotes from the *Financial Times*; about the use of *Alice* imagery to advertise toilet paper; about the work of experimental fiction whose every tenth word comes from *Alice*; and about the semaphore version of *Jabberwocky*. And as all these facts came thick and fast, and faster and thicker, and thicker and faster, everything seemed to blur.

'Wake up,' someone said. 'Why, what a long sleep you've had.'

'Oh, I've had such a curious dream about a very strange party,' I replied. 'At least, I *think* it was a dream . . .'

CONTACT
Sarah Stanfield
Little Folly
105 The Street
Willesborough
Ashford
Kent TN24 ONB

Limbo-dancing

After 'Kilroy was here', the most widely used piece of lavatory graffiti is 'Beware limbo-dancers'. When I met Della McKenzie, who has worked as a professional limbo-dancer all around the world, she confirmed that people often ask her whether she gets into toilets without paying. In principle, I suppose she could save a penny or two – because in her time she has limboed under a bar that was just 10 inches from the floor; while one man she knows has gone even lower, managing 7 inches. 'But he's male,' she said. 'He's got no boobs.'

Della set up the limbo-bar in her front room: She passed me a glass of Jamaica rum and orange to give me confidence, and she put on a cassette of Caribbean music. 'Hot! Hot! Hot!' went the lyrics of the song, and I took off my shoes. I was ready for my first attempt at the anti-high jump.

If you stretch your legs too wide under the bar, you will lose control, topple over and probably fall on your back. I know this from experience. But if you have your legs too close together, you'll never get under. Della also told me to avoid advancing my feet in rhythm to the music: the lower heights are attained by easing oneself continually forward, without jerking.

I tried many times. My chest went under, my head went under – and I was desperate to straighten up as soon as possible. Though, when I reached the other side, I didn't exactly spring up. I creaked up, clutching my back. I am afraid that I could go no lower than 3 foot 6, the second rung of the bar. Della told me I shouldn't be ashamed. Even people who are extremely fit, like footballers and boxers, can find limbo difficult – it requires such a general flexibility. All I could do was watch her at work: she went under, she trembled her hands for extra showmanship and, as she came up, her head straightened itself smoothly and effortlessly.

I guess I'll still be paying in the gents, then.

CONTACT
Della McKenzie
Tel: 081 689 0549 (home)
or
c/o The Norman Jackson Agency
35 Seafield Road
Arnos Grove
London N11 1BR
Tel: 081 368 0516

The Maledicta Society

I feel like running my finger up and down the symbols keys and making statements like !#"£?$%'!&*@!! and *&'%$£!!"£$, or worse still, !??##!!"&!@!£($*%!!. There is no such coyness in the journal of the International Maledicta Society, and if you're offended by swearing and X-rated vocabulary, then *do not* join this organization. Taking its name from the Latin *male* (meaning bad) and *dicta* (meaning words), the society is concerned with the academic study of abusive language, curses, imprecations and general verbal nastiness. This is what you will see if you run your eye down the contents page of the society's journal:

> Talking Dirty in Cuban Spanish
> Swearing in Australian Football
> Black Excremental Poetry
> Greek Fist-Phallus Gestures
> Glossary of Fart Euphemisms
> Elementary Georgian Obscenity
> Offensive Rock Band Names – a Linguistic Taxonomy
> Pet Names for Breasts and Other Naughty Body Parts . . .

The Maledicta Society was established by Dr Reinhold Aman, an American linguistics scholar, who sees it as his life's mission to collect and analyse every obscenity ever uttered by man. This quest to put his ear in the gutter began in 1965, when Dr Aman was translating an obscure nineteenth-century Bavarian text. He came across a sentence which, he says, jumped out and struck him like a lightning bolt: 'I'm going to hit you over the head with a spoon, you monkey.' Dr Aman wondered why a person would call another person a monkey. That night, he made a list of other animal insults: dog, pig, rat, snake. Then he went on to food-related offensiveness: you meatball, you cabbage head, you silly sausage. Once he got going he couldn't stop, making lists of insults relating to professions, nationalities, body parts, etc. 'I found it very intellectually stimulating,' he says. Here, after years of study, are some of his favourite curses:

Yiddish 'May all your teeth fall out, except one – so that you can have a toothache.'

American South 'Yo' breath is so foul it would knock a buzzard off a manure wagon.'

Ghanaian 'You smell like a white man's armpit.'

American 'He couldn't track a buffalo in four feet of snow!'

Swahili 'God curse you, and the curse is that you be what you already are!'

Thai 'Talking to you is like playing violin to a water buffalo.'

Reading the Maledicta journal gives fascinating insights into the slang used by certain social groups and professions. Amongst medical ancillary staff in San Francisco you will find the use of a term like 'code brown' – which is the name given to a copious, foul-smelling bowel movement in an inappropriate place (bed, floor, corridor). The term is modelled after the official codes – 'code red' for fire, and 'code blue' for cardiac arrest. (The staff also use 'code yellow' for urinary incontinence.) If we change profession and place to focus on servicemen in a Kentucky artillery battalion, we find that there are expressions to describe people who are too genteel, or too crude, for the group. Thus, of a rather uppity girl, it might be said, 'She thinks she shits strawberry ice-cream,' or, 'She thinks her shit comes out wrapped in cellophane.' While a very crude man might be described as 'the kind of guy who'd fart in the bathtub and bite the bubbles as they come up'.

During a phone conversation I had with Dr Aman, he tried to summarize the results of his investigations. In general, he told me, Anglo-Saxon cultures prefer insults dealing with excrement and body parts, while Catholic countries are fond of blasphemy. Cultures of the Middle and Far East have a penchant for ancestor insults. There are also curses which make sense only within the context of a particular culture; in parts of New Guinea, for example, the worst thing you can call someone is a yam thief. But Dr Aman admits to a particular liking for Yiddish insults: 'A good Yiddish insult will begin in a way that gets you to drop your defences – and then poke you right in the eye,' he said. So, you might have an expression like: 'May you have three shiploads of gold – and it should not be enough to pay your doctor's bill,' or, 'May you become famous – they should name a disease after you.'

According to Dr Aman, the people who have the worst insults in the world are the Hungarians and the Romanians. The inhabitants of those two countries utter curses so vile, so poisonous, that if I want this book to escape impounding by the police, I'd better not repeat them here. Should you wish to pollute your vocabulary by using these expressions, I suggest you contact the leading source of effluent, Dr Aman himself.

CONTACT
Dr Reinhold Aman
Maledicta
PO Box 14123
Santa Rosa
CA 95402-6123
USA
Tel: 0101 707 523 4761

Marbles

From Ash Wednesday to Good Friday it's marbles season in Sussex. There's the rolling of spheres and the downing of beers at the Black Dog, the Red Lion, the Half Moon and the Bush. But on the season's last day, go to the Greyhound. The biggest marble of all – no less than the blue-and-green one, the planet – may be said to be at stake in the game; for every Good Friday, the Greyhound at Tinsley Green hosts the marbles championships of the world. One Sunday, I went for beer and sandwiches there to meet Sam McCarthy, the secretary of the British Marbles Board of Control.

He told me that at Tinsley Green the game goes back centuries. There is a legend that in Elizabethan times two young men were rivals for the hand of a local maiden; they tried to settle the matter by competing against each other in various sports – archery, falconry and the like – but always came out equal. In marbles there has to be a winner, so it was the obvious solution to their problem.

The object of the game is straightforward: to knock marbles off a raised, 6-foot-diameter ring, using your tolley or shooting marble. The best players can put topspin, backspin and sidespin on to their tolleys, and just like snooker professionals, they can manoeuvre themselves into the best position for the next shot. But it came as a surprise to me that it's hard to master the simplest of marbles' skills – namely, the flicking of the thumb.

'There's an approved way of doing it,' said Sam, 'which gives you maximum control over shots.' So I did as instructed, and with the tip of my index finger I cradled the tolley on the joint of the thumb. I flicked. And the tolley dribbled out.

Sam wasn't surprised. 'Why *should* you have a strong thumb?' he asked. 'Unless you're a marbles player, you won't have any need of strength.'

He recommended a series of exercises. I could start by flicking a marble against the skirting board at home. Then I could change the angle at which I flicked, and then I could flick from further back. If I kept up the training, there might come a day when I'd be as strong as one of the greats of the game, Jim 'Atomic Thumb' Longhurst, who could shatter a beer glass with a single tolley. Jim believed in constantly flicking his thumb – even when he didn't have a marble – to keep it in shape. But he did not take as much care of his equipment as the fabled Wee Willie Wright, a 5 foot 2 Welshman, who had a hot-water bottle specially sewn into his overcoat to keep his thumb warm and to help the circulation.

Realizing I wasn't going to be good enough to compete for several years, I asked Sam whether he'd seen any moments of drama in marbles. He reminisced about various classic encounters, but the story that intrigued me concerned the sand, the game's 'baize', which is sprinkled over the surface of the ring. 'I've seen a time when a marble was on the edge of the ring, held on by just a grain,' he said. 'People were stamping on the ground to try to make it fall off.'

But for Sam the marbles themselves are of interest, as much as the game. 'I love marbles, I collect them,' he said. 'I have a demi-john full of them on my windowsill. It's the nearest I'll ever get to having a stained-glass window.' Though he mentioned that materials other than glass have been used for marbles: stone, clay, metal. And that isn't all. 'In the 1950s,' said Sam, 'a lot were made out of old toilet bowls. I've got about half a dozen of those.'

CONTACT
Sam McCarthy
Secretary The British Marbles Board of Control
c/o The Greyhound Pub
Radford Road
Tinsley Green
Sussex RH10 3NS

Masks

The mask enclosed, rather than fitted, my face. I had a sense of being inside a box, or a sweaty room. It made the eyeholes somehow reverse direction and purpose: they were *peepholes*, not for me to look out but for another, a woman, to spy in. She too wore a mask, something like a crescent moon, or a wan Mr Punch. As she stared at me, peeped at me, came closer, glimpsed my nakedness, I backed away; but unlike a room, from which you could run out and escape a voyeur, I carried my peepholes with me. I backed into a corner and it seemed that my body needed angularity. My elbows stuck out. Needed anxiety. My fingers were spikes. Perhaps here, in the corner, cowering, shivering, my state reflected my mask: with its mouth paralysed in the shape of an 'O', it resembled rather closely 'The Scream', the well-known painting by Munch.

After the audience had clapped and I'd taken off my mask, Brige Bidell said that my technique wasn't quite right. I had interpreted what the mask should be, whereas the whole point was to allow the mask to take over, to bypass the brain. She recounted an experience of her own which had convinced her of the power of masks. 'Once,' she said, 'I was organizing a masked ball. I had the choice of all the masks and I picked one that looked like a cat. But about half-way through the evening I started feeling a great sadness coming over me, for no apparent reason. Then I went and looked in a mirror, and I noticed something I hadn't seen before: the cat's face was sad. I thought, Wow!'

She couldn't explain that experience, except to say that she believes every piece of matter holds information. 'I think masks have a life of their own,' she said. 'Even when I'm making them, they just somehow evolve. I don't consciously design them.'

I watched two other participants at Brige's workshop, a man and a woman. The woman had a flirty mask. The man's was more ambiguous: some people thought he looked cocksure, but I saw him as a person who would blunder through, rather helpless, meaning no harm, innocent enough to have some hope. The woman attracted him, swayed her hips, made him follow her, then walked away. This was repeated around the room.

Although you could regard Brige's mask workshops as drama classes, where roles do not come from play scripts but from papier mâché, she believes that participants can touch deep inside themselves. Put on a mask and you may reveal the personality kept hidden behind your *normal* mask. Maybe you'll see the dark side: I can murder, I can be cruel, I can steal, I can lie ... Brige's intention is that we will reach a better understanding of ourselves and others. And we can always pull off the mask if we feel we're going too far. 'Something so artificial gets to the truth about things,' she said.

And my hidden self? All right, I admit it. A woman *did* remark that my performance had reminded her of an imbecile.

CONTACT
Brige Bidell
6 Shaftesbury House
Trinity Street
London SE1 4JF
Tel: 071 378 7933

Mazes and Labyrinths

There is a brick path on the village green at Saffron Walden, inlaid like marquetry into the grass. To walk it is to walk a very long and very winding road. I would call it a second cousin to a spiral: you start at the edge and let the whirlpool suck you in. Yet it is not a spiral, nor a spiral's sibling, nor even a first cousin. It has a different dizziness *en route*. I must invoke fairgrounds: the corkscrew of the helter-skelter, the up and down of the roller-coaster, the direction changes of the dodgems. Yet somehow, for all this disorder, it manages to resolve itself and take you to its core. This is a labyrinth.

I did not say maze. A maze has dead ends; the path at Saffron Walden is unnecessarily long, but it never once leads you astray.

The person who taught me the difference between a maze and a labyrinth walked one step behind me on those bricks. He was Jeff Saward, one of the country's foremost authorities on circuitous routes. Jeff runs Caerdroia, which will signify little to you unless you speak Welsh. It is a pun, meaning both City of Turnings and City of Troy – the latter being a continental name for a maze or labyrinth. As you will have guessed, Caerdroia is a society for people who would like to hunt minotaurs for a living and spend their holidays at Hampton Court.

Jeff told me that he clips out magazine advertisements like the one for financial services: 'Find your way through the money maze'; that he keeps records of psychological experiments on animal learning: the old rat-in-a-maze test; and that he stores videos of TV programmes which are in any way labyrinthine. 'One day,' said Jeff, 'a video of Channel 4's *The Crystal Maze* will be an historic document.' Even Christmas presents from his wife can be related to Caerdroia – she gives him children's games, such as 'Heroes of the Maze' (enter at your peril . . .).

Behind all this lies a serious interest in history and archaeology. Labyrinths and mazes are ancient symbols which have appeared in virtually all human societies. Their patterns were etched on Syrian pottery in 1300 BC and on rock faces in pre-Columbian North America; Scandinavian fishermen used the symbols to give magical protection against trolls; and the Romans used them as graffiti. Where there are humans, you will find mazes and labyrinths. Why, though?

Jeff believes people are fascinated by the distortion of space and time. How long will you be trapped inside? You do not know. Which direction will your journey take? You do not know.

Some members of Caerdroia have built labyrinths on the sides of hills to increase the sense of confusion. 'My centre of gravity changes so rapidly when I'm running along one of these hillside mazes,' writes a member in Caerdroia's magazine, 'that I don't know where I am.'

So, you have to take the path and follow it wherever it goes. The path, of course, can easily become a metaphor for life. There is one member of Caerdroia who uses mazes and labyrinths as problem-solving tools: he sits and stares at the designs, asks spiritual questions and relates the twists and turns to the turmoils of his own existence. Jeff keeps an open mind on the effectiveness of mazes when used for such purposes. 'If you stare closely at them, I'm sure you'll see all sorts of funny things,' he said.

Caerdroia offers many other approaches to the subject. It may be that your liking is mathematical analysis: one member has calculated a formula, involving *pi*, to determine the length of a labyrinth, given a certain path width and a certain radius. Or maybe you'd like to use the symbols for artistic inspiration, perhaps to write a story with a labyrinthine plot? Or maybe you are interested in modern developments in maze technology, such as mazes with time-dependent doors that open only at certain intervals, or randomly.

Jeff himself goes on field trips. Prior to the fall of Communism, he went to inspect mazes 30 miles from Leipzig. 'We were followed by the Stasi for several days,' he said. Another time, he donned full caving gear and went down a disused mineshaft in Surrey – a six-hour dangerous climb. After several hours' walking along underground galleries, he saw a chalk drawing of a labyrinth, probably sketched by a miner. Was it worth it? 'Oh, yeah,' he said. 'I have the only photographs.'

Jeff and I were at the end of a much safer pilgrimage: the Saffron Walden labyrinth. We had walked a mile, crammed into an area 35 yards across. It seemed an appropriate moment to ask how his interest in mazes and labyrinths had begun. 'It was seventeen years ago,' he said. He happened to be in Winchester and went out for a stroll. 'I was near a ruined chapel and I came across a strange pattern marked out on the top of a hill . . .'

You never know where a path might lead.

CONTACT
Jeff Saward
Caerdroia
53 Thundersley Grove
Thundersley
Benfleet
Essex SS7 3EB
Tel: 0268 751915

The Meccanomen

There are people who have memorized the part number for every part produced in the entire Meccano range since the toy's inception in 1901. Pick any one of the hundreds of gears, brackets, strips with holes and axle rods and they are able to comment without a moment's hesitation: this is part 20a, the 1916 version of the 2-inch pulley with turned lugs; or that is part 30b, the bevel gear with twenty-four teeth. Sometimes they can give a historical perspective, pointing out that part 159 was only around from 1927 to 1935. Or that part numbers changed: 117 became 168d; 170 became 130a; and, most intriguing of all, 217a (1¼ inch) became 24a (1³/₈ inch).

These are not ordinary men, but Meccanomen; and in 1990 they formed themselves into an international society.

'I wanted to make my retirement interesting,' said John Westwood, the editor of *International Meccanoman* magazine, when I visited him in Streatley. We were talking in a room devoted to his pastime, surrounded by working models of water mills, traction engines and numerous other mechanisms with axles and gears – all having that sprayed with machine-gun bullets look that characterizes matter in the Meccano universe.

When John bought himself a No. 10 set in 1974, it was the first time he had touched Meccano since he built a human skeleton in 1936. Yet a gap of nearly forty years is not unusual in a Meccano career, and in the International Society of Meccanomen wise old friends of the little bolt quite happily exchange exploded drawings with youngsters who could be their grandchildren.

Now, when I was a child, I was never much taken by Meccano. I can remember putting together a few models with a junior set – with its girders of safe yellow plastic and its unswallowable blue nuts and bolts – but it never grabbed my imagination; when it came to models, I preferred Plasticine. But from my discussion with John, I have learned that you need not build *any models at all* to be a Meccanoman, for he has written a booklet purely on Meccano collecting. The idea is to snap up job lots of Meccano at jumble sales. You may also strike it lucky in the lofts and attics of elderly friends and relatives. 'Meccano parts have a distinctive aesthetic quality which makes them a pleasure to sort and examine,' he writes in his booklet. Though he advises that this should always be done on a tray with sides about half an inch high; then, any grub screw or other small part which falls accidentally from your fingers will not roll on to the floor and vanish in a dark corner. 'If this does happen', he says, 'rummage with a magnet.'

Undoubtedly, I am skewing this article, for the main interest of Meccanomen is to use the stuff – to build the racing cars, cranes and thousands of other models that Meccano makes possible. So before I finish, I shall mention my favourite application. It was devised by a member whose new spectacle

167

frames were late in arriving at the optician's. I don't need to tell you what he did next, do I?

CONTACT
Don Sawyer
Treasurer
International Society of Meccanomen
32 West Street
Marlow
Bucks SL7 2NB
Tel: 0628 483331
or
John Westwood
Editor *International Meccanoman*
The Malt House
Church Lane
Streatley
Reading
Berks RG8 9HT
Tel: 0491 873001

Mediumship

'I've always been aware of the spirit world,' said Dell Round. 'Even as a little girl I saw people who looked just like us.'

'So how did you know they were spirits?' I asked.

'I didn't.' She realized the truth only when she saw her godmother, whom she knew belonged in the grave.

For the past ten years, Dell Round has been running the British School of Mediumship in Swansea – an academy where, you might say, the ouija board meets the blackboard. Dell teaches all aspects of communication between this world and the next, including trance mediumship (where, as she puts it, 'the spirit uses the medium's mind as a typewriter') through to psychic art (where the spirit moves a pencil in an artist's hand). 'Anyone can be a medium, in principle,' she told me.

Although I didn't have the time to attend a full week-long programme of studies, I dropped by the school one afternoon. Sixteen trainees had reached the 'Doris Stokes' part of the course: one person would go up front, on to a stage, and act as an intermediary between the spirit world and the rest of class. Some of this mediumship remains in my memory:

FIRST TRAINEE: The name Beryl is coming to me. A young woman. She's got plaits.

MAN IN AUDIENCE: My mother's named Beryl.

FIRST TRAINEE: Did she die young?

MAN IN AUDIENCE: She's still alive.

And then:

SECOND TRAINEE: I see a young boy with science-fiction posters on the wall. Can anyone take that?

WOMAN IN AUDIENCE: Yes.

SECOND TRAINEE: He wasn't all that strong.

WOMAN IN AUDIENCE: No, he was strong.

SECOND TRAINEE: (Pause) I'm telling you how he felt, not how he looked.

And then again:

THIRD TRAINEE: I've picked up the image of a farm labourer.

DELL: (Coming forward) Speak to the audience, in front of you.

THIRD TRAINEE: But the spirit's behind me.

I decided to play along and went up on stage: I let my imagination flow. The first thing to come to mind was a name, Robert. Then a man with a beard. A red beard. Then a Scottish connection. Then birds . . . caged birds. A caged bird set free. Then drink. Alcohol. Uncorking a bottle. Some problem with feeding, with diet . . .

Now, when I mentioned the red beard, a woman from the audience put up her hand. She said the beard and Robert meant something to her. With each additional piece of information, she nodded and said yes, though she didn't elaborate. When I dried up and stepped down, she caught my arm. 'The man with the red beard was the father of a friend of mine, Robert,' she whispered. 'Robert was my lover for ten years, but it didn't work out. We used to go to Scotland together. And he used to draw pictures of birds on stones. He called me the bird who got away. He's now hitting the bottle and not eating properly. I still see him sometimes.'

A coincidence? Or was the woman making it up? Maybe I should just start boasting about my powers of clairvoyance. Medium? I was excellent.

CONTACT
The British School of Mediumship
Tel: 0792 460620 or 0792 646545

Model Rocketry

If you were now to stare at nothing but pointed objects for half an hour – packets of needles, sharp pencils, marital aids – you might acquire an after-image on the retina so that, wherever you looked, you would have a haunting impression of the inside of Trevor Sproston's shed. Trevor is one of the country's leading model-rocketeers – his vehicles blast off and they leave the earth. Yes, these rockets are small, but their principles are pure Cape Canaveral.

Until 1988 the British government took the view that private rocketry was a crime – an unusual position, since even Iron Curtain countries were happy for their fettered citizens to build *models* that broke the chains of gravity. Perhaps the British just don't like to be reminded of the V2. It means that in Britain today, model rocketry is underdeveloped. There is no official national society for rocketeers, but instead just a loose association of individuals and local groups who gather together for competitions and events. But should you want to break into rocketry, Trevor is one of the best contacts. 'I'm a space-race baby,' he said. 'I've been into this since I was a kid.'

Trevor's rocket factory, or his garden shed in Letchworth, sets the right atmosphere for space exploration. On a shelf, I noticed a model of Robby the Robot from the film *Forbidden Planet*, as well as another robot, the one that used to say 'Affirmative' in *Lost in Space*. These rubbed shoulders with the three-legged Martian from *Quatermass and the Pit* and the Ice Warrior from *Dr Who*. 'I don't know who came up with the idea for the Ice Warrior's hands,' said Trevor – I looked at those terrible tongs – 'but he can't exactly pick his nose with those things, can he?' Aside from such monsters, it was rockets, rockets, rockets.

Although Trevor has made replicas of standard designs, like Saturn Fives, I was more interested in his own creations, especially a series of models based upon 'national characteristics'. So, there was the Islamic rocket, essentially a minaret in space; and the German rocket, black, stark and efficient. There was also the British Victorian rocket, like the Albert Memorial. And Trevor mentioned some future designs: the Russian, like St Basil's; the American, like the Empire State Building; and the Italian, like the Leaning Tower of Pisa. 'I could make the Eiffel Tower fly,' he said.

Model rocket designs do often embody a strong element of

humour. Trevor has seen a flying toilet (with a man sitting on it), flying stepladders and flying stoves. I asked the obvious question. 'Yes, all sorts of flying dicks,' he replied.

When it comes to payloads, such as model astronauts, people have been known to send up Garfields, but there is a code of ethics that nobody should launch a pet or any living creature. Not much of a gerbil would survive an acceleration of 20g.

So, with Trevor telling me about possible speeds of 300–400 mph, and possible altitudes of 14,000 feet, he drove me to a field. The model he thought he'd demonstrate was a flying saucer, about 10 inches in diameter.

We stood by his mission control, the launch box that sends an electrical current to the motors. There was a fizzing sound. The saucer went straight up, and then came straight down. It was in the air for less than ten seconds and went to a height of 50 feet. Well, I know I only wanted a taster, and I know that this was a short-range vehicle, but it seemed to me you could get more fun from shaking up a lemonade bottle. Trevor wasn't surprised by this reaction. A non-rocketeer, who hasn't had the pleasure of building a vehicle, will typically say, 'Does it just go up and down, then?' To which Trevor's standard answer remains, 'If it just went up and stayed there, it would look very silly indeed.'

CONTACT
Trevor Sproston
180 Icknield Way
Letchworth
Herts SG6 4AE
Tel: 0462 686134

The Monarchist League

'The Monarchist League isn't pressing for America to become a monarchy,' said Donald Foreman, their secretary. 'But people forget that America does have a royal family – the former Hawaiian monarchy. And there are some people who would like it back.'

Wherever a monarch once reigned – not only in Hawaii, but also in Romania, Bulgaria, Albania, Uganda, Brazil, or any other former kingdom – the Monarchist League would like a monarch back. So they will note with the greatest of interest a recent poll in Germany showing 59.9 per cent in favour of the restoration of a Kaiser; or the news that feminists in Latvia are pressing for a woman to rule as Queen. 'I still haven't given up on Greece,' said Donald. 'Perhaps even Italy isn't a lost cause.' He told me that in 1946 a referendum in Italy revealed that 11 million people were in favour of retaining the monarchy, with 12 million against. 'But large parts of the country couldn't vote because they were under foreign occupation.' And with a smile he offered me a piece of Battenberg cake. 'It was the most royal cake I could find.' His smile broadened. 'Though I think I might have some Bourbon biscuits somewhere . . .'

The Monarchist League has been in existence since 1943, when it was established along quasi-chivalric lines. Obviously, the league could not have a president, so there was a chancellor; but also the treasurer was called the receiver-general. Today, it has about 1,000 members, including, I was surprised to discover, some members who support the principle of *absolute* monarchy. 'Yes, well, the fact is you can't say to someone, "Our monarchy is all right but yours isn't,"' said Donald. 'In the Middle East, it works rather well. And there are certainly Russians who would like an absolute monarchy – it's part of the Russian psyche.'

Donald found it difficult to say why the principle of monarchy was such a fundamental part of his psyche. 'It's just something I've had with me. It's difficult to know when it began. Perhaps because my father was on duty at the Coronation as a civil servant.'

I mentioned the troubles of the House of Windsor, but he brushed these aside. 'You shouldn't see individual failings as making the institution any less valid,' he said. He recounted the principal arguments in favour of a monarchy: a monarch is a non-party-political head of state, and therefore can be supported by people of all points of view; furthermore, a monarch does not have to intrigue his or her way up the political ladder.

'Name me a country that's ceased to be a monarchy and is better off,' he asked. 'If the Kaiser had been there, would there have been a Hitler?' And, he added, 'A lot of people in Thatcher's era were glad she had to report to someone.'

CONTACT
The Monarchist League
BM 'Monarchist'
London WC1N 3XX

Mu Sum Ba

He calls his work Mu Sum Ba – the name of a South African dance rhythm – because the sound of the words relates to the beat of his heart. Thomas Christen told me this, and then, just as others would copy farmyard sounds or bird-song, he turned himself into a stethoscope – a mimicry of ventricles. So I ask you now to put your hand on your chest and, when you've found the rhythm, to pump words as well as blood – to say in time: 'Mu Sum Ba, Mu Sum Ba . . .'

Thomas Christen's Mu Sum Ba workshops are about *poly-rhythms*: the combination of two or more separate rhythmic structures into one overall whole. The workshop begins simply enough. You sit cross-legged and start tapping out a double-time rhythm on one knee. All right, I thought, I can handle this. Then, without stopping the first rhythm, you have to tap a triple-time on the other knee. Rather more difficult, but by no means impossible: the brain recognizes that the two and the three have a lowest common denominator of six, and you soon produce a rhythmic pattern which allocates the right fractions of time to each knee. But when Thomas made us stand and requested that we move our feet in a rhythmic dance step – somewhat reminiscent of the Shadows' famous stage walk – while clapping in a second rhythm and making Zulu vocal sounds in a third, my brain turned to liquid and gushed like a geyser from the hole in my ear.

Everyone else was coordinated – but they had worked with Thomas before. My only rhythm was of repeated failure. I would get out of step, abandon the exercise, wait, re-enter and get out of step once more. And this was one of Thomas's easier workouts. I was informed that we could, if we wanted, make a polyrhythm of seven, nine and eleven beats. By this time, I was mentally dead-beat.

What is the purpose of Mu Sum Ba? It seems like a tongue-twister in body language. Or it might remind you of that child's game where you try to pat the head while also rubbing the stomach. But what does it add to the quality of life?

Thomas told me that anyone coming to a Mu Sum Ba workshop would increase their 'rhythmic consciousness'. He cited the example of someone who, prior to attending, hated the sounds of the city. After some Mu Sum Ba, the noises of the cars, the people and everything else suddenly became structured – as if the city was a concert. 'Rhythm isn't just a musical element; it's part of existence in general,' he said. 'Think of day following night. And the movement of the weeks, the months, the years. I want people to relate to rhythm.'

With that, he took me through a simpler exercise: drawing a triangle in the air with one hand and a circle in the air with the other. As you might imagine, my triangles were very circular and my circles were very triangular . . .

CONTACT
Thomas Christen
Green Hedges
Nash Street
Nr Hailsham
East Sussex BN27 4AA
Tel: 0825 872453

The Muzzle Loaders' Association

The shot was muffled by the ear protection I wore, so smell was the sense, not sound. Clouds of smoke billowed around the barrel and I had the whiff of the powder in my nostrils. Remember that odour of caps from a toy gun when you were a child? Only I was firing no toy.

'Your line was perfect,' said Alan Bell, my supervisor on the rifle range. 'It's just that you were a bit high.' When I rose from prone and looked through a long-range lens, I could see what he meant: the hole in the target was aligned in a vertical axis with the bull's-eye, but a couple of inches above the scoring circles. It is appropriate to say that had I been at Balaclava, I might, with a bit of luck, have dislodged a helmet.

For I had fired no ordinary rifle. I had used an 1853 Enfield, a type that saw service in the Crimea. If you draw back the cock, it isn't difficult to imagine the weapon defending the honour of the Empire against flashing sabres and charging cavalry. And more than 100 years later, the lock, stock and wrought-iron barrel are still in perfect working order.

I had gone to Bisley rifle range as a guest of the Muzzle

Loaders' Association – a group dedicated to firearms that have a loading ritual. First, you take your flask and pour the black grains down the barrel; next you drop in a bullet which has been lubricated with tallow and beeswax; and then you use the ramrod. Because of the antiquity, it's more endearing than loading a modern weapon, and also more relaxing, allowing a break of concentration between shots. But muzzle-loading can be physically demanding. Any lengthy session means that you're continually standing up and then lying down, loading and firing. 'I always sleep well after a muzzle-loading session,' said Alan.

The association's journal, *Black Powder*, is full of fascinating historical trivia. I read how in 1522 a Bavarian philosopher denounced gunpowder – anything to do with sulphur and fire just *had* to come from the devil. The said Bavarian even believed that tiny demons rode the bullets, sending them this way and that, spoiling the accuracy of a shot. He conceded that if the barrel were *rifled*, with an internal groove to make bullets spin, it would improve matters – but only because demons couldn't hang on to a spinning projectile.

'We're all basically amateur historians,' said Alan. 'It's a learning society as well as a shooting club.' He reminded me that during the Indian Mutiny there were rumours – probably untrue – that the British Army had employed an alternative to the tallow and beeswax lubricant I had been handling: namely, a mixture of cow and pig fat, greases to outrage both Hindus and Muslims.

It was time to lie down for another shot. I felt more confident with the gun and pressed it against my cheek for a firmer hold. This time I did better, scoring 'five at four o'clock' – that is, low down on the right-hand side of the fifth of the ten target rings. Respectable enough for a complete beginner, but a real sharpshooter using the same gun would expect to hit the bull's-eye three times out of four at 600 yards (six times the distance of my target).

Such accuracy requires a thorough understanding of how ambient conditions affect the projectile. Unlike a shot from a modern rifle, a muzzle-loader's bullet travels very slowly – through a lens, you can actually see it approach the target, like a bumblebee of metal – and the expert needs to know how factors such as humidity will affect the flight. 'But if you've had a bad day,' said Alan, 'you can always blame the gun.'

As we walked back to reload, Alan began talking about the

law and its treatment of muzzle-loading – a subject which irks the association, because an antique weapon is regarded in law as simply another firearm. 'It gets a bit ridiculous,' he said. 'Who's going to hold up a bank with a flintlock?' Certainly, as I rammed home another lubricated bullet, it struck me as unlikely that a bankrobber would fire one shot at the ceiling and say to the cashier, 'Could you hang on a minute while I reload?'

CONTACT
The Muzzle Loaders' Association of Great Britain
Membership Records Department
PO Box 154
Rickmansworth
Herts WD3 2GB
Tel: 0923 771398
Fax: 0923 771462

The Narrow Bandwidth Television Association

It was a black and white photograph of a human face, but the features were dissected by vertical lines, like one of those automated billboards at the moment when the slats have started to turn.

If I told you the picture was taken from a television screen, you would guess that atmospheric conditions had affected the broadcast, but the truth is that the lines would be there come what may. It would be wrong too to talk about broadcasts: the picture was transmitted no farther than the width of a room – and faces are the only images the set ever receives – images of members of the Narrow Bandwidth Television Association, a group which aims to promote the development, study and widespread use of *low-definition* TV. That is to say, the members build obsolete devices that cannot pick up signals from modern television stations. Their passion is mechanical television, as pioneered by John Logie Baird – technology abandoned in 1935 when cathode-ray tubes replaced spinning discs.

The group was founded by Douglas Pitt, a physics teacher (now retired), who was nostalgic for the very early days of television. 'I built my own TV when I was fifteen,' he told me, as he put one of his creations on the table – a set capable of receiving a picture the size of a cigarette card. Many years later, in 1975, Douglas put an advert in *Practical Wireless*, asking whether anyone else was still interested in Baird-style TV. 'A surprising number of people replied,' he said. 'They were reminiscing about the old days, saying they wished they'd bring mechanical television back again, in spite of the fact that the pictures weren't a patch on modern TV.'

Douglas told me that one of the men who got in touch had also built a mechanical TV as a teenager, but in his part of the country there was no electricity. To solve the problem, an electricity-generating turbine was hooked up to a tap, making a water-powered TV. 'When it was working,' said Douglas, 'you couldn't go to the lavatory – otherwise the picture went.'

Douglas sees building obsolete televisions as having a similar romanticism to driving steam locomotives. And even if the technology is outmoded, it can still improve, for the members are constantly striving to find better-quality thirty-two-line pictures. This leads to the paradox that digital-enhancement techniques that are state of the art may be applied to technology that went out with the ark. That isn't all. At the group's annual convention, when members transmit and receive their own faces, an astounding array of home-made TVs are put to work, combining rotating drums, tilted mirrors and goodness knows what else. Given the existence of the water-powered TV, you cannot even exclude the kitchen sink as a component part! 'Some of the devices you wouldn't recognize as televisions unless you were told,' said Douglas. You might think they were death-rays, or hypnotism machines, or pieces of modern sculpture.

Douglas admits that those who join the Narrow Bandwidth Television Association are the dedicated few. 'Essentially, we're a sect,' he said. Membership has never reached the 200 mark and a large chunk of members – about one-fifth of the total – is based in Holland. The Dutch interest is connected with the Nazi occupation, when all radio receivers were confiscated and it was illegal even to own a crystal set. Consequently, there is a yearning in the low countries for pre-war technology.

Douglas told me that at one exhibition organized by the Radio Retailers' Association, a boy of about fourteen approached the Narrow Bandwidth stall. The boy peered for a long while at the spinning disc of a mechanical TV, then he went away. But he came back. He kept on going away and coming back, and on his fourth visit to the stall, Douglas asked whether there was a question that he wanted to ask.

'Well, where's the cathode-ray tube?' asked the boy.

'There isn't one,' said Douglas.

'Cor,' said the boy, 'whatever will they think of next?'

CONTACT
D A Gentle
Treasurer
The Narrow Bandwidth Television Association
1 Sunny Hill
Milford
Belper
Derbyshire DE56 OQR
or:
D B Pitt
1 Burnwood Drive
Wollaton
Nottingham NG8 2DG

178

Narrow Bandwidth Television: The Sequel

'No matter what your age,' said Andrew Emmerson, 'there's some era of TV you've got a soft spot for.'

If you have just finished the previous entry, you'll know that the Narrow Bandwidth Television Association is devoted to obsolete television technology. The NBTVA is not the only organization with such an objective. There is also 405 Alive, a society concerned with the obsolete technology of the succeeding era – namely, black and white 405-line TV, the age of valves. A member of 405 Alive, though, has broader interests than a Narrow Bandwidth fan, because apart from an attachment to the technology of their chosen period of obsolescence, a 405 Aliver also hankers after the old programmes. 'For me,' said Andrew Emmerson, who runs the society, 'black and white is a totally viable medium. Nobody criticizes Charlie Chaplin.'

I was sitting in Andrew's lounge next to one of his proudest possessions: a pre-war set with a 5-inch screen and burr-walnut cabinet. In 1939, it would have cost twenty-nine guineas – about six weeks' wages. 'It still works,' he said. He added that it was quite possible to obtain replacement valves, for they continue to be made in China. 'Whereas when a modern TV goes wrong,' he said, 'the spare parts are unobtainable.'

Andrew said that he saw a magic in television which perhaps could not be understood by anyone under forty. 'In the 1950s,' he said, 'TV was like a forbidden fruit. It was only on for a few hours a day and your parents had to be fairly well off even to own a set.' It was a lost era, a time of going next door to the neighbours to watch *Andy Pandy* or the Coronation. 'Though I'm not attached to the period overall,' he said. 'People forget the butter that went rancid because you couldn't afford a fridge.'

We settled down to watch a video of black and white adverts from the 1950s and 1960s. In between the old white sun sign that was the symbol of Associated Rediffusion, were petrol adverts: 'The Esso sign means happy motoring', Bing Crosby singing 'You can be sure of Shell' and 'Getaway people get Supernational'. Then up popped Simon Dee advertising crisps. Followed by an old Sugar Frosties ad which suggested that if children ate their cereal they would get their sums right at school. 'You wouldn't be allowed to put out an advert like that today,' said Andrew. Every so often, the face of a has-been actor would crop up to promote a product. 'He was in *Z Cars*, wasn't he?' I said. Neither of us could remember his name.

Andrew passed me a stack of television yearbooks from the late 1950s and early 1960s. Here were the faces you don't see any more: Norman Vaughan, Hughie Green, Frank Ifield, Ronnie Carroll, the Springfields. The photographs, though in colour, were actually tinted black and whites, and so the skin tones were unnatural, morbid. Yet such books are much sought after. 'To get them without kids' scribbling in isn't so easy,' said Andrew.

405 Alive's magazine reflects the group's twin concerns with collecting old televisions and using them to watch old programmes. You might find a small ad offering for sale outdated set-top VHF aerials, and hard-to-find connectors and leads, as well as an article in praise of the interlude films like *The Potter's Wheel*, *The Kitten* and *London to Brighton in 4 Minutes*. 'Ah! What memories of those early days,' says the author of an article, 'when my family and I watched everything on a single-channel Pye set with a 9-inch screen.'

CONTACT
Andrew Emmerson
405 Alive
71 Falcutt Way
Northampton NN2 8PH

Origami (with feet, etc.)

It was a rogues' gallery of politicians: Hitler, Stalin, Castro, Nixon. Shame that Mao wasn't there – given his famous comment about a paper tiger, I'm sure he would appreciate the irony of being made out of paper himself.

The possibility of portraiture had never occurred to me, but origami evolves, and grows more powerful over time. A recent development is the modelling of sea creatures, with their antennae, claws, fins, flukes, legs and spines. New 'ultra-complex' folds have emerged over the last few years which allow the construction of twenty-five legs from a single sheet of paper. Obviously, I wasn't going to *start* with a crayfish or a shrimp, but Gwyneth Radcliffe, of the British Origami Society, said she would show me how to do a box and an envelope, and, if I managed those, a swan.

Yet despite the fact that it was only a piece of paper, that the lesson was in origami not diamond-cutting, I felt nervous as I copied Gwyneth and slid a fingertip along a fold. 'People *are* nervous about folding,' she said. 'I'm teaching some members of the Women's Institute next week and someone is sure to panic and say, "I can't do it, I can't do it."' Gwyneth herself is so relaxed that she scarcely has to think about the models she makes. She can fold while watching TV, or while holding a conversation. But then, she has been at it since the age of eight, and at the age of fifty-four she can still remember that first model, a paper kettle. From then on, it was pandas, monkeys, rabbits, even strawberries.

What I particularly like is eccentric origami. For at meetings of the society, there are competitions for folding behind the back, with one hand, with the non-dominant hand, or even with the feet. (I have taken off my shoes and tried, and yes, I can make a paper hat.) Then there is micro-origami: the smallest paper crane was made from a 1-millimetre square using a needle and a microscope. The folder was a surgeon who normally worked with blood vessels.

I asked Gwyneth whether she kept her models. 'To me, they're just temporary things made of paper,' she said. 'I have no compunction about chucking them away.'

I looked at the politicians' faces. There was Hitler, with his fringe and moustache made from two-coloured paper, one side white, the other black. And Nixon, with his nose and furrowed brow. All consigned to the dustbin of history.

CONTACT
Penny Groom
Membership Secretary
The British Origami Society
2a The Chestnuts
Countesthorpe
Leicester LE8 3TL
Tel: 0533 773870

Overtone Chanting

Two. Two musical notes: do, re. Human voices sing them only one at a time, is that not so? Yet I find myself singing a duet ... with myself. I am singing chords. *Chords*.

There are thirty singers in the room, and sixty notes. Maybe someone here remembers Duane Eddy's old hit 'Play Me Like You Play Your Guitar'. The song begins to seem plausible, now our voice boxes have more than one string. But unlike the riffs of Duane, ever a-twanging, these sounds are crystalline, bell-like, rising right above our heads. One person calls it the music of the angels, and it is indeed unearthly. It is part of a sound workshop run by Jill Purce, one of the world's few teachers of the singing techniques of Tibetan and Mongolian overtone chanting.

Jill, a former musical associate of Karlheinz Stockhausen, studied overtone chanting in the Himalayas with the chantmaster of the Gyuto Tibetan Monastery and Tantric College. 'Overtones are produced by modulating the resonant cavities,' she explained to us, 'thereby bringing out component notes, like rainbow colours.'

One begins by creating a bass note like a bagpipe's drone and then, after adjusting the shape of the mouth – it helps if you say the French name Henri – the eerie overtones start to emerge, octaves higher than the original, fundamental note.

For some, this chanting and its strange beauty might be worth knowing as a party trick – an outstanding novelty and nothing more. For Jill, there is a much deeper significance. She remains attracted to the Tibetan tradition because of its interpretation of the voice as an intermediary between the realm of the mind and

182

the realm of the body. As she puts it, 'Through singing you can unite the material with the immaterial.' Moreover, she is convinced that overtone chanting is therapeutic. 'After participation,' she says, 'some have said that dark clouds that have long affected their lives have lifted.' Others have found that nagging fears and pain – both physical and emotional – have disappeared.

Whether or not you subscribe to the spiritual underpinning of the musical overtones, Jill's classes are an interesting experience, with attendees ranging from duchesses to signers-on at the DSS. At my own two-day workshop, participants included a professional opera singer, one of Michael Jackson's backing vocalists, a man who said he was there to escape 'the horror' (without saying what the horror was) and a woman who was living in a Native American-style tribe. Vegetarianism seemed to be the only common characteristic. 'I don't know anyone these days who eats meat,' said one overtoner. Now, I have been known to enjoy the occasional pork chop and so, being brave, I said, 'Well, I do.'

'What!' she exclaimed. 'You know someone who eats meat?'

CONTACT
Tel: 071 607 5819

The Peashooting World Championships

'Choose a nice straight one. And remember to blow, not to suck.' This was the advice as I chose a 15p pink plastic peashooter in the village hall at Witcham, near Ely – home of the peashooting world championships.

Peashooting has been a part of Witcham's summer for the past twenty years ever since it was decided that an unusual contest would help raise funds to build the village hall. Though most entrants see the championships as just a pleasant afternoon – a journey back to childhood – some take the event seriously, and pay particular attention to the factors affecting pea-ballistics. I saw fingers rolling peas on a table-top, choosing the ones which were the most uniformly spherical. Size matters, too – a small pea, rattling in the barrel, will not be accurate, whereas a well-fitting one will come out like a bullet.

Soon, the air was full of the noise of phut, phut, phut. In the first round, competitors fire five peas at a circular target and the sixteen highest scores progress to a knockout phase. I wasn't good at judging the required amount of puff. (Too much and you'll overshoot the target, too little and you'll fall short.) So after I was eliminated, all I could do was watch.

I observed differences in style – one-handed versus two-handed grips and most important, the method of loading the pea. Some favoured loading one at a time, while others went for five in the mouth and, by deft tonguing, managed to fire all five in machine-gun succession. One prominent advocate of five in the mouth is Mike Fordham, five times world champion. 'It allows you to establish a winning stance,' he said. 'Get one pea on target and you can fire the rest in the same way, without having to reload.'

Championship contenders like Mike would not be happy with cheap plastic shooters; they make their own from metal piping. Sighting mechanisms are allowed, and some competitors have a metal V on the end of their shooters. But nobody had expected that the sights rule would be taken to its limit; this year, one competitor strapped on to his shooter a £250 laser-optic sight – the type favoured by snipers and hit men.

Purists were outraged, and many of the more experienced

competitors remained sceptical. 'There's no substitute for natural talent,' said Mike. Events proved him right, for although ruthlessly accurate, the laser sight was also extremely heavy – it was wobbling all the time and did not secure victory. Whether this approach will lead to a tripod launcher in future years, or perhaps a shoulder-held pea bazooka, remains to be seen.

In the knockout phase, a contestant fires alternately with his opponent. This is designed to stop five-in-the-mouth tactics, thereby proving ability at re-establishing aim and posture. As the contest reached the final, we knew it would be a shoot-out between Mike Fordham and the 1990 champion, David Trent.

The village hall was hushed. You could have heard a pin – make that a pea – drop. Mike was hungry for success. With ten peas he scored eight perfect fives and two threes, compared to David's six fives and four threes. 'He deserved to win,' said David, very sportingly.

I thought I detected a tremor of emotion on David's face, the natural disappointment of the man who comes second. Was that a lump in his throat, or had he just swallowed some of the peas?

CONTACT
Judy Phillips
Tel: 0353 778363

The Pipe-smoking Contest

It was not an ordinary briar pipe but a long clay churchwarden. 'Dip the end in your beer,' said the man next to me, 'otherwise it'll stick to your lip.' He followed up with more advice, such as, 'You don't want to go too strong early on,' and, 'Try to get it alight all the way around, not just in the middle.'

I struck a match. The bowl is so far from the mouth it's difficult to see what's happening. I sucked, had a taste of tobacco, and then there were a few hairs of smoke. I sucked again. Nothing. 'Fifteen seconds to light your pipes,' said the referee. I panicked. Another match. This time Satan smiled on me: there was a glow ... for a few seconds.

I was eliminated even before the contest had begun.

Every Shrove Tuesday, while the rest of Britain thinks pancakes and lemons, Harpole in Northampton thinks pipes and tobacco. The village's pipe-smoking contest is thought to have started in the nineteenth century. Certainly, not a person alive in the village today can remember the time pre-contest. The rules are straightforward: pipes containing a thimbleful of tobacco are issued to competitors; two minutes is given for lighting up; after that, the aim is to keep the pipe going as long as possible – and if a competitor has to leave the room, the pipe has to be left behind.

At 8.30 in the Bull Inn, the contest began.

You sometimes hear people talk about deals struck in smoke-filled rooms. We are talking about one helluva deal – like negotiations to end a third world war – to find fumes on a par with the Bull on Shrove Tuesday. It's funny how people are willing to enter. Offer a non-smoker a cigarette and they'll refuse, but offer a non-smoker a churchwarden and they'll have a go. Though there are problems if you're not used to it: I heard about an entrant one year who had to leave the room to vomit because of the pipe's juice. Apparently, though, he returned refreshed and actually won the contest.

As I was out, all I could do was listen to the coughs and observe the styles and stances. Some held the bowl in the palm of the hand; others, the stem, like a dart. In one or two cases, I thought I'd glimpsed the pose of Noël Coward in that pub.

And since the contest does take place in a pub, drink is a factor affecting performance. There was drama when a man had to run to the toilet, and then dashed back, hoping he could save his pipe. 'I ain't washed my hands,' he said. He sucked furiously, but to no avail. 'I won't drink next year,' he said. 'But I've got a weak bladder. I couldn't stop.' A woman beside him suggested that he could have done something with a plastic bag and a rubber band.

The number of the pipes alight dwindled, as if a vigil were winding down. A certain honour is attached to the manner of one's exit. 'It's better to smoke it out than for it to go out,' said Stan, a champion of thirty years ago. He'd had a bad night, being eliminated shortly after myself. One man complained that he'd been coming for five years and had never lasted more than a minute.

After an hour, we were left with just two competitors. Suddenly, one said, 'I'm going,' and he was out. The other blew smoke and said, 'I'm gone.' It was the closest contest in living memory, won by a single puff.

CONTACT
The Bull Inn
Harpole
Northants.
Tel: 0604 830666

The Police History Society

One hundred years after the murders in Whitechapel, the mystery of Jack the Ripper was solved – by democratic means. 'That was our most popular conference, when we had the ballot about the Ripper,' said Martin Stallion, the secretary of the Police History Society. The candidates included a man associated with sceptres rather than knives, and someone known for the painting of flesh, not its dissection. So who was Jack? Before I pull off his cloak, let me explain about the society.

The Police History Society is open to anyone with an interest in British law enforcement. You don't have to be on the beat to join. All aspects of police work are covered: the history of truncheons, police dogs, uniforms, transport, what you will. But like most casual observers of police matters, I am intrigued by serious crime, so my examination of this society's work is biased. For instance, in the society's journal I was attracted to a piece about Charlie Richardson, the notorious London gangster, who in 1966 was sentenced to twenty-five years at Her Majesty's Pleasure. Actually, it was a review of Richardson's autobiography, and was especially interesting because the reviewer was a detective chief superintendent. He noted that the book said little about Richardson's current employment. 'I suppose it was stretching optimism beyond the limits,' he remarked, 'to expect that Charlie Boy would save criminal intelligence officers the trouble of keeping tabs on him by actually saying what he is up to these days.'

Or if you take Dr Who's police-box time machine back into the nineteenth century, there is plenty of true-crime material to enjoy. I was struck by an article on a Victorian policeman who had a photograph taken of a dead girl's eyes in the hope that they would contain her last view of the murderer. And there is a

188

frightening account of a nineteenth-century mob attacking a policeman at a steel foundry. The mob were carrying iron bars so pliable that they became entangled with each other. They burnt the policeman's uniform. He was held on the floor and there was an attempt to force a glowing bar down his throat. He wrote in his memoirs, 'Someone brought a bar and, placing a foot at either side of my head, and grinning like a fiend, he put the bar to my mouth.' The policeman escaped only by grabbing the metal with his bare hand.

Further back still, there are the Peelers. A silhouette of one of these original policemen, wearing a top hat, was on the mug of coffee Martin handed to me. Martin himself is a librarian, though he did spend a few years working in a civilian capacity for the Metropolitan Police, and it was whilst with the Met that he had his first look at the contents of the Black Museum. 'At one time, they wouldn't even let women police officers in there,' he said. The general public is still denied admission, though Martin did say that society members stand a better chance of getting in than anyone else. So we spent a while talking about the exhibits: the cooking pot where Dennis Nilsen boiled heads; the rigged binoculars which shoot out spikes when raised to the eyes; the body parts in formaldehyde. 'There was a British murderer who fled to Germany,' Martin said, 'and he died over there. So the British police asked the Germans to send back the murderer's fingerprints. But the Germans went a bit further than that.' The severed hands now float in a jar in the museum.

But let's return to the murders in Whitechapel. Martin said that a couple of slaughterhouse workers were arrested on suspicion of carrying out the atrocities. 'In those days,' he said, 'forensic science was so underdeveloped that it wasn't even possible to tell whether blood was human or animal.' An employee at an abattoir, even if dripping red, would have the perfect alibi. So who was Jack?

In the end, the society voted overwhelmingly for one Montague Druitt, an insane barrister who killed himself when the murders ceased. I thought it would be in bad taste to enquire whether Druitt won on a first-past-the-post system or by single transferable vote.

CONTACT
Martin Stallion
Secretary
The Police History Society
18 Cornec Chase
Leigh-on-Sea
Essex SS9 5EW
Tel: 0702 528480

The Polite Society

I asked Ian Gregory whether he ever swore. 'I invent my own swear words,' he said. 'Things like "breadmug". It's got a "b" and a "g" in it, it's all you need.'

Six years ago, Ian saw the truth about Britain. People put their feet on the seats in trains, there was belching, there was burping, there was talking in the library, there was spitting in the street and, overall, a general rudeness and lack of courtesy in the realm. Something had to be done. He decided to launch the Polite Society.

The society, whose badge has a picture of a man doffing his hat, has a code of good behaviour which every member pledges to uphold. It includes rules like, 'I will exercise the maximum self-control in all situations likely to test my patience and temper,' and, for males, the rule continues, 'to treat women with especial courtesy, observing habits of chivalry towards them.' Couldn't the latter cause problems with feminists? 'Our chairman opened a door for a lady,' Ian said, 'and she told him, "You don't have to open a door for me because I'm a woman." So, he replied, "No, not because you're a woman, but because I'm a gentleman."'

Ian gave me a copy of the society's manifesto, *The Good Manners Guide*. The book makes good sense. Who has not suffered a waspish rebuke? A harsh word when none was needed? A lack of basic consideration? Or had an unanswered letter? The trouble is, when you read a text spelling out the ways to avoid committing these sins, when you read something like, 'Kindly, polite people stand at the mirror before they go out

190

every morning and practise their smiles . . .', isn't the natural reaction then to want to smash the book's author in the face?

'Doesn't it ever grate on you,' I asked, 'when you go to a pizza restaurant and they always say, "Enjoy your meal"?'

'I'd rather hear that,' he said, 'than nothing at all.' He told me that society members carry out 'courtesy audits', when they go to shops incognito and see whether staff are observing the correct niceties.

Presumably, on the way to these shops, the members follow *The Good Manners Guide*'s advice on walking with a straight back: 'Try it. Practise it. Stand in front of the mirror and make yourself 2 inches taller. Look in shop windows and see how you are doing as you walk along.'

It's not that I disagree, but . . .

CONTACT
The Polite Society
18 The Avenue
Basford
Newcastle under Lyme
Staffordshire ST5 0LY
Tel: 0782 614407

Pranks

I understand now the anxieties of crime reporters: you can only say so much, for fear of copycats.

Some of the material in *Hoax!* magazine, a publication which chronicles pranks, describes practical jokes so beastly I would not dream of repeating them here. (The magazine itself carries a disclaimer saying that its 'sole purpose is to entertain and inform readers by documenting various forms of "pranking" phenomena' and that it is not intended to serve as 'a prankster's field manual' or a 'trickster's cookbook'.) Still, in spite of my qualms, I'm not going to condemn *Hoax!*, for I think it's both a funny and an important publication. Pranks are part of human life and leisure, and we've all played them, even if only on 1 April. Surely these cruelties, often as inventive as a sting-in-the-tail short story, should be recorded somewhere? So let's have a few examples – the milder examples – of the material you'll find in the pages of *Hoax!*

From a feature on frauds involving mystery animals: An American noticed a rhinoceros's foot in a friend's apartment – it doubled as waste-paper basket. He appropriated it and one snowy dawn he put it to good use. The local press soon covered the story about the footprints of a large four-legged animal whose tracks were found leading across the grounds of Cornell University campus and down to the shores of Beebee Lake, which supplied the university with its water. Fifty yards from shore was a large hole in the ice. Zoologists were called to explain what had happened. They identified the footprints as belonging to a rhinoceros and concluded the creature had gone for a midnight stroll and had fallen through the frozen lake. Half the population immediately stopped drinking the water. Of those who persisted, many said they could taste the rhinoceros.

From the letters page: Two people who were fairly unpopular at work got married and the reception took place at the company's 'function room'. In a vicious stroke of genius, one of their colleagues went into the area the night before with several hundred stinkbombs. (The glass type you crush underfoot.) He placed one under every single carpet tile in the room. The next day, as more and more people entered the room and moved about, the smell got more and more intense until the whole thing had to be moved to another room amid tears and gagging.

An assortment of postal pranks: (1) Send a postcard anonymously or under an assumed name to a randomly selected person, saying how you're enjoying your holiday, wish you were here, etc. This can really wind some people up as they rack their brains for weeks afterwards, trying to remember who you are. (2) Write to an old third-rate, has-been celebrity, telling them how great they are, how they have changed your life. Request an autographed picture or some other personal memento you could treasure as a permanent reminder of how special they are to you. You will probably receive a very tacky photo from over a decade ago, when they were at the height of their popularity, and a warm personal letter thanking you for your kind support. (3) Post a kipper. (Or, as one contributor to the magazine admitted: 'Recently my girlfriend sent "kitty krap" to a book-club company who pestered her in one of their postage-paid envelopes.')

Advice for successful pranking: (1) Never trust or confide in anyone. (2) Always bide your time. Whenever you have to get even with someone, never say, 'I'm going to get even with you.'

Wait until things cool down, and then strike. (3) Most fake food provided by joke manufacturers – for example, hot pepper sweets and garlic chewing gum – usually comes in suspect packaging. So remember to repackage so as not to arouse suspicion.

Clippings from the national press: 'A Scrooge hoaxer has written to householders telling them their gas will be cut off at Christmas'; 'A hospital porter who thrust the head of a man decapitated on a railway line into a workmate's hands was fired yesterday'; 'A street's residents were horrified when official letters announced their homes were built on a Black Death burial pit. Archaeologists said they planned to sink shafts through their living rooms to retrieve some of the 600-year-old skeletons . . .'

When I spoke to *Hoax!*'s editor, John Quel, I raised the question of responsibility. He conceded that it was a very important matter, particularly as some pranks can go horribly wrong: the latest issue mentions how a prankster lay in the road pretending to be dead . . . and was run over by a car and killed. There are also sick pranks, like fake offers of help to dying children. 'A future issue of *Hoax!* may explore the ethics of pranking,' he told me. Though overall, he saw pranks as a civilizing influence, especially in the context of revenge. 'It's more intelligent to send someone 100 copies of a mail-order catalogue than to punch them,' he said. He was also interested in the sociological and psychological implications of pranks. 'Phone pranks are often a ten-year-old's rite of passage,' he said, 'and it's the same with the pranks carried out on stag nights. They are unwritten customs that happen even though the participants have no control and don't know why they are compelled to carry out such actions.'

So I asked John whether I should put his phone number as well as a contact address. He thought for a moment, then said, 'No, you'd better not put the phone number . . .'

CONTACT
John Quel
Aux
64 Beechgrove
Aberhonddu
Powys
Wales LD3 9ET

The *Prisoner* Appreciation Society

I would prefer to explain nothing to you. I would like you to be confused. That might make you understand his situation. Unfortunately, the rules of writing say that I must explain myself. But who makes those rules? How dearly I would love to break free.

I'll begin again. Recently, I met David Lally, one of the leading members of Six of One, *The Prisoner* Appreciation Society. For those of you who don't know about *The Prisoner*, here's some information. Back in the 1960s Patrick McGoohan, Britain's highest-paid actor of the day, created a television series so enigmatic that he admits, 'I myself am still getting new interpretations of it.' The series has been described as 'television's *Waiting for Godot*', 'a plea for the freedom of the individual in modern society', and an allegory that 'sums up life in seventeen episodes'.

Strange, then, that it begins as a spy story. McGoohan plays a top-notch British agent who resigns from the Service, but he refuses to say why. Returning to his London home, he starts packing, failing to notice that a hearse has pulled up outside. A jet of vapour comes through the keyhole and he falls unconscious. When he awakes, he is in a room which is exactly the same as his lounge in London. But looking through a blind, he realizes that he is in a completely different location, 'The Village', where people have no names, only numbers. He is Number Six. He has become the Prisoner.

'The series plucks a responsive chord in the psyche,' David Lally told me, 'and it's amazing that McGoohan got away with it. You couldn't do it today. The accountants would move in and stop you. And then there'd be the broadcasting standards people on your back. McGoohan pushed it right to the brink.'

For in *The Prisoner* there are no answers, only questions. 'Where am I?' McGoohan asks. In real life, it's no secret that the village is Portmeirion, in Wales. I visited it some years ago and as I wandered past the strange statues of Atlas and Buddha, I was struck by the village's dreamy quality – even in the real place in Wales, things don't quite add up. But in the Village (capital V), it's like a sinister Butlins. There is an announcer

194

whose voice is so nice she might easily say 'Good morning, campers'. But at the same time, everyone is under electronic surveillance. There is Village-brand soup, with cans bearing the distinctive penny-farthing symbol, and there are also white killer balloons that patrol the beaches. Where is the Village? Who runs it? Is it perhaps in Number Six's mind?

Superficially, Six's captors want to know the reason for his resignation. In reality, they just want him to be compliant, to conform. 'I am not a number, I am a free man' – the most famous line in the series, and, as Six says it, the Village authorities laugh in his face. Anyone who has ever clashed with the forces of conformity can identify with *The Prisoner*. It's a eulogy for the lone wolf.

But who is the ultimate authority in the Village, who is the mysterious Number One? In the seventeenth and last episode, McGoohan pulls off Number One's mask – and reveals his own face. Viewers, disgusted by the absence of a traditional climax, jammed the ITV switchboard. McGoohan was assaulted in the street. With the show's descent into Theatre of the Absurd a cult was born that persists to the present day. The members of Six of One hold an annual convention in Portmeirion, where they re-enact the remarkable chess scene with human beings as pieces. (During the game a rook makes an unauthorized move and is taken to the Village's hospital for 'treatment'.) David told me that there are some members of Six of One who even go to work dressed like McGoohan.

And now I shall let you into a secret. Some years ago I myself was a member of Six of One. I left. And I'm certainly not going to tell you why I resigned!

CONTACT
Six of One
PO Box 60
Harrogate
North Yorks HG1 2TP

Psychic Questing

There was a cinema-sized audience in the hall in Holborn and on the screen at the front a slide projector cast an image: two brushstrokes of red on a white background, suggesting a sword. Everyone there would have known the significance. In 1979 Andrew Collins, the meeting's organizer, travelled to a secluded part of the Worcestershire countryside, where he unearthed a sword bearing Mary Queen of Scots' personal monogram. He used no metal detector, nor a map where marks the spot; he was led to the sword by 'psychic clues'. Andrew, who has told the full story in his book *The Seventh Sword*, has in effect created a new form of psychical research: psychic questing, the retrieval of hidden artefacts located by psychic means.

Since 1979 literally dozens of objects have been found by psychic questing. Or so it has been *claimed*. The fruits of the questers' labours are so impressive that one is entitled to ask whether they come from a genuine fruit tree or were purchased at a greengrocer's. But whatever the degree of one's scepticism, it's well worth attending the Psychic Questing Weekend, which is held every year in London. I went to the 1992 event, and heard questers from all over the country give lectures about their latest discoveries: jewellery, silver boxes, crucifixes, daggers and much more besides, all exhibited in a display cabinet at the back of the hall. Such a rich and varied jetsam has been found by these psychic beachcombers that Andrew Collins himself has now become rather jaded. 'I don't get a lot out of it any more,' he told me. 'I've seen it too often.'

Psychic questing can be carried out in many different ways. It could be that a quester will have a dream or a hunch about a hidden artefact. Or maybe a group will start the quest by meditation. When Andrew Collins addressed the meeting, he said, 'You could have a psychic vision in the bath, on the loo, or down the pub.' However, the initial insight is unlikely to give the precise whereabouts of the object. Additional research will probably need to be done in libraries and local archives, so even if you're not terribly psychic, you can still play a role in a questing group. And if you're very lucky, the spirits themselves might lend an ethereal hand. One speaker told of a quest which led to a churchyard in Cumbria. There, he followed an other-worldly trail of pinpricks of light until he found a golden ring – a trinity ring, or three rings joined – which, he believed, once belonged to St Bega. He referred us to the display cabinet for a better look.

196

Most spectacular of all is the phenomenon known as the apport. This is an object which isn't dug out of the ground but instead materializes out of nowhere. Apports fall into our world like mail through a letter-box. So, at the meeting I heard about the lump of amethyst which just *appeared* on a ledge in a church – and it was hot to the touch. There was also the quartz crystal which materialized in a quester's car. Oh, and the car was an Astra, which suggests Astro (or star), and the quartz appeared in the boot. I mention this because the quester did. He thought it extremely relevant. Because at the time of the materialization, he happened to be doing research work on the star constellation of Bootes.

The spirit of Frankie Howerd suddenly impels me to say, 'What a very good thing he wasn't doing research work on the planet Uranus.'

CONTACT
SKS
St Aldhelm
20 Paul Street
Frome
Somerset
BA11 1DX

Pun Intended

There is the odd time in life when a pun is useful, such as when inscribing a card that bids farewell to a colleague. Someone called Ruth, say, moving on to a better job, might merit a comment like, 'You have no pity, to leave us so Ruthlessly.' Once in a while, a pun is OK. It leaves the right taste in the mouth.

But once in a while is not good enough for some people. There are persistent punsters, whose favourite hobby is making cheap *jeux de mots*. They even have their own specialist quarterly newsletter, because *Pun Intended* is written in nothing but puns. Let's hear some examples, taken from its pages:

> I've heard that plants will grow better if you talk to them. I can't do that because I never studied any fern languages.
> Bill Clinton says he smoked pot in the 1960s. Someone asked, 'Did you smoke it in the rain?' 'I may have smoked it in the

rain,' he said, 'but I didn't in hail.'

My friend had some trouble with the starter on his car. 'Solenoid?' I asked. 'Of course!' he replied. 'Why should it bother anyone other than me?'

I might have been a psychic televangelist but I couldn't find anyone to fund a mentalist preacher . . .

Et cetera, ad nauseam. The magazine is an offshoot of the American pun-making championships, the O. Henry Pun-off (named after the American short-story writer who was himself a notorious punster), and every year in Austin, Texas, a crowd of up to 2,000 gather to hear habitual punsters duel. A topic is chosen at random and then a contestant is given up to five seconds to make a pun. Suppose, for instance, the topic is 'real estate'; the puns go back and forth between the two duellists like this:

I wanted to learn to fly a plane but there were more gauges than I could deal with.

Let's see. I've got a hat, shirt, pants and socks. That's four clothes.

I'm sick of these glasses. I'm getting contracts.

It's the lease you can do.

I've got some puns left in me, eight, nine, maybe tenement left.

So it goes on, to the accompanying groans or even boos of the audience, until one competitor is gonged out for taking too much time, and the other goes through to the next round. Though in one case, when the topic was 'oil business' (when the competitors made comments like, 'Have you seen my wife, Ethyl?' or simply sighed, 'Oh, well'), neither competitor showed any signs of exhausting his stock of impromptu puns, and after fifteen minutes both were allowed through to the next round.

Such contests have now been running for fifteen years and the people involved are said to have developed a real sense of camaraderie – possibly because they would not be tolerated anywhere else.

Me? I have a problem. Or rather, had. I have been trying to come up with a pithy ending to this piece – an ending which is itself a pun, hopefully of some sophistication, and one which summarizes everything in the previous paragraphs. My salvation came when I opened a dictionary of synonyms and discovered that an alternative word for pun is calembour. The solution was then obvious. Some people make lots of puns and others call 'em bores.

CONTACT
Pun Intended
1124-A Clayton Ln
Austin
Texas 78723
USA

Punch and Judy

It was an elocution lesson, but banish all thoughts of the rain in Spain. For in this class, any approved vowels were made as if by comb and paper, while favoured diphthongs shared something with the cries of parrots and crows. 'Try, "Judy, Judy, Judy,"' said the tutor, himself squawking. Then, 'Kissy, Kissy, Kissy.' And, 'Walky, walky, walky.' I did my best, but the words came out not so much as units of language but as a root-ti-toot-ti-tooey stream. It's not a simple art, this mastery of received pronunciation according to Mr Punch.

I was at the Worcestershire home of Glyn Edwards, a television producer (responsible for shows like *Tiswas*), who also happens to be one of Britain's leading Punch and Judy 'Professors'. Glyn is indeed the only one of the men of the booths to be in any way professorial, for he, unlike the rest, is prepared to teach students the traditional skills of Punch and Judy in regular 'that's the way to do it' courses. Even so, he is wary about too many people knowing the secret of Punch's squawk; and can tell you only that a *device* is involved, and there is a knack to using it. 'Some people get the voice straight away,' said Glyn. 'With others, it takes six months. But when people do learn the trick, they walk around like bullfighters, full of pride.'

So I looked down at my toreador course notes. I read that an aid to clarity is to have other characters repeat Punch's lines. ('You don't want to look after the baby, Mr Punch? Of course you

199

do.') But that's too easy a way out. It reminded me of that wimp of a puppet, Sooty, whispering all the time in Matthew Corbett's ear.

Of course, the voice is just one aspect of the professor's art. Glyn led me to a backroom, where he had set up a blue and white striped booth. With the crocodile stuck on my left hand, Mr Punch on my right and a string of sausages on my forearm, I walked past the 'next show begins at' clock and stepped into the canopied anarchy of the Punch and Judy world. I proceeded to learn the rudiments of a 'behind you' sketch – the crocodile steals up on Mr Punch but, as soon as old red nose turns around, it vanishes. This happens again and again, until, as you would expect, Punch gets to work with his stick. And the crocodile snaps at his nose. 'Kids do get a bit frightened of the crocodile,' said Glyn. 'They feel as if it could jump out and get them.'

Glyn is especially concerned that his students should learn the history of the show, and all his courses trace the development of the Punch and Judy tradition, from the Italian puppet Pulcinella, through Samuel Pepys's diary entry in 1662 that he was 'mighty pleased' to see a street show featuring a Punch marionette, and onward to the Crimean War, when the crocodile was replaced by a Russian bear. The show is still developing. In our own era, there are often guest appearances by puppets based upon characters like Arthur Scargill, Frank Bruno or even Salman Rushdie.

The one thing that never changes is Punch's contempt for society's conventions. As everyone knows, a baby gets thrown about a lot, and for Punch there would be no problem in answering the question, 'Do you still beat your wife?' But Glyn has no time for those who would bowdlerize the script. 'Condemning the violence of Punch and Judy is about as sensible as the RSPCA condemning the violence of Tom and Jerry,' he said. He holds that the violence is part and parcel of Punch's individualism. 'For all his wickedness,' he said, 'you can't imagine Punch joining the Nazi party, or the Stalinists, or the religious extremists. Punch wouldn't join anything. Punch does the things we dare not do. He's an anti-authoritarian figure – it's just that violence is the way his anti-authoritarianism is expressed.'

In any case, sensitivities about the show appear to be subject to fashion. In Victorian times, the wife beating and child abuse passed with few comments, while to the church-going audience of the day the appearance of the Devil puppet was a cause of considerable disquiet. Similarly, twentieth-century campaigns against capital punishment have led to qualms about the scene in which Mr Punch tricks a hangman into executing himself. 'What next?' Glyn asked. 'Will animal rights activists protest about the mistreatment of the crocodile?'

I closed those jaws with a satisfying snap. I think the crocodile's safe. But what about the sausages? It can't be long before the veggie lobby calls for their omission.

CONTACT
Professor Glyn Edwards
Punch's Oak
Cleobury Road
Far Forest
Worcestershire DY14 9EB
Tel: 0299 266 634

Punk Singing

The older generation has always got it wrong. In spite of what your parents said, you knew in your young, ardent heart that rock 'n' rollers had plenty of talent. After all, Elton John wrote his own stuff, and as for Yes, Led Zep and ELP – well, they were brilliant, almost virtuosos. Then along came the Sex Pistols and suddenly your parents were right. Here was a band that couldn't sing, couldn't play and weren't ashamed to admit it. OK, they had honesty, and all right, they had energy, and maybe in their own way they had genius – but let's face it, the Pistols were dreadful.

Which is why my fingernail stopped its slide down the small ads column. A music teacher was offering tuition in punk singing. Was it for real? Punk suggests chaos, broken rules; yet the ad implied that it could be worked upon, could be improved, that musical anarchy could be taught. Intrigued, I made an appointment and travelled to Edgware, to the music room of Sybil Esmore.

Sybil, whose main love is grand opera, knows Pavarotti. His inscribed photograph sits on her piano – indeed, she has the distinction of being an honorary member of the Pavarotti Society of Great Britain. She also believes that the Sex Pistols 'definitely had something', and she maintains that the techniques of good singing are applicable to all the forms of music she teaches, from punk to opera.

For the first hour or so, she taught me how to breathe. I expanded in the area of the diaphragm and learned how to control the air I inhaled. Then there were scales and other vocal exercises. Very quickly, I realized that her teaching worked. I was sustaining notes as I had never done before.

Then it came to the song. For me, there could be only one choice: the tune – if I can call it that – that started punk, 'Anarchy in the UK'. 'Oh yes,' said Sybil, in a refined voice, 'I've got the *Never Mind the Bollocks* LP . . .'

During the next hour, she proceeded to strip away my received pronunciation vowels. 'No,' she said, 'it's not "I [as in eye] am an Antichrist", it's "Oi yam an Antichrist-tuh".' Similarly, 'I wanna be' became 'Oi wanna bay', 'Coming' became 'Comin', and so on. I would need the full resources of the international phonetic alphabet if I tried to write down how Sybil murdered my speech.

She next emphasized that I needed more contrast in my version of 'Anarchy' – I was becoming too uniformly horrible in my singing. 'I would do the "Oi wanna bay" a little less heavily,' she said. 'The important word is *anarchy*'. By the time we had been through the whole song, I was as rotten as Johnny.

I cleared my throat.

Scientists refer to a *ceteris paribus* change when they alter just one factor in their experiments. Sybil did something similarly scientific in her dealings with me: we kept the song exactly the same, the only difference being that I would now be singing 'Anarchy in the UK' as an operatic recital.

Sybil made me sustain every note and perfectly pronounce every word. 'Cos Oi wanna bay' became 'Because I want to be'. It was hard to shrug off Rotten's influence. 'You've got a bit of an "Oi" in there,' Sybil would say. At one point, my brain became so addled with the change that I found myself slipping back involuntarily into punk mode – like a strange musical Jekyll and Hyde, with Johnny Rotten and Luciano Pavarotti fighting to gain possession of my soul.

My session ended with an operatic flourish on the last word of the song – *destroy*. Sybil had proved her point about the universality of singing techniques. And I finally realized the

202

truth about the Pistols: Rotten and Co had nothing to do with chaos and everything to do with music . . . Good music.

CONTACT
Sybil Esmore
Tel: 081 958 9323

Pyramidology

Ten miles south-west of Cairo, at the desert's very edge, stands the largest, the heaviest and, so some would say, the most wonderful building on earth. That the Great Pyramid at Giza is the largest and heaviest has never been open to question. Containing the masonry for thirty Empire State Buildings; possessing four facets each with an area of 5 acres; being over 2 million individual blocks – who would deny this pyramid its wonder? Not I. Probably not you. And definitely not the 600 members of the Institute of Pyramidology, for whom the building at Giza has no one but God as its architect, and for whom the pyramid's complex mathematical structure reveals the Almighty's plan for our world. Full of wonder about the institute itself, I travelled to Chesham, to meet its organizer, Fred Binns.

Fred had already posted me four volumes – handsomely bound, tooled in gold – containing the heart of the institute's message, so I felt well prepared. Written by the institute's founder, Adam Rutherford, the pages of *Pyramidology*, Books I to IV, greet you with an extraordinary mixture of square-root signs and biblical prophecy. 'There's enormous interest in pyramidology in the USA,' Fred told me. 'I get asked obscure questions on measurements from all over the world. I'm hoping to get one or two of the more mathematically minded brethren working on answering them.'

It is no exaggeration to say that an ardent pyramidologist will carry out trigonometric calculations to five decimal places in an attempt to prove the veracity of the book of Daniel. Pyramidologists believe that God's will is encoded in the building's dimensions and that a careful study of the Giza geometry reveals such divinely known data as the spheroidical shape of the earth (that is, the amount by which the earth deviates from

203

a true sphere by 'flattening at the poles'); the mean distance of the earth from the sun; and the volume of the earth's crust above mean sea level.

'Do you ever wonder whether you're reading things into the pyramid that simply aren't there?' I asked Fred.

'Always possible,' he answered, 'and you can quote me on that.'

The reason for all this interest can be found in the book of Isaiah, 19: 19–20: 'In that age there shall be, in the centre of Egypt and yet at the border, a monument that shall be a sign and an altar to the Lord.' Could this be Cheops's pyramid at Giza? It stands at the centre of Egyptian life – to this day, Cairo buses run out to the pyramids – yet also it is on the country's border, for beyond lies the Sahara. But a true pyramidologist will seek and find further confirmation of Isaiah. For instance, in Hebrew the letters of the alphabet serve also as numbers, so it is possible to calculate the numerical value of the words used in any biblical passage and arrive at a total. For the Isaiah quotation, this turns out to be 5,449 – which happens to be, in ancient inches, the exact height of our good old friend at Giza! Just in case you think this is coincidence, then you must explain another fact: if you take a map of the world and find the exact centre of the earth's landmass – including North and South America, unknown to the ancient Egyptians – it turns out that your marker pin will have its point in the middle of . . . you guessed it.

Most astonishing of all is the pyramidologists' claim that the building has an inbuilt calendar predicting major events in human history. By measuring the pyramid's passageways and adopting a scale of 1 inch to a year, and by a careful interpretation of the building's geometry and architectural symbolism, pyramidologists claim they can find predictions of the rise of Napoleon, the 1848 European revolutions, the Great War of 1914 and so on. Even the invention of esperanto is foretold – and its 'mention' in the pyramid indicates, according to Rutherford's books, that esperanto will probably be the official language in the kingdom of heaven. It is worth noting too that in one interpretation of the pyramid's chronology the year 1979 has special significance – for back in the 1950s pyramidologists predicted that in that year would come the end of the world. I asked Fred how the institute's members felt when 1979 came and the cataclysm didn't happen. 'Very disappointed,' he said.

I left Chesham thinking that the equations of God are not that easy to solve and that divine geometry is probably non-Euclidean.

CONTACT
Fred Binns
The Institute of Pyramidology
108 Broad Street
Chesham
Bucks HP5 3ED
Tel: 0494 771774

Qigong

The floor was of polished wood. There was a pot plant in the corner. The only complexity to be seen was an acupuncture diagram on the wall, showing a naked oriental man, back and front. In the middle of this studio two men stood facing each other, their eyes closed, their feet a shoulder width apart, their arms hanging down. I was one of those men.

Simon Lau, the other, had told me to breathe slowly and to imagine that my feet were on the earth while my head was touching the heavens. Also, I had to believe that water was running down my body, as though I were under a waterfall. After some time standing motionless, my leg muscles began to shake. I rocked on my feet to try to make the spasms stop. My eyelids fluttered. Then my eyes opened and Simon's seemed to open at the same time. He smiled. We had been through the simplest of qigong exercises.

What is qigong? It is difficult to know. When I phoned Simon, who teaches this 4,000-year-old Chinese exercise system, he told me that it was impossible to learn about qigong in one session. How long would it take? 'Three months,' he said. Oh. But he agreed to meet me for a couple of hours to try to impart what understanding he could.

Qigong (which means 'vital force') is a series of physical, mental and breathing exercises which improve one's general well-being. What is special is that after about 100 days of these exercises, a strange energy starts to circulate around the body. 'You know when the energy is there,' said Simon, 'but you can't describe it. It's a physical sensation. Maybe you're used to waking up in the morning with a cold, empty stomach, but after qigong you won't feel it. You'll get tingling and palpitations in the stomach. You'll stop having cravings. Maybe you used to have a bottle of wine. You'll go down to one glass, then no wine at all.'

To give me further insights into qigong, Simon showed me a few written testimonies by his students. Amongst the comments about calmness, health, optimism and contentment, there were descriptions of the onset of the energy.

The first testimony said, 'It felt as if my whole body was about to explode. My head, which was whipping around in a frenzy, seemed set to rip off my shoulders and rocket into orbit. And all the while I moved around the room dribbling, panting and fighting an imaginary opponent. In short, I must have resembled a drug-crazed evangelical epileptic.'

Another said, 'I felt like the boy with the red glow around him from the old Ready Brek ad.'

And a third, 'After the first few months, I noticed that my physical coordination was sharper. When I threw things into the waste-paper basket, my aim was consistently more accurate.'

I watched Simon do some advanced qigong, including a rippling arm movement which I've seen break-dancers do, and a head movement which reminded me of a tortoise emerging from its shell. 'Do qigong daily,' he said. 'Do it first thing in the morning, before you answer the phone, before you watch the news, before anything. Just do it, not for any specific reason.'

That's about it. I don't understand qigong, except that the muscular spasms in my legs *may* have been the merest indication of what it's like when the energy flows. Yet in spite of my dissatisfaction with this threadbare account, I feel the most profound satisfaction for having met Simon: at last I had a Q for the book.

CONTACT
Eastern Horizon Studio
28 Old Brompton Rd
South Kensington
London SW7 3DL
Tel: 071 581 1118

The *Randall and Hopkirk (Deceased)* Appreciation Society

'If I could afford to retire,' she said, 'I'd devote my life to *Randall and Hopkirk*.'

It was late evening in a front room in Edgware, and Vanessa Bergman, the founder of the *Randall and Hopkirk (Deceased)* Appreciation Society was telling me of her devotion to the show. I was lucky to see her: running the society occupies so much of her time that it was difficult to squeeze in an interview. '*Randall and Hopkirk* has taken over my life,' she said. 'I try to watch at least one episode every night. I never get bored with it. I turn on the news and it's so depressing, so I put on a video of *Randall and Hopkirk* instead.'

Randall and Hopkirk (Deceased) was first broadcast in 1969. ('On 21 September, on Sunday evening, at 7.30,' said Vanessa.) It features two private investigators: Jeff Randall (played by Mike Pratt), who is craggy, chain-smoking and poor – a gumshoe who is very much down at heel – and his partner, Marty Hopkirk (played by Kenneth Cope), who is a pleasant sort of chap . . . and who also happens to be dead. 'It was so different,' said Vanessa, 'the way it linked a fantasy, a ghost story, with crime.'

Such is Vanessa's involvement with *Randall and Hopkirk* that, without realizing it, the show's script is beginning to influence the way she speaks. So she will ring up her mother and say, 'I'm on my way. Right now –' which is the last thing that Marty said to his wife, Jeannie, before he was killed. Or somebody at work will ask whether she's busy and she'll answer, 'Frantic!' using precisely the same intonation as was once used by Jeff.

The society aims to uncover every piece of trivia about the dead-and-alive detectives. Vanessa told me that Irish comedian Dave Allen was originally considered for the role of Jeff. (Would Frank Carson have been a suitable choice for Marty?) There are also activities such as *Randall and Hopkirk* quizzes, where two teams face questions like, 'What is Marty's plot number in the cemetery?' Or, 'What is Jeff's bank?' But at least these questions have answers. There is one member who writes to Vanessa with enquiries of a more philosophical nature, such as, 'Why doesn't Jeff have a dog?' Or even, 'Why didn't Marty and Jeannie write a song together?'

Vanessa spoke of how she felt when the series was repeated in 1988 – her big chance not only to refresh her memories but also to capture the whole series on video. Thames Television transmitted sixteen of the twenty-six episodes and then there was a break for the Olympics. 'I was going demented,' she said. 'It was like somebody telling you a joke and not giving you the punchline. Then Thames said that they had no plans to show the rest of the series and I thought, you can't do this to me.'

Eventually Thames *did* show the remaining episodes, so now Vanessa has the whole series to watch again and again. 'If I won the pools,' she said, 'I could fill the day with *Randall and Hopkirk*.'

CONTACT
Vanessa Bergman
RAHDAS
10 Brook Avenue
Edgware
Middlesex HA8 9XF

Rat Fancying

It is probably the only magazine in the world with an obituary column devoted to rodents. For in *Pro-Rat-A*, the official journal of the National Fancy Rat Society, mourners can find an opportunity to share their grief. 'I was heartbroken when Ricky and Percy died two years ago. I still get a lump in my throat every time I look at the holes in my curtains and the gnawed speaker leads.'

Yet all is not sad. There is coverage too of marriages and births: 'On 14 May, to Gudrun Freyasdottir and Kevin, six sons and five and a half daughters' (the half being a runt). On further examination of the journal, we can discover the spirit of entrepreneurship – the selling of rat-related merchandise, such as keyrings, mugs and sweatshirts – plus the fun of the design-a-rat-Christmas-card competition. Why, there is even a Health Hints column, devoted to all aspects of the well-being, both physical and mental, of fancy rats. 'Dear Editor,' writes one concerned reader, 'I have a black-capped white rat called Gem. She doesn't often squeak but she often makes a quacking noise. She also snores. Is this unusual?'

Needing to experience such rats myself, I arranged a meeting with Malcolm Cleroux, president of the National Fancy Rat Society. 'The relationship of fancy rats to sewer rats is like the relationship of domesticated dogs to wild dogs,' he told me. 'Our rats are very affectionate. There's absolutely no truth in the myth that they jump for your throat.'

He proceeded to place a rat on my shoulder. 'They love cleaning your ears,' he said. 'They put their snouts in and they sort of wriggle around.'

I have to say that in a very short time I too became a rat-fancier. They let you stroke them, they'll take chocolate drops from your fingers, they'll crawl up and down your arms. One of them scampered across my shoulders and tickled my neck with its claws. It's hardly surprising that they're now becoming a top person's pet. It was Malcolm himself who told me of the society's ultimate seal of approval: 'We now supply rats to Harrods,' he said.

But for many people the mere thought of touching a rat would bring on a screaming fit. Why? Malcolm believes it could have something to do with the tail, so naked, so worm-like. 'If rats had furry tails they wouldn't have such bad press,' he said. 'They'd be like squirrels. Though in reality squirrels are very, very aggressive, not like rats at all.'

In Malcolm, the rats have found their perfect PR man. I sat on his sofa, with a rat on my lap, as he sold me their virtues: 'Hamsters are a bit vicious, and ferrets, oh my goodness, do they smell. But rats are wonderful to hold and very clean. Some of our members have them running around the house.' He told me that rats will quite happily sit with you and watch TV, and there are even rats that like music. 'I used to have some rats that seemed to enjoy Ray Moore on Radio 2,' he said. 'When he took a couple of weeks' holiday and there was a stand-in on the show, they weren't the same at all . . .'

CONTACT
Joan Branton
Membership Coordinator
The National Fancy Rat Society
71 Groome Court
Regency Walk
Croydon
Surrey CRO 7UT

The Richard III Society

He was the wickedest wicked uncle of them all – a monster who killed his own nephews as they slumbered in their beds. A king? Yes, he was that, but one who schemed and murdered his way to the crown; a fiend, twisted in body as in soul – worthy only of stinking rags, never ermine. For this was Richard III, Richard Crookback: the foulest toad, the cruellest snake in all of English history, the most rat-hearted, ravenous *wolf*.

Or maybe, you know, he wasn't so bad after all.

The idea that Richard III (1452–85) has had a raw deal from history is what unites the members of the Richard III Society. In London I met Elizabeth Nokes, the society's general secretary. 'He was almost certainly not a crookback,' she said. She told me that the famous portrait of Richard has been doctored, with a raised shoulder painted in afterwards. 'And there's no evidence he had a withered arm,' she added.

According to the society, Richard was quite an enlightened ruler. In his two-year reign, he helped the poor, fought injustice, reformed the machinery of the law and administration and was a patron of Caxton. He showed unshakeable loyalty to his brother, Edward IV, and had the good fortune to marry his childhood sweetheart. Could such a man *really* have killed the Princes in the Tower?

'We're not short of candidates for the murderer, like Henry VII or the Duke of Buckingham,' said Elizabeth. 'I suppose it's *possible* that Richard murdered the princes, but I wouldn't put any money on it.' As for his brother, the Duke of Clarence, being drowned in a butt of Malmsey wine – well, that might be true,

212

but once again there's no evidence at all that Richard was involved.

Richard, it seems, was the victim of a propaganda campaign mounted by his successors, the Tudors, who would do anything to blacken his name to strengthen their hold on the throne. They were ably assisted by the man who wrote Richard's biopic, William Shakespeare. At one time, the society would put articles into theatre programmes, telling the audience that Shakespeare had written a pantomime version of history, with Richard as a boo-hiss villain. Nowadays, they have moved on to other activities, such as holding a commemorative service at Bosworth, where Richard was defeated and killed, and in their specialist journal, *The Rickardian*, they re-examine Richard's life and times.

Gradually, the society seems to be winning the argument. Twenty or thirty years ago you could pick up a schoolbook and find Richard as a murderer-monarch with a bludgeon for a sceptre and a babe's cracked skull as his orb. Today, we have a more open-minded approach, and there have been reappraisals of Richard, such as the Channel 4 television programme *The Trial of Richard III*, in which Richard was found not guilty. 'I think there are an awful lot of closet Rickardians out there,' said Elizabeth. 'We get people writing in saying, "I've always thought he was badly treated. I'm glad to know there's a society – I thought I was the only one."'

Yet if Richard wasn't too bad, then just how *good* was he? Elizabeth counselled a degree of caution. There are some people who go too far in the other direction. She mentioned in passing one book in which Richard was portrayed as so heroic he was almost St George.

'For his time,' she said, 'Richard III wasn't too bad a chap.'

CONTACT
Membership Department
The Richard III Society
PO Box 247
Haywards Heath
West Sussex RH17 5FF

Runes

There was a time when Wednesday was called Woden's Day, when the middle of the week – and not just the middle – was an offering to a pagan god.

The twenty-four earthenware tablets on my desk are squares the size of chessboard squares. Each bears a letter of a long-gone alphabet; each is a cameo of a long-dead script. They belong to the era of Woden. As I say the names of these symbols aloud – *thurisaz, algiz, laguz* – they make me think of gemstones, like lapis lazuli. In their own way, they are precious. For these are runes, tools of occult power and fortune-telling since Viking times. To understand them better, I travelled to north London to meet Freya Aswynn, teacher of runecraft.

When I entered Freya's house, the sound of Wagner's 'The Ride of the Valkyries' was shaking the speakers and rising up the stairs. Freya replaced the heroics of Teutonic opera with a cassette of her own voice singing the runes: '*Kenaz, hagalaz, nauthiz,*' she wailed. 'The runes are energies,' she said. 'They are very good in aggressive combat.' I asked what she meant, and she told me that she once used the power of the runes to put a curse on a man who had threatened her husband with an axe. 'In front of at least five witnesses this man showed signs of possession,' she said. 'He was foaming at the mouth.'

Freya has had a sense of her own occult powers from a very early age. Even as a four-year-old child, she believed that she had, or had once, the power of flight. As she grew up, she often seemed to know what would happen before it actually occurred. 'In all honesty, I believe that I am a naturally born or chosen priestess of Woden,' she told me.

She explained that the runes are a means of shifting probabilities, not simply a method of foretelling the future. They can make the future happen – or at least make it more likely. 'Suppose, for instance, you're out of work,' she said. 'You cast a rune spell, and later that day you're on a tube train – and on the seat next to you is a paper with the perfect job. That's the power of the runes. They're no mere fortune-telling device.'

For centuries people have asked questions of the runes. There is a record in the works of Tacitus, the Roman historian, of how a priest would inscribe the runes on strips of wood, then close his eyes, face north, invoke the gods and cast the runes on a white cloth. The priest would take three and interpret them in the light of the questions posed. I learned from Freya's book *The*

Leaves of Yggdrasil (named after the tree where Woden sacrificed himself) that to obtain maximum benefit from interpreting runes requires a thorough knowledge of the Norse legends. In drawing a *thurisaz*, for instance, one has to know that this rune represents Thor the thunder god's clash with the ice giants that feed on human flesh – *thurisaz* is about the fundamental conflict between order and chaos. The rune *pertho*, on the other hand, is a little more down to earth. When a direct question is asked and *pertho* is the answer, this often means you're not supposed to know. Posing further questions will only result in *pertho* turning up again. 'Because of this irritating habit of *pertho*,' said Freya, 'we call it the "fuck off" rune.'

Back to the earthenware tablets spread upon my desk. I decided to ask the question, 'What must I sacrifice this year in order to be successful in my work?' I put all the runes in a bag, shook it up and thought of the three Norns, the ancient women in dyed wool cloth who dictate the fates of men and gods alike. I plunged my hand into the bag and made my choice.

One of the runes that emerged was an upside-down *ansuz*, which may be interpreted as meaning misjudgement. It struck me that one can aim to sacrifice, or discard, one's poorer qualities, such as, of course, misjudgement. This was useful advice, striking a very positive note. It was also unexpected, because when I posed the question I had been thinking entirely of the sacrifice of desirables. I realized that the runes had been wiser than I, for with their upbeat, positive attitude I was more likely to succeed. The runes had caught me out, and just for a moment I imagined three old women nodding knowingly . . .

CONTACT
Freya Aswynn
43 St George's Avenue
Tufnell Park
London N7
Tel: 071 607 9695

(The Followers of) Rupert

I had forgotten about the origami features in the *Rupert* annuals: those paper fowls, those foolscap beasts. So when Raymond Cassidy, the secretary of the Followers of Rupert – an appreciation society for the *Daily Express*'s little bear – said that the Followers had held a special origami meeting where paper frogs had been made, it was like looking through a peephole at my own childhood. Years ago, I made those very creases and folds, brought forth an angular amphibian which would jump if you stroked it in the right way.

Yes, as a child I was a follower (with a small f) of the little bear – he of the yellow scarf and trousers, and the jumper in pillar-box red. 'We get people writing in,' said Raymond, 'asking why he's kept the same clothes for the last seventy years. But you couldn't really imagine Rupert in denims, could you?'

Indeed, you could not. For Rupert lives for ever in the world of Nutwood, a world of wireless and politeness and countryside. Judging from the designs of the cars in the drawings, he seems to be stuck in about 1937, though part of Nutwood's appeal is the way that things seep through from other periods. Bill Badger's clothes could come from *Tom Brown's Schooldays*, while Mr Anteater, in his morning dress, spats and pince-nez could be a fashion plate for 1890. There are also the elements which hark back to the dark ages – castles, dwarfs, cobblers. In so far as the passage of real time has ever been marked in the adventures of Rupert, it is done in a profoundly conservative way, such as by acknowledging the coronations of George VI and Elizabeth II.

I asked Raymond whether he'd seen *any* changes in the strip over the years. 'I think Rupert's become more of a goody-goody,' he said. 'In the early days, he was sometimes naughty and occasionally punished – like the time when he and Bill Badger ate all the Christmas pudding and were sent to bed.' Also, Rupert has become a little more wordly-wise, a little less naive. 'He used to be a bit trusting of witch-like women,' said Raymond. He recalled how, as a child of five, he had found a story of a witch turning into a wolf rather disturbing. But a more obvious change in the stories is the expunging of racism – today, there certainly wouldn't be a yarn like *Rupert on Coon Island*.

In a typical Rupert adventure, the fantastic impinges upon the mundane. Mr Bear, Rupert's father, might be trimming away his hedge, shaping a peacock with his clippers, when suddenly Tiger Lily weaves a spell and the bird comes alive. Or, as in the story *Rupert and the Sands of Time*, Rupert wakes up one morning and finds that all the clocks in Nutwood have gone wrong. He goes to see Father Time and discovers that the master clock controlling Nutwood's timepieces is near an open window and sand coming in has clogged the mechanism. Rupert's is a world where crows can take you flying to meet the King of the Birds; where you may be asked to rescue the last herd of unicorns from the clutches of an upstart magician.

It is very easy to criticize all this. There is no mention of birth, death, marriage or religion in the strip, though there is crime of a certain sort, such as when a burglar wants to steal an old man's gold or when foreign spies attempt to kidnap a boy-king. 'People say that Rupert is middle class, polite and élitist,' said Raymond. 'But I'm wearing a Mensa tie, so I *am* an élitist.'

In the Followers' *Nutwood Newsletter*, a beautifully printed magazine, one can read accounts of how a yellowing *Daily Express* was discovered lining a drawer, or find advice on safe storage of a Rupert collection, or read comments on the recent reappearance in the strip of the Wise Old Goat. 'It was good to see him again,' says the *Newsletter*. And a Follower can always be relied upon to spot a mistake in continuity: 'In *Rupert and the Stone Fiddler*, the small statue left indented footprints wherever he went, but when there is an entire gathering of statues dancing in the woodland, not one blade of grass seems to be crushed.'

Ah, Rupert. I wish I had lived in a world like yours. As Mrs Bear once remarked, as she tucked her ursine son into bed, 'We'll see what adventures are waiting for you tomorrow . . .'

CONTACT
Shirley Reeves
31 Whiteley
Windsor
Berks SL4 5PJ
Tel: 0753 865562

The Sacred Relics Research Group

If a comparison is obvious, it's unnecessary and shouldn't be made, but some comparisons are *so* obvious they are simply required. It would be peculiar – like a breach of etiquette – if I did not make a connection between Jonathan Boulter and Indiana Jones. Oh, there's no dust on Jonathan's hat – for the good reason that he doesn't wear one – and when we met, he didn't put the coils of a bullwhip down upon the table. What he shares with Indiana is a goal: Jonathan Boulter, a twenty-six-year-old librarian from Willesden Green, intends to be the man who finds the Lost Ark.

At the time of our conversation in Ye Olde Swiss Cottage pub in London, Jonathan had just formed the Sacred Relics Research Group. As examples of the relics of interest to the membership, he mentioned King Solomon's ring and King David's golden harp. But central to the group's endeavours is the search for the most famous filing cabinet in history: the Ark of the Covenant – the box of acacia wood and gold containing the tablets of the Ten Commandments.

'The Ark could be in Egypt. Or in Iraq,' he said. 'Some people claim it's hidden in the Vatican. Or on Mount Nebo. Or under the Temple Mount in the centre of Jerusalem. Or in Calvary – two American archaeologists claim to have seen it there. It could even be in Rennes-les-Châteaux in the south of France. Last year, it was reputed to be in northern Ethiopia.'

It seems to get around a bit, then. 'Ah, but there could be more than one Ark,' he said. 'There could be replicas.'

Since the group has only just been established, Jonathan's plans for tracking down the Ark (or Arks) are obviously sketchy. But he is serious. For a long time, he has been intrigued by both the occult and antiques, and he is quite open in his admiration for the Spielberg films. 'The initial task is to make contacts and trade information,' he said. Longer term, he plans a visit to Ethiopia. 'There are rumours that the Ethiopians carried it on to the battlefield when they were fighting the Italians in 1896,' he said. 'And they won. Just as the Israelites were always victorious when they carried it into battle.'

So the Ark could be a weapon, a sort of divine bazooka. Or perhaps even a *nuclear* weapon. According to the Bible, you had to be careful not to touch it – the Ark was carried on poles, for a finger on its sacred surface meant instant death. Jonathan told me that if he found the Ark he would ask scientists to check it over with a Geiger counter. If necessary, he would put on protective clothing. However, he would as willingly open the Ark as he would a present at Christmas – he had no qualms, no fears, even though in Spielberg's film the Nazi raiders were melted by guardian spirits. He went on to speak about the group's forthcoming newsletter, which would feature a profile of Otto Rahn, the German archaeologist upon whom the character of Indiana Jones was loosely based.

I think it's time to return to obvious comparisons. I think we have to talk in terms of finding a slender metal thing, used in sewing, within a pile of dried grass. Jonathan isn't put off, though. 'I do believe,' he said, 'that I'll see the Ark one day.' He paused for a moment. 'I'm open-minded as to when that might be.'

CONTACT
Jonathan Boulter
4 Huntington House
St Paul's Avenue
Willesden Green
London NW2 5SR
Tel: 081 459 5520

The Saint Club

It's when he's doing nothing in particular that you know an adventure is about to begin. He'll be sitting in a bar, and a man is shot with a blowpipe. He'll be walking along a bridge, and the wind carries top-secret documents into his hand. He'll be making a phonecall, and the man in the next booth drops down dead. (Heart-attack? No. A small, broken glass phial is found on the booth's floor.) As Simon Templar puts it himself, 'Trouble is one of the things that sort of happen to me, like other people catch colds.'

But any man who had blown his nose *that* often, *that* much, would have worn away his sinuses long ago. Because Templar has encountered continual trouble ever since 1928, when Leslie Charteris, his creator, penned the first Saint novel, *Meet the*

Tiger; and in television series, radio plays, films, comic strips, pulp magazines, as well as in fifty-four books, Charteris fleshed out the career of an adventurer with no flesh at all – a stick-man with a halo.

Everyone has heard of the Saint. Most people of a certain age will be able to whistle the theme tune from the Roger Moore television series, but not so many will have heard of the Saint Club. One of the oldest surviving appreciation societies in the world, the Saint Club was founded in 1936, by Charteris himself. Today it has about 1,600 members, 60 per cent of whom are women, and in its official magazine, *The Epistle*, it is still possible to feel the presence of that earliest generation of fans. 'I was one of the first members,' writes one lady, as she talks about the effect of fifty years' inflation on the price of the club's stick-man neckties. 'I'm almost seventy-seven years old now,' she writes, 'and I *still* have my rule book.'

The man running the club today is a twenty-three-year-old broadcasting engineer, Ian Dickerson, who became hooked on the Saint at the age of nine. In central London I met Ian in accordance with clause no. 9 of the Saint Club's rules: 'Any meeting place where two or more Saints are gathered together shall be known as a Heaven. If they start talking politics it will probably look more like Hell. In any case, it will probably be called a Bar.'

'The one thing about the Saint,' said Ian, sipping his Guinness, 'is that you can't take it seriously. A lot of it is tongue in cheek – like at one point in the books, Templar talks about "My friend Charteris".' Well, the whole scenario of Roger Moore inspecting his halo is enough to indicate that the Saint is not exactly *film noir*. 'And the Saint doesn't take *life* seriously,' Ian continued. 'You won't find him reading the politics section of a newspaper – he'll be studying the racing form.'

But what distinguishes the Saint from other crime-fighting heroes is the downright disreputable side to his character. Ian showed me a club membership card:

Notice to the Police: the bearer of this card is probably a person of hideous antecedents and low moral character and upon apprehension for any cause should be immediately released in order to save other prisoners from contamination.

For the Saint is no goody-goody. He carries two ivory-handled knives – one called Anna, strapped to his arm, and one called

Belle, on his leg. He will steal and he will murder. He can be considered a latter-day Robin Hood, taking from the unworthy rich and giving to the deserving poor, but he will keep 10 per cent for himself as a fee. Above all, the Saint is no Sherlock Holmes. 'As a general rule,' Templar remarks, 'problems in detection bore me stiff. It's so much more entertaining to commit the crime yourself.'

Yet this is not to say that Templar lacks moral values. 'The Saint,' said Ian, 'feels that there is a need for a justice outside the law. Though it's also his way of enjoying himself.' Ian proceeded to illustrate Templar's code of morality by referring to the story *The Sleepless Knight*. This tells of the Saint's encounter with the boss of a haulage company who has been overworking staff to the point where they fall asleep at the wheel. The Saint decides to strap the haulier into a driving simulator and make him drive . . . and drive . . . and drive, long into the night and to the point of exhaustion. Whenever the haulier's eyelids start to droop, Templar wakes him up with a sound beating.

As Ian and I discussed the Saint and the Saint Club, we kept coming back to the man who started it all, Leslie Charteris, who, right up to the time of his death in 1993, aged eighty-five, maintained an active interest in the club's affairs. 'He used to phone me most weeks to keep an eye on developments,' said Ian. 'I had dinner with him the week before he died.'

Charteris had stopped writing Saint novels some years before – Ian joked that subsequently the only thing Charteris wrote were cheques – but any future biographer will find the last flourishes of an astonishingly successful writing career in the letters of Charteris to club members. Hence, when apologizing for an increase in subscriptions, Charteris wrote, '. . . next year we are going to double the price, just to catch up with inflation. Even so, it will still be a fabulous investment for those who lead clean, sober, healthy and smoke-free lives, few as they may be amongst the membership we have.'

Aside from its longevity, what sets the Saint Club apart from other appreciation societies is that it is also a benevolent organization. This was Charteris's idea right from the start and, like Templar, the club is dedicated to helping the less fortunate. Every penny of its profits from subscriptions and the sale of merchandise goes to a good cause. Currently, it is helping the Arbour Youth Centre in Stepney, East London, to provide social and sporting amenities to underprivileged young people. As Charteris put it in a letter to members, '[These youngsters] might otherwise be tempted to compete with you in whatever dubious earners you are trying to get away with.' The club is also assisting a man actually named Simon Templar, who has dedicated his life to the rescue of mistreated and cruelly exploited chimpanzees. 'I am sure you will agree,' said Charteris, 'that this is the kind of monkey business to which the Saint Club simply had to contribute . . .'

'TV drama lacks a hero,' said Ian, as we finished our drinks. 'And those it has are so serious. Inspector Morse is very cerebral. All the fun's gone out of TV.'

I thought back to my childhood. I remembered Roger Moore's fights, when fists fell to the accompaniment of the most strident chords an orchestra could manage and afterwards he would dust himself off, adjust his cuffs and walk away. Yes, TV bosses should make a new series – the Saint may be hokum, but it's good hokum.

CONTACT
The Saint Club
c/o Arbour Youth Centre
Shandy Street
Stepney
London E1 4ST

The Sausage Appreciation Society

'Some of the letters I receive do demonstrate *such* an obsession for sausages that sometimes it borders on the worrying.'

Robert Metcalfe, the man who runs the Sausage Appreciation Society, went on to describe different types of enthusiast. There are quantity appreciators, eating sausages at just about every meal; there are questing appreciators, who will travel hundreds of miles, just to get hold of their favourite banger; and finally, quality appreciators, who can identify the contents of a fry-up with the expertise of a connoisseur of fine wine.

Meanwhile, my own mouth was full of a singularly delicious

sausage: the prize-winning Porkinson Banger, flavoured with a mouth-watering blend of honey and lemon juice. As I swallowed, I asked Robert whether the society had any advice on cooking.

'Ah, to prick or not to prick, that is the question' he said. The society's advice is not to prick. Far better to cook with the juices in the skin; though the cooking should not be rushed, so as to avoid splitting. 'But pricking has its defenders,' he said.

The Sausage Appreciation Society was launched in October 1992, when Barbara Windsor was the guest of honour. 'It's impossible to talk seriously about sausages,' said Robert. So that's why they invited Barbara? 'It seemed a natural association,' he said.

Eating is just one aspect of the society's work: when it calls itself the Sausage Appreciation Society it means exactly that. Even before the society was fully up and running, Robert was responsible for organizing a sausage song contest. 'There were 450 entries,' he said, 'in every musical genre.' With that, he turned on a cassette of sausage music. There was a reggae track, which had the lyrics:

> Don't want the stone age, the bronze age, the iron age
> I want the sausage
> I want to share my sausage with you.

Then an oompah piece:

> Don't drop a clanger
> Bang a British banger!

Then a moody Irish ballad, of considerable beauty, which spoke of men who had

> Strings of chipolatas
> For their inamoratas.

Yet music is not the only food of love for people with this love of food. Robert spoke of organizing an exhibition of sausage *paintings*.

'Will you accept avant-garde?' I asked.

'Any style will do,' he said, 'as long as there's a sausage in it.'

CONTACT
The Sausage Appreciation Society
26 Fitzroy Square
London W1P 6BT

The Shakespeare Oxford Society

My copy of the *Complete Works of Shakespeare* is leather-bound and in the centre of the cover is a gold-leaf portrait of Stratford-upon-Avon's most famous son. Or rather, there used to be a portrait, for three-quarters has worn away. To the members of the Shakespeare Oxford Society, that means a quarter too much is still left, for if they could, they would scratch with sharp fingernails until not a flake of Shakespeare's features survived. Then, they would have the book regilded with a new, aristocratic face: that of Edward de Vere, the Seventeenth Earl of Oxford, whom they believe to be the true author of the greatest body of work in the English language.

When I wrote to the society's headquarters in the USA, I received a stack of information on the case for Oxford. Though I have not met any of the members in person, in their own literature they reprint a comment, critical of the society, which says: 'The Oxfordians I've talked to remind me of Moonies. They get a crazed glint in their eye when they start talking about their beloved Edward de Vere.'

You see, once you start acknowledging that de Vere is the author, it does make a difference to the enjoyment of Shakespeare. The text becomes a hunting ground, because events from de Vere's life, or his family history, may be alluded to within the plays. One member writes of how he watched the Kenneth Branagh film of *Henry V* in which there is a scene in the French camp when a nobleman asks a constable of France, 'The armour that I see in your tent tonight, are those stars or suns upon it?' This may be an allusion to an historical episode during the War of the Roses, when the de Veres, wearing the star of the Lancastrians, were shot by their own side's archers by mistake – a mist had descended upon the battlefield and made the star seem like the sun of York.

At its most extreme, the search for de Vere references leads the Oxfordians to re-examine Shakespeare's use of words like 'every', 'ever' or 'never', because he might be punning upon his own name. But why is this? What is the case for Oxford?

It begins with the mysterious life of William Shakespeare of Stratford. Scholars have scoured Elizabethan documents and have uncovered reams of information about major poets and many minor poets, but all they have about Shakespeare are three dozen references, not one of which describes him as a poet or playwright. Also, Shakespeare is supposed to have spent twenty-nine years in London, yet there is not a single record of anyone seeing the great actor or playwright in the flesh. Strangest of all, in an era when the death of an English poet meant a lavish funeral and the composition of eulogies, Shakespeare's demise went completely unnoticed. Even Ben Jonson, who later claimed to have been a great admirer and friend of Shakespeare, expressed not the slightest regret when the Swan of Avon died. He didn't even mention the event.

In contrast, de Vere is *known* to have written poetry. It is also known that he wrote under a pseudonym (though that pseudonym is not recorded). Furthermore, being an aristocrat, he had personal experience of royal courts and so just the right background to describe the events in the plays. And it is intriguing that the family crest shows a lion holding a spear.

Well, who knows, the Oxfordians may be right – and opinion may be swinging their way. Recently, I saw a copy of the book *The 100: A Ranking of the Most Influential Persons in History*, by Michael H. Hart, and in this revised second edition Hart has become so convinced by the Oxfordian arguments that he has handed Shakespeare's place to de Vere.

A thought occurs to me: if the Shakespeare Oxford Society eventually comes to represent the received wisdom, will I one day find myself writing an article about a fringe group called the de Vere Stratford Society?

CONTACT
The Shakespeare Oxford Society
71 Spit Brook Road
Suite 107
Nashua
New Hampshire 03060
USA
Tel: 0101 603 888 1453
Fax: 0101 603 888 6411

226

The Sherlock Holmes Society

You will know what he wears on his head and what is lodged between his lips. You will probably know his address – and you will certainly know the name of his sidekick. It is a measure of Sir Arthur Conan Doyle's achievement that I can assume all this knowledge on your part. What you are less likely to be aware of, however, are the activities of the British society that honours Conan Doyle's creation. A society which ensures that its newsletters are printed in Baskerville type . . .

Not so long ago I went to Southsea, the town where Conan Doyle practised medicine for eight years and where he wrote the very first stories about Sherlock Holmes. By an improbable coincidence, a coincidence which probably would not have brought a single crease to Holmes's brow – did he not say that once you have eliminated the impossible, whatever remains, however improbable, must be the truth? – Southsea is also the home town of the secretary of the Sherlock Holmes Society of London, Commander G S Stavert.

When I visited the Commander's house, one of my first questions was whether the society members dressed in deer-stalkers and smoked Meerschaum pipes. 'We do dress up for certain functions,' he said, 'but not just as Holmes.' Indeed, the society has arranged five costumed trips to the Reichenbach Falls in Switzerland, where Holmes and Moriarty had their life-and-death struggle. 'About seventy or eighty of us go on a procession to the Falls, dressed as characters from the canon. I went as Dr Thorneycroft Huxtable, a dotty headmaster who appears in *The Adventure of the Priory School*. I already owned a mortar board and gown.'

The society was founded in London in 1951 with the aim of studying 'the life and work of Sherlock Holmes and Dr Watson'. For some members, this means acting as if the tales are real and trying to determine the date when an adventure occurred: a story's references to the weather and other contemporary events are vital clues, which are then compared to records of the time. Other members will establish that *mistakes* are made in Watson's chronicles: a passing mention of, say, Thursday, 14 October will lead some members to check and discover that the 14th was *not* a Thursday. Even grander forays into the borderland between fact and fiction have taken place at some society meetings, such as enquiring into the methods Holmes would have used to solve the Jack the Ripper murders.

In a sense, Conan Doyle encouraged readers to regard the text as a starting point for all sorts of further considerations. Many readers of the tales, myself included, are tantalized by the allusions to the unchronicled adventures, like 'the story of the politician, the lighthouse and the trained cormorant' or 'the story of the giant rat of Sumatra, for which the world is not yet prepared'. Commander Stavert has himself written his own interpretation of an unchronicled story, 'the singular tragedy of the Atkinson brothers at Trincomalee'. In his account, Holmes is faced with the mysterious death of a boy who is crushed under the wheels of a Hindu ceremonial chariot. 'I'd served at Trincomalee with the Navy,' he said, 'and I had pictures of all the temples and the religious ceremonies, like fire-walking. So I put on a slide show for the society while I told the story.'

And I sit and wonder about Mycroft Holmes, the detective's more intelligent elder brother, who could have solved all the cases far more efficiently than Sherlock if only he'd had the inclination to shift himself out of his armchair at the Diogenes Club . . .

CONTACT
Commander G S Stavert, MBE, MA, RN (Retd)
Honorary Secretary
The Sherlock Holmes Society of London
3 Outram Road
Southsea
Hants PO5 1QP
Tel: 0705 812104

The Simplified Spelling Society

The word 'said' was spelt as 'sed' while 'police' was 'polees' and 'precious', 'preshus'. However, there were some mistakes in the booklet; these were duly pointed out on an errata slip. 'Replace "boy" with "boi",' said the slip, 'and "merger" with "merjer".' Anyway, let me offer you the first sentence of a story, *The Star* by H G Wells, which the booklet renders thus:

> It woz on the ferst dae ov the nue yeer that the anounsment woz maed, aulmoest simultaeneusli from three obzervatoris, that the moeshen ov the planet Neptune, the outermoest ov

aul the planets that weel about the sun, had bekum veri eratik.

The booklet was amongst literature passed to me by the Simplified Spelling Society.

You will have already gathered that this society wants to perform plastic surgery on the face of the English language; but that doesn't mean there is any agreement on the operation required. For some members, it's a nose job, for others a chin lift, while still others want the bags removed. So, although the passage above has 'was' spelt as 'woz', this is not accepted by all. 'I feel the best spelling for "was" is "wz"' writes one member in the newsletter. Bob Brown, the society's secretary, told me that he is sent new spelling schemes at a rate of one a month, though the various suggestions do differ in the degree of their radicalism. For example, the Drop Useless 'E' (DUE) scheme merely involves the deletion of the 'e' at the end of certain words, leaving us with a lexicon of amputees like 'giv' and 'hav'. Or there is the Drop Redundant Initial Letters (DRIL) campaign, so one has 'nit', 'nolledge', 'ritten' and 'hoo'. Or there is the version which has 'th' replaced by dh: Bob showed me a children's book, *Dhe Litl Red Hen*, which began, 'Wun dae dhe litl red hen found a graen ov wheet.' There are even those members who favour revolution. For these spelling Lenins, that means a completely new alphabet – I have seen the squiggly pages of Shaw's *Androcles and the Lion*.

'I joined in 1973,' said Bob. 'Simplifying spelling just seemed like a damned good idea. Not that I have any problem with spelling. Though some members do. You get people joining saying that poor spelling has blighted their whole life.'

The trouble is, one's natural sympathy towards dyslexics is tempered when 'apple' is written as 'apl'. Bob assured me that I would soon get used to it. 'The feeling that it looks like children's writing soon goes,' he said.

Simplified spellers don't fail to tell you that English is behind the times and out of step. After all, *other* languages periodically revise their spelling rules, so that orthography reflects changes in pronunciation. The mere mention of this argument makes me worry that some EC directive could actually bring simplified spelling about.

Meanwhile, I take pleasure in writing plough, rough, cough and through – and I am especially proud of the eccentricity and character of 'eight', where only one of the letters, 't', takes its normal value.

CONTACT
Bob Brown
133 John Trundle Court
Barbican
London EC2Y 8DJ
Tel: 071 628 5876
Fax: 071 628 9147

Snail Farming

We do not eat snails and they do, that is the difference between the British and the French.

All right, I exaggerate. The tongue of Albion does stick itself in the odd shell. In fact, I can give you a figure: 200 tonnes of snails a year are eaten in this country. Which is nothing really, for in the same period 300 times as many will be eaten by the thrush-like French. 'Eat *snails*?' says John Bull. He will consider the trail of slime, which reminds him of unwiped noses. He will think of the horns tickling the roof of his mouth, as if the creature is still alive when consumed. 'Eat *snails*?' That is me speaking. I have done many things but, like a true-born Englishman, I cannot swallow a gastropod.

One man who has no time for my disgust is Roy Groves. As a gift, he gave me the book he has written, *Snail Cookery*, within the pages of which I saw an array of recipes, including Snail Omelettes, Snail Fondue, Snails in Champagne and Snail Curry. Yet Roy's cookery is just a sideline. His supreme achievement is that he is one of the world's leading authorities on keeping snails, being the first man in Europe to set up an indoor snail farm. And he is anxious to pass on his expertise to others. In the courses that he organizes, you can learn how to start a snail farm in your garage and turn a hobby into a profit-making business. The economics of the snail game aren't bad: by selling to restaurants, you can make £20,000 a year. A case of where there's mucus there's brass, I suppose. It's like compound interest. 'If you start with 100 snails,' he told me, 'you'll have 25,000 in six months.'

Which led us to a consider the sex life of these creatures – which is intriguing, because snails are both male and female at the same time. They do seek mates, though, and they impregnate each other. Roy explained that in the case of the common garden snail, there is a courtship ritual: the two boy-girls wander around in a ballroom of slime, and shoot bony love darts at their partners' body, thereby increasing the urge. But a different breed, the *Achatina*, doesn't do any of this. 'It gets down to the job much quicker,' he said.

Roy took me to see a few snails. Though he has now retired from active farming, he still keeps one or two for research purposes. In a plastic container was a peculiar specimen whose shell was not tightly coiled but unwound, like a spiral staircase. This was a freak, a mutant. 'I'm going to put it in with some normal ones to see whether it'll breed,' said Roy. I noticed that on the wall was a photograph of a giant snail covering much of a man's palm. Was that another mutant? 'Oh, that's Charlie,' he said. Charlie was an African land snail who even made an appearance on TV. 'Believe it or not,' he said, 'Charlie received fan mail.'

That captures the essence of the British. We don't eat snails, we write to them.

CONTACT
The Snail Centre
'Chestnuts'
Billingshurst Road
Wisborough Green
West Sussex RH14 0DX
Tel: 0403 700650
Fax: 0403 700160

Snuff-taking (Competitive)

My eyes streamed and again I spluttered. Meanwhile, Arthur Albin clicked the lid of his silver box and calmly tucked it back into his jacket. 'The first time I tried snuff,' he said, trying to sympathize with my distress, 'it blew my bloody head off. But I've been taking it for sixty years now.' By this time I was busy blowing my nose ... and watching two mahogany-coloured streaks appear on the handkerchief.

I had travelled to the hall in Feniton, Devon, to meet the contestants at the snuff-world's night of the year: the United Kingdom snuff-taking championships.

Championships? Granted, human nature has ever tried to parade vices as virtues, but is this the first example of a filthy habit becoming a competitive sport? Mr Albin, the secretary of the British Society of Snuff-blenders, was defensive. 'There's nothing filthy about snuff,' he said. 'I've sat watching people at dinner – and when you see the way that some people eat, *that's* what you call a filthy habit.' He told me that in Regency times, snuff-taking was regarded as such a refined activity that a gentleman was judged by the richness of his box and the grace with which he took a pinch. (Just the right bend of the elbow, precisely the proper action of wrist and hand, and certainly no grimace with the sniff.)

But by the later part of the twentieth century, snuff-taking needed a better reputation and a higher public profile, so in 1973 the annual snuff-taking championships began.

'Do you feel like entering this year's contest?' asked Mr Albin.

Now, my nose was a total novice, whereas the hardened snuff-addict would probably take three pinches before breakfast. I weighed up the odds. I'd finish last, but it might be an interesting experience. Thus, without knowing what I was letting myself in for, without even knowing the rules of this peculiar-sounding sport, I accepted the challenge. Only the presence in the hall of some women from the St John Ambulance Brigade indicated that this might be an act of folly, that snuff is not to be taken lightly.

Already, my thoughts were, I need some training. Ken Wilson, who called himself the Western Counties Snuff-taking champion, helped by offering me samples of all manner of brands from a tiny chest of drawers. The names were seductive, like words from exotic reveries: Masulipatam, Morlaix, Old Paris, Orange Cardinal. And yet ... 'Here, try some of this,' said Mr Wilson, smiling a little too much. He offered me a pinch of an Indian make. 'Don't you think it smells of –' I do not intend to quote the precise words of his description. Suffice to say, a dog-owner could be fined for the substance that was put on the back of my hand.

Mr Wilson said that if I wanted to do well in the championships, I would have to learn to take the grains up in short, sharp sniffs. He spread a gunpowder trail from my thumbnail to my wrist and invited me to go ahead. This time, the snuff was more pleasant – an odour of raspberries – and somehow I managed to ingest it all. I felt quite proud of myself, though I was beginning to feel decidedly woozy. Then Mr Wilson put my achievement in perspective. 'I wish I had my sword here,' he said. He told me that one of his party pieces is to spread snuff all along the blade, from tip to hilt, and rapidly move his nose along, taking up every speck. However, he *had* brought along another training aid: his snuff gun. This peculiar German-made device consists of a palette, with a spring-release mechanism, which literally *fires* a quantity of snuff up the nose. As a nasal bullet, I tried an Indonesian brand which smelt like fish oil. I realized that if I wanted to be on my feet when the competition started, I'd better stop training. Thanking Mr Wilson, I went to meet someone I'd heard so much about, Mr Jack Pope.

As Pelé is to soccer, so Jack Pope is to competitive snuff-taking. Mr Pope's devotion to powdered tobacco can be judged by the fact that he sleeps with a box under his pillow just in case he wakes up in the middle of the night. It is not simply that he has been UK champion five times; it is that he stands at the heart of Britain's first family of snuff-taking. For when Mr Pope gave up his crown, he passed it on to his son, Larry, who became six-times champion; and when Larry himself retired, the title was passed to Mr Pope's younger son, Roderick. Even Mr Pope's wife has been champion in the ladies' event. But just as he was reminiscing about the time he captained the British team at the world championships – for yes, snuff-taking is now an inter-national sport, complete with national anthems and flag waving – the MC called everyone together for the start of the evening's contest.

Competitive snuff-taking involves edging along a lengthy table, snorting as you go. Behind this table sit twenty-five official servers, holding in their hands two spoons, each containing a pinch of snuff – so, in all, fifty different brands are represented. As a competitor moves along the line of servers, snuff is placed upon the back of his hand; the snuff is to be cleared as fast as possible – and every grain must go up the nose and not drop on the table or remain on the hand. An eagle-eyed referee, who carries a stopwatch and follows each competitor, will allocate penalty points for spillages and uncleared pinches. In a way, competitive snuff-taking resembles show-jumping, for both the total time taken for the course and the faults incurred will play a part in determining one's score. Though show-jumping does not have snuff-taking's rather unique disqualification rule: a sneeze, cough or splutter means you're out.

With the rules made clear to everyone, the referee blew a whistle and the first competitor was away, steaming down the table in a couple of minutes – nose down, elbow out and accompanied by the crowd's traditional encouragement: 'Up! Up! Up!', whooped out like a tribal war cry. One by one, the contestants came forward. I asked Ken Wilson how he thought he'd done. 'I dropped a few,' he said, 'but I'm pretty pleased with my performance.'

Then my name was called. Still in a haze from my training, I was unsteady as I got to my feet. 'Think of England,' said Mr Wilson.

Off went the whistle. 'He'll never do it,' I heard someone say, and that was a goad. I knew I couldn't compete with the vacuum-cleaner nostrils of the serious contenders, but I was determined to complete the course. 'Up! Up! Up!' went the crowd, drowning out the sounds of my sniffs. All the perfumes of the snuff – strawberry, peppermint, lemon, eucalyptus – merged into one; my nose felt like it was being rubbed raw with a test-tube brush and bleach. With that much tobacco being taken so rapidly into my system, I was virtually passing out. When at last I reached the fiftieth spoonful and took it all up, I got the biggest cheer of the evening.

Later, as the winner, Roderick Pope again, received his trophy and glory, I stood elsewhere, slumped over a poorly lit backroom sink, bringing up a yellow-brown liquid that looked like a mixture of egg yolk and naval shag. No, I thought, as I emptied myself, as I came near the point of fainting, this is not a filthy habit, no, not at all . . .

CONTACT
Arthur Albin
20 Carclaze Road
St Austell
Cornwall PL25 3AQ
Tel: 0726 66857

Somewhere in Time Enthusiasts

There are few great quests that end in Golders Green, but the search for the video of *Somewhere in Time* is one of them. After calling at half the video outlets in London, I had found a store, the Video Palace, that had a copy of this now deleted movie.

'Now deleted', what terrible words. *Somewhere in Time*, a romantic fantasy, may have been a box-office disaster when it was released in 1980 – somehow, the star billing of Christopher Reeve and Jane Seymour never captured the public's imagination – but is that any reason to allow the film to be forgotten? The 700 members of INSITE, the International Network of *Somewhere in Time* Enthusiasts, would have much to say on this matter. Because it produces its own quarterly magazine, campaigns for the cinema re-release of the movie and, even as I type these words, is holding a weekend *Somewhere in Time* convention in turn of the century dress at the Grand Hotel, Mackinac Island, Michigan, USA.

For those of you who have never seen *Somewhere in Time*, I'll try to sketch the plot. Christopher Reeve takes the role of a playwright who, at a backstage party in 1972, is approached by an old woman. He has never seen her before. She presses into his hand a pocket-watch and utters the words, 'Come back to me.' She walks away. Eight years pass and Reeve is staying at the hotel on Mackinac Island. Killing time before lunch, he visits the hotel's Hall of History, where he spots a photograph of a beautiful young woman (Jane Seymour), whom he learns was an early twentieth-century actress. For Reeve, obsession begins. After much detective work, he discovers that, sixty years after the picture was taken, the actress had aged into the very woman who handed him the watch! By sheer force of will, Reeve sends himself back in time to meet the young Jane Seymour – and the two fall in love. The spell is broken when the sight of a 1979 penny, that Reeve had been carrying in his pocket, sends him hurtling back to the future. He pines for his lost love and wastes away. The two are reunited after death.

I decided to write to INSITE's founder, an American, Bill Shepard. 'I find myself fascinated by the notion of going back in time,' he replied, 'not as a sterile scientific experiment, but out of an obsession for a woman seen only on an antique portrait on a wall.' He said that when he first saw the film in 1980, it produced in him 'a feeling of being on the verge of tears, not from sadness, but from an indescribable sense of beauty'.

Is *Somewhere in Time* an undiscovered masterpiece? It's an unusual film that's worth a look. The 1912 scenes are well crafted – the long dresses and parasols re-create pointillist paintings. (In the group's magazine, I discovered that two different film stocks, one made by Kodak and one by Fuji, were used to shoot the contemporary and period sequences – the slight distinction in coloration helping to emphasize the differences between the eras.) And yes, the film's portrayal of the culture clash between lovers from two ages is poignant, in an amusing sort of way. 'You will marry me, won't you?' asks Jane, having been to bed with Reeve for the first time.

On the negative side is Reeve's performance. There are moments when he looks lost, speaks too quickly, and makes you wish you were watching *Superman*. (At times, you think you *are* watching *Superman*.) During one of the most important scenes – when he finds a dusty hotel register, signed by himself, thereby proving that he had travelled to the past – his acting is, to put it charitably, understated. Had I discovered that I'd booked into a hotel years before my birth, I think I would have shown some kind of reaction.

Not that this will deter the members of INSITE. 'I've never really thought of INSITE as a fan club,' writes Bill. 'To me it's more of a cause. We have a particular goal, that of influencing public and media perception of the film, to assure its recognition as the classic we know it to be.'

Maybe Bill's dream will come true . . . somewhere in time.

CONTACT
INSITE
PO Box 1556
Covina
CA 91722
USA

See also Superman – *The Adventures Continue*, page 242, for more on Reeve's acting.

The Street Lamp Interference Data Exchange

The gutter was yellow, now black; the lamp it had reflected was dead. Looking along the street, this was repeated all the way down, off into the distance. Lamps were failing one by one – the tiger flees, the panther chases. Vandals, vandals. Yet they wield no sticks – if they did, they couldn't stretch. They hurl no stones – their aim's not true. We are dealing with a different kind of lout. One with a catapult not in his hand but in his mind.

Psychic vandals may exist. The possibility occurred to me after meeting Mr Hilary Evans, a paranormal researcher and founder of the Street Lamp Interference Data Exchange, or SLIDE. This is a forum for anyone interested in the alleged ability of some people to switch off (or in a few cases switch on) the lamps on our streets by mental power alone. I should say that you don't have to possess this power to join. Hilary doesn't. He hasn't even witnessed it. But since establishing SLIDE, he has received well over 100 letters from human switches. 'In 99 per cent of these letters,' he said, 'there's a sentence which says something like, "I'm so glad that somebody is taking this seriously at last."'

Hilary gave me examples of the people he calls Sliders. There was the man who would drive to a meeting every Thursday evening. On the way home, a lamp would go off when his car passed underneath. *And it was always the same lamp.* 'In most cases,' said Hilary, 'the people have a history of affecting other electrical apparatus.' One woman who has communicated with him says she has to be careful whenever she flies. She'll be sitting on a plane, waiting for take-off, and the captain will apologize for an unexplained electrical fault. 'She *knows* that she is responsible,' he said. Another Slider claims to have knocked out the hi-fi system at a Greek taverna. And one American correspondent even says that he's 'done' the lights at his local football stadium.

Hilary has discovered that few factors correlate with the blackout power: age, sex, class, profession, marital status – all these are irrelevant. The factor that *does* seem to be significant is state of mind, but there is no agreement on *which* state of mind. Sometimes, tension and anger are responsible; but one correspondent claims to put out street lamps whenever he makes love to his girlfriend.

Yet is not wiring failure the most obvious explanation? Or

perhaps a light source, such as car headlamps, triggers the photo-electric cells inside the street lamps?

Hilary believes that some examples of street lamp interference do have a normal cause, but the vast majority do not. 'If the car headlamps theory is right,' he said, 'how could that explain the fact that the lamps stay on when someone else drives the same car? Or what about when someone is just out walking?'

Coincidence? I suggested. Surely with millions of people walking the streets every day, under hundreds of thousands of street lamps, there will be lamp failures? Hilary agrees that coincidence has to be taken into account, especially as the power is erratic, but he thinks there's much more to street lamp interference than a statistical fluke. He told me about two paranormal researchers who were walking back at night, discussing SLIDE, when suddenly a lamp went off. 'That has to be a coincidence,' said the more sceptical of the two. They walked further down the road and the next lamp they passed went off as well.

Hilary is currently in touch with electrical engineers who have an interest in street lamp interference – one of them has sent him a twenty-five-page analysis of the phenomenon – and before long he hopes to conduct empirical research. 'The great thing about street lamp interference,' he said, 'is that it can be put to the test. In the case of someone like Uri Geller, there's always the *possibility* of sleight of hand being involved, even if he's genuine. But who's going to tamper with a ruddy great street lamp?'

I wonder whether the talent could be nurtured? What if I practise? This Christmas, I shall be gazing long and hard at the fairy lights on my tree. The following Christmas? Oxford Street, watch out.

CONTACT
Hilary Evans
59 Tranquil Vale
London SE3 OBS
Fax: 081 852 7211

Subterranea Britannica

There was an electric light upon the walls, where centuries ago there would have been candlelight. What there was not, what there had never been, was a single ray of sunlight.

I was 30 feet underground in a mysterious and unnatural cave. Unnatural, because no geological process, no erosion, no seeping water action could have given it such a shape – like an upright wine bottle, with a neck that narrowed the higher it went. Mysterious, because when you are standing at its base and staring upwards, you cannot help but ask yourself, who built it? And when? And why?

'Coming down here changed my life,' said Sylvia Beamon, who had accompanied me along the passageway that led to Royston Cave. It was a chance visit to the cave with her children in 1974 that started Sylvia's fascination with the achievements of the human mole. The experience led her to found Subterranea Britannica, a group which studies and explores man-made and man-used underground structures.

Members of Subterranea Britannica tend to be spotted at land collapses, such as the well-publicized event of a few years ago, when a double-decker bus fell through a road in Norwich. And Sylvia reminisced about the time she and a male colleague were summoned to a collapsed churchyard. They climbed down the hole into a crypt and then a little boy came along and peered over the edge. 'Hey, mister,' he shouted, 'there's a football down there.' It turned out to be a skull.

But your cranial capacity would be enormous if you were an expert on the full range of Subterranea Britannica's research interests and concerns. The group examines everything from prehistoric burial chambers to nuclear fall-out shelters, including, along the way, shafts and wells and sewers; and drains and tunnels and dungeons; even underground mushroom farming and the homes of modern-day troglodytes, or cave dwellers. 'I'd love to have a cave,' said Sylvia, as she spoke about there being several hundred troglodytes in modern France. 'There's no decorating. And you can always tunnel backwards and create another room.'

In the meantime, I was becoming aware of the change in temperature to something suggesting the grave. One begins to feel ill at ease. There is an atmosphere . . . and I remembered the Morlocks, the sinister subhuman subterranean race of H G Wells's novel *The Time Machine*.

'You lose all sense of time underground,' said Sylvia. 'You can go down at ten o'clock at night or in the daytime, and it's always dark.' Was it ever dangerous? She admitted that it could be. 'But if you go into an area with cracks,' she said, 'you just don't speak.'

Fortunately, the roof of Royston Cave seemed sturdy enough for the conversation to continue. Sealed up and forgotten for centuries, the cave was rediscovered in 1742, when a workman hammered a stake into the ground in the market-place – and the stake went straight through. At the time, the cave was thought to contain treasure. What it actually contained was a set of medieval wall carvings: pictures of martyrdoms, crucifixions and other religious symbols. But why had the cave been sealed? For that matter, why was it built at all?

Members of Subterranea Britannica can suggest some answers. For example, in Britain there are underground follies, grottoes built by hermits. Could that be what the cave is? Or is it an ice-house? There are 3,000 of these structures, which by careful use of insulation could preserve ice chipped from lakes and ponds for up to five years. Or perhaps the cave is associated with some religious cult that met underground?

Sylvia's own belief is that Royston Cave was built by the Knights Templar, initially to store market goods (the temperature would have kept them fresh) and then was turned into a chapel. The Knights were disbanded in 1308, amid accusations of heresy – they had begun dabbling in witchcraft and freemasonry – and the discrediting of the order would account for the cave being sealed.

Is Sylvia right? My own knowledge was just too meagre to judge. I knew of only one thing concerning the Knights Templar: were they not rumoured to possess the Holy Grail? And could the Grail *possibly* – just possibly – have been stored in this strange cave at Royston?

'Ah,' said Sylvia with a smile, 'you're flying a kite with that one . . .'

I had been too long underground. My brain needed all the fresh air it could get.

CONTACT
Malcolm and Barbara Tadd
65 Trindles Road
South Nutfield
Redhill
Surrey RH1 4JL
Tel: 0737 823456

The Sundial Society

I did know one technical term and was eager to flaunt it. 'Isn't the thing that casts the shadow called the *gnomon*?' I asked.

David Young smiled, pleased that I should know even this. He told me that in 1989, when he and a few others founded the British Sundial Society, they had originally planned to call themselves the British Gnomonic Society. 'But we realized pretty quickly that most people would think we were interested in garden gnomes,' he said.

In the age of quartz crystals and Stephen Hawking, an age when it's not unknown to hear talk of nanoseconds, it may seem peculiar for anyone to be attracted to telling the time by shadows. The interest becomes understandable, akin to collecting clocks, when you realize the range of gnomonic devices.

There are dials that tell time by moonlight, there are ultra-modern dials with photo-electric cells and a digital read-out, there are helical structures, circular structures and even human structures, where a person has to be the pointer, as well as primitive scratchmarks on the side of Saxon churches and electronic dials for the blind that give the hours in Braille. Not all of the 15,000 sundials in the UK are in good condition, though. Some are little more than lichen-encrusted birdtables and, sadder still, some old dials are now in permanent shadow, beside newly erected buildings. But whatever the state of a dial, wherever it is, the Sundial Society will never let it be forgotten.

'Some of the members are attracted to the mottoes,' said David. He quoted a few examples, most of which were to do with human transience, like 'Man fleeth as a shadow' and 'What you look at are minutes, not what you lose', as well as the punning 'We must die-all'. 'We also have quite a few mathematicians as members.' He showed me a copy of the society's bulletin, with pages of trigonometrical alphas, betas and thetas, all to determine the position for the pointer. 'But sundials can be studied in so many ways,' he said. 'Art, science, geography, astronomy, craftsmanship – sundials are a combination of all these things.'

Looking through the literature, it was easy to see the multi-disciplinary approach at work. There was a feature on medieval Hungarian dials, a poem or two – 'Here is Time in heavenly grace / Hither brought from outer space' – and an analysis of the use of dials for navigation at sea. I noticed a booklet for schoolchildren, telling how to make a dial out of a broomstick and bicycle wheel, and yet there were also highly technical works, such as 'The Accuracy of Using Polaris to Align a Gnomon'.

David told me that he started taking notice of sundials when he was a teenager, soon after the war. 'I cycled all over the country, in one big circle, looking for them,' he said. But the seed of fascination may have been planted even earlier. I asked him whether he had ever relied upon a dial to tell the time, and he said, 'I can remember when I was a young child, playing in the park. I looked at a sundial to find out when to go home.'

And to this day, he remains impressed by the accuracy of shadow and pointer. 'One of our members came across a dial that was reputedly made by Sir Isaac Newton,' he said. 'It was made in 1620, and it was accurate to within ten seconds. Yet the nearby station clock was ten minutes slow.'

CONTACT
David Young
Brook Cottage
112 Whitehall Road
Chingford
London E4 6DW
Tel: 081 529 4880

Superman – *The Adventures Continue*

Jim Nolt is a forty-six year-old teacher from Pennsylvania. This is what he said to me in one letter:

There is no way I can describe to you the influence he has had upon my life. He was there when a young boy needed a hero and has continued to guide me and help me through my entire life. I feel he is with me constantly. It was his sense of fair play, honesty, quiet strength, courage and stick-to-itiveness that continues to challenge me every day.

And in another:

I feel he is partly responsible for my becoming a teacher.

There are many days in the classroom when I think of him and wonder if he'd appreciate my efforts. He has inspired me to help children, to devote a portion of my time, money and energy to helping others.

The person who has inspired Jim is not, as you might be tempted to think, Jesus Christ, but another figure with extraordinary powers – Superman. Or, to be strictly accurate, *one interpretation* of Superman: the 1950s low-budget television series featuring the less-than-musclebound George Reeves. Ever since he was a kid, when he would put on a T-shirt with a towel pinned to the back, when he would pretend to fly and bend steel bars (aluminium foil rods), Jim has been influenced by George Reeves's – and *only* George Reeves's – version of Superman. When I asked him what he thought of near-namesake Christopher Reeve's interpretation of the Man of Steel, the answer was a curt, 'George Reeves was Superman, Christopher Reeve was a man portraying Superman.' Jim even starts using inverted commas when referring to Christopher Reeve's work, such is the contempt he feels. 'His "Superman" lacked spark, his "Clark Kent" lacked absolutely everything.'

I managed to track down a video of a George Reeves performance, *Superman and the Mole Men*, a cinema film shot in less than a month on a budget that wouldn't even stretch to shoestrings. The special effects? You *won't* believe a man can fly. It also struck me that George Reeves's interpretation of Clark Kent is far too strong; there are times he seems more powerful than Superman. The effect is emphasized by the clothes worn by the two-men-in-one: sharp suits for Clark, while for Superman's costume, the seams are as prominent as the S symbol. Surely something is flawed here? Jim doesn't see it that way. 'George's Clark was indeed a strong character,' he told me, 'in fact, so strong that I often thought I'd like to see a series based solely on Clark Kent.'

To keep the memory of the late George Reeves alive, Jim publishes a magazine, *The Adventures Continue*, devoted exclusively to the 1950s Superman and featuring interviews with the stars, writers and anyone else connected with the show. It is a well-produced magazine, but also rather sad – I don't like to see photographs of an ageing Lois Lane. There is even a roll call of those actors who have died since appearing in the series – over eighty are listed in my copy of the magazine along with the year of demise. Of course, the magazine's subscribers themselves aren't getting any younger; there is a page showing pictures of grandchildren in Superman romper suits.

The fact that George Reeves didn't really look the part doesn't seem to bother the true fan. 'He was strong, but it was not the violent strength of Arnold Schwarzenegger,' writes Jim. 'Instead, his was a quiet, gentle strength.'

He may have leapt tall buildings, but he landed softly.

CONTACT
The Adventures Continue
PO Box 26
Stevens
PA 17578
USA

Survival Training

SAS SOLDIERS BEHEADED IN CLASH WITH YEMENI REBEL FORCES

This was one of the newspaper cuttings in Mick Tyler's scrapbook, the book of his twenty-seven years with the SAS and the Paras, a tale of Cyprus, Jordan, Kuwait, Malaysia and the Borneo jungle. 'The survival techniques I teach do work,' he said. 'I've done it for real. They're why I'm here.' He mentioned some of the food he'd eaten in the jungle, like iguana, which he described as 'good eating'.

'Would you eat it raw?' I asked.

'No problem.'

He said that when you've trapped an animal, the first thing to do is drink its blood. 'Get those minerals down you,' he said. He then discussed the merits of eating flies, grasshoppers, crickets, grubs, slugs and ants. 'If you're fucking hungry, you'll eat them,' he said.

I must make it clear that Mick's courses in Survival Training do not demand starvation as an entry requirement, so unless you really want to, you won't be asked to stick your tongue down an anthill. But he will teach you how to skin a rabbit, and gut an eel; he'll show you which fungi to avoid and which greenery to seek. 'Stinging nettles contain a lot of roughage,' he said.

244

'And you can make coffee out of dandelion roots.'

Now, you may be wondering whether I have tried this activity? Have I, like Mick, done it for real?

Well, sort of. Mick takes his students out into the wilds – and this has a similarity to a week-long course I took five years ago. I've abseiled down mountains, I've read maps by the moon, I've waded across mudflats and been sucked in to my thighs. Those experiences had a certain value: I think they changed me – maybe I wouldn't have done half the stuff in this book without the syringeful of bravado they injected. Still, as an inveterate dabbler, I didn't want to repeat the exercise – and anyway, I like civilization's warm sleeping bag too much. So I've only done part of the training, and I have never learned the pure techniques of *survival*. Like firelighting ...

Mick painted a grim picture of what it can be like on the Brecon Beacons if you haven't got a fire. 'It's a wet kind of cold up there,' he said, 'with a chill factor. It will get into your bones and lower your inner temperature. Your blood starts to thicken. The oxygen won't get to your brain. You'll start slurring your speech. Your vision will blur. You'll start stumbling. If you sit down and fall asleep, you won't wake up.'

He fetched a belt with pouches containing different types of fire-making equipment: a magnesium block, flint and steel, a burning glass. He took a frying pan, put it on the floor and threw in a screwed-up newspaper. He added chemicals from the belt and there was spontaneous combustion: we had a campfire in the lounge. Smoke was filling the room, enough to make us cough.

After he'd opened a window, Mick moved on to the subject of natural medicines, like the fungus Jew's ear, which can be used as a sore throat cure. And if you put a polythene bag over an oak-tree branch and seal it, you will collect a dark liquid which combats diarrhoea. 'Or,' he added, 'you can eat charcoal from your fire to bind your motions together.' I wondered whether our burnt *Daily Mail* would have quite the same effect.

He spoke of how to make a longbow out of a yew tree, arrows out of hazel twigs and a bowstring out of plaited grass; how to catch trout by hand and how to build shelters in the snow. But unless civil order breaks down, is any of this relevant? Mick had a response to that question. 'You are going to end up in a survival situation whether you like it or not,' he said. 'You are going to get old.'

I only hope I can rely on Meals on Wheels.

CONTACT
The Breakaway Survival School
17 Hugh Thomas Avenue
Holmer
Hereford HR4 9RB
Tel: 0432 267097

Talking to the Trees

The last time mankind mucked around with a tree of knowledge, we all got into quite a bit of trouble. Like greatly increased pains in childbearing, having to eat our food by the sweat of our brow, and being hurled out of Paradise. With Chapter 3 of Genesis serving as a warning, I went to visit Martin Blount, founder of the group Tree Spirit. This is a society with the laudable aims of protecting and conserving woodland – though many of its members go further and ascribe a certain wisdom to wooden friends.

At Tree Spirit's stall at Kingston's Green Fair, Martin passed me a free copy of the society's magazine. I flicked through to find passages like the following: 'When we travel we talk to the trees where we camp. We tell them of the beautiful trees where we live, of how the Dorset hills look, or the Welsh mountains. We tell them of the weather in places other than their own.' Another passage advised readers to share their 'deepest feelings and secrets, treating the tree like a close friend. You can trust the tree, it will never tell anyone else.'

Martin took me along to a sycamore. He and I sat beneath a bough and began a conversation. Perhaps we were overheard by ears that rustled . . .

SJ: In your magazine, there are people saying they communicate with trees. Tell me about that.

MB: You show the tree respect. You open up, show affection. You try to get on to the same wavelength as the tree. It helps if you imagine you've got a root.

SJ: What do you say to a tree?

MB: Occasionally, if I've got a problem, I ask the trees for advice. We hug trees as well.

SJ: You hug them?

MB: There's nothing wrong with showing affection. One of our members has so much respect for trees that she changed her name to Hazel Birch. You see, a lot of our members believe in dryads. They're the unseen spirits of trees. The souls of trees.

SJ: And do you believe in them?

MB: Yes. In a forest there would be one dryad for all the oaks and another dryad for all the birches. But if someone brought along another oak from a different forest and planted it there, that would bring in a second oak dryad.

SJ: How would the two of them get along? Would they fight?

MB: I think they'd give each other some hassle.

SJ: Tell me about how Tree Spirit got started.

MB: It all began in 1984 with a campaign to save some local oaks. Now we've got about 100 members nationwide.

SJ: I can't resist asking whether you're organized in regional branches.

MB: (*Laughing*) No. But we get involved in a lot of tree planting. We concentrate on native species.

SJ: What would those be? Sorry about my ignorance, but I'm just a symptom of the general lack of tree education in modern society.

MB: Oak, silver birch. They're best suited to our climate, soil and landscape.

SJ: So what's the appeal of trees?

MB: You can learn a lot from them. I always feel good when I'm with trees. Mind you, they're not always peaceful. Sometimes they're aggressive.

SJ: And what are your favourite trees?

MB: Silver birches are very feminine and happy and joyous. But they don't live very long – seventy or eighty years. Nothing for a tree. Yews can live for 1,000 years. They grow so slowly, they've seen a lot of things. They're very wise trees.

SJ: I see. What do you think of wood as a raw material?

MB: I think it's excellent.

SJ: But doesn't chopping down a tree pose some ethical problems for you? Doesn't it make you feel guilty?

MB: What you have to do is go out and explain the situation to the tree. You have to tell the tree why you're doing it. You show the tree respect and then you thank it for its timber. Some time ago, I went and talked to a walnut before I cut it down.

SJ: What message do you have for my readers?

MB: Go out and hug a tree. The more you do it, the more

natural it becomes. Millions of people hug and talk to cats and dogs – it's the same thing.

CONTACT
Tree Spirit
Hawkbatch Farm
Arley
Nr Bewdley
Worcs DY12 3AH

Tarantula Breeding

Fraction by fraction, I moved my finger forward, closer to the bristles. On the table in front of me lay the skin of a very large spider. It looked like a broken-up wheel – no rim, but an axle and spokes. Or perhaps it lay like hand-me-downs; being just a skin, it was really a garment. Whatever, I was afraid. I touched one of the legs and moved my fingernail up and down the bristles. They were gingery. My heart went faster, my lips tightened. I was acting as if the ghost of the spider were about to return, as if one of those dead limbs were about to twitch. Arachnids may cast off their hides but I don't think I'll ever cast off my arachnophobia.

I was in a plain room, but one that smelt of rotting fruit. 'That's to feed the flies,' I was told. There were also boxes of chirping crickets and boxes of locusts and boxes of maggots ... All the choicest food. And I was in the home of Paul Carpenter, whose hobby is breeding tarantulas. Indeed, Paul's fondness is for a particularly aggressive strain, African baboon spiders, which have legs as thick as pencils. As he opened a container – and as I stood as far back as possible – I saw a prize specimen. 'Look at those fangs,' Paul said with glee, 'you could catch a trout with one of those.' I kid you not, the spider's eight eyes were staring at my two, and until that moment I hadn't known that spiders made a noise – this one was hissing like a steam kettle.

As soon as the lid was on and not before, Paul and I began talking about the joys of spider sex. As you may be aware, for the male there is always the possibility of ending up as a post-coital meal. 'I've got a female up there that's eaten four of her husbands,' Paul said, pointing to the top shelf. Given the costs of buying replacements, it's not surprising that he sometimes resorts to prising the couples apart with a knitting needle. Rather them than me, I thought.

Mind you, in the British Tarantula Society, of which Paul is the vice-president, there is much more to enjoy than the de Sadean pleasures of sex followed by cannibalism. Every year, the society holds a convention at which members compete for the Best Spider trophy, like an arachnid equivalent of Cruft's. Some members even give names to their non-incy-wincy pets, Adolf, Attila and Webster being fashionable at the moment.

Paul and I spoke of spider digestion – and how this involves injecting venom, crushing the prey and sucking its innards like soup. We spoke of the black widow, and its habit of building webs in Australian outside toilets, particularly favouring the environment under the seat. And we spoke of the Mexican redknee spider that lived for a record twenty-eight years – and then only died because the lab assistant forgot to feed it. Still, I must not give the impression that Paul, a pest-control officer by profession, is interested only in spiders. For in other plastic boxes he keeps his giant Madagascan cockroaches and his venomous centipedes. 'One of these centipedes will open up an adult locust like a tin of beans,' he said.

I hope there isn't a locust appreciation society out there anywhere.

CONTACT
Ann Webb (Honestly, that's her name!)
Secretary The British Tarantula Society
81 Phillimore Place
Radlett
Herts WD7 8NJ
Tel: 0923 856071

The Test-card Circle

'It first hit me when I was about four years old, about 1963. I tuned into the schools programme and on came this strange black and white pattern of circles and lines. I was transfixed.'

So says Paul Sawtell, the chairman and founder of the Test-card Circle, a group of eighty-five enthusiasts devoted to the study and appreciation of test cards and test-card music. No, the horizontal hold of your brain has no need of fine tuning, and yes, your eyesight is indeed giving you a perfect picture of these words. For I tell you, there are people out there who swap videos and tapes of the card and its soundtrack; people who admit that in their youth they would hurry home from school to get in some serious viewing before the programmes started; even people who are nostalgic for the television strikes of the 1960s, when the test card was shown all day. 'The only thing missing from a perfect day's viewing,' says one member, reminiscing about those long-ago strike-ridden times, 'was the lack of the national anthem at closedown.'

Now you, reader, will probably know of the card that shows the little girl and the clown and the noughts and crosses board. But at the chairman's home in Stourbridge, I watched a wealth of videos, featuring other test cards, including regional variations, Christmas specials (with holly in the corners) and reduced-power versions. Paul also explained to me the rudiments of the card's engineering functions. The well-known 'letter-box' in the design was used to test for high-frequency streaking, caused by a misaligned aerial; the centre circle was a check on the curvature of the picture's geometry; and as for that seemingly innocent noughts and crosses game – well, that was really a test for static convergence. Such a treasure chest of fascination is embedded in the card and its soundtrack that at the group's annual convention there is a test-card quiz. Contestants are asked about television installation and about obscure pieces of music: for example, 'Which types of aerials are most likely to cause ghosting?' and, 'Who played the music in the middle section of the 1985 BBC tape featuring Markhu Johansen?' The competing quiz teams have buzzers set to operate at the tone frequencies associated with the BBC1 and BBC2 transmitters – 1 kHz for BBC1, 440 Hz for BBC2.

Now, it is possible you are asking yourself what sort of person gets their thrills from the test card. Do they have no boredom threshold? Are their attention spans the length of the Humber Bridge? The truth is a little more complicated and, I am afraid, rather more sad. Paul admits that if test-card enthusiasts have anything in common, it's probably an unhappy childhood. 'Most of us were the ones in the classroom who were picked on,' he told me. He admits to having few friends at school and said that, against a background of being bullied, he found a certain comfort in the screening of the card. What particularly attracted him was the music, which he maintains was more varied and of a higher standard than most of the sounds of the era. By turning on those circles and lines, he had access to an extraordinary musical diversity: jazz, big band, classical – 'even a man imitating the bark of a dog'. Today, Paul works as a professional musician and composer, and as he played me a tape of his tunes it struck me that they bore a resemblance to card music – an influence which Paul does not deny. It seems that in his work, just as much as in his leisure, Paul Sawtell's whole life has been affected by a means of checking that televisions are correctly installed.

What is clear is that the Test-card Circle fulfils a need. Paul told me that prior to its foundation there was 'a bubble of frustration about to burst' – and then there was enormous relief, as people across the country suddenly realized that they were not alone. At last it was possible to meet others who shared a belief that the rest of television's output was 'a mindless deluge'. With the coming of the Test-card Circle, with the forming of contacts, you could ring someone up and hum the 'Trains and Boats and Planes' tape down the telephone line.

Sadly, the test card is now almost a thing of the past. Replaced by CEEFAX, the good old card is shown only for six or seven minutes a day in the very early hours of the morning. However, with the Test-card Circle in existence, it will never be forgotten. I opened the group's magazine and read a report of last year's convention. 'We thrilled to the showing of the colour-receiver installation film,' a member writes. 'Not a dry eye in the house . . .'

CONTACT
Stuart Montgomery
Membership Secretary
The Test Card Circle
2 Henderson Row
Edinburgh EH3 5DS
Tel: 031 556 2092

Tiddlywinks

It was whilst watching Charles Relle in action at the table that I began reflecting on the significance of the sci-fi movie *The Incredible Shrinking Man*. If only real people could step into strange vapours and emerge ant-sized . . . Charles's sport would suddenly zoom into view, with huge, aerodynamic discs sailing through the air, crashlanding into causeways of other discs or dropping into a Mount Etna-sized crater. Because Charles, a middle-aged classics master from Catford, plays a sport which operates on a scale far too small for most people. It can be dismissed as a kindergarten pastime, or derided in the words of St Paul: 'When I became a man, I put away childish things.' For Charles Relle is one of the country's foremost players of tiddlywinks.

Laid out on the felt playing surface, the brightly coloured counters, or winks, look as innocent as the contents of a tube of Smarties. But within minutes of reading the rules and struggling to follow Charles's advice on tactics, it became clear to me that this was a game of considerable depth, a game to be taken seriously.

Although the pot is the focal point, the object is not simply to sink one's winks as fast as possible. Tiddlywinks has elements of attack and defence, as a result of the so-called 'squop' rule: if, at any stage, a wink is covered by another wink, it is said to be squopped and cannot be played. Basic strategy, then, involves immobilizing or outmanoeuvring one's opponent, with the successful player establishing a military-style domination of the playing surface. Modern tiddlywinks thus combines skills both of the hand and of the mind. Even potting has its subtleties: try putting away a wink using a backspin shot. It's not easy.

Not surprisingly, a winks subculture has emerged. At its heart is the English Tiddlywinks Association, which publishes the magazine *Winking World*. Its American counterpart publishes a rival, *Newswink*. The pages of these publications are awash with terminology: squidgers, gromp shots, nurdled winks and cruds – words which themselves seem designed to provoke public ridicule. In fact, it is the game's embarrassing image which seems perversely to attract many players. 'Most people start it as a joke,' Charles admits, 'but eventually they see there is much more to it than they had thought.'

Tiddlywinks has spawned a world championship – currently dominated by the Americans – and at the highest level it is extremely competitive. 'The best players have the ability to ride a crisis,' said Charles. What is endearing, in a quaint way, is that there is no scandal and not the slightest suspicion of cheating. Tiddlywinks is simply not important enough. As Charles puts it, 'You might cry if you lost the varsity boat race, but not the varsity tiddlywinks. After being soundly thrashed by your opponent, you would probably go down to the pub together.'

Whereas most sports can bring out the seedier sides of human nature, tiddlywinks remains innocent and apart: a metaphor for a simple, almost Christian confrontation. This may appeal or it may bore. Its strength or its weakness, depending on how you look at things, is that no one could ever have a misspent youth down the tiddlywinks club.

CONTACT
The English Tiddlywinks Association
26 Canadian Avenue
London SE6 3AS

The *Titanic* Society

There was no hour hand on the pocket watch. If you looked closely, there was a tiny arrow of rust, the hand's silhouette, marking the last time to be told.

'That's my father's watch,' said the old man. He pressed his finger against the showcase. 'I often come into the museum to see the time when it stopped – when the water got into the works.' He meant the time when his father died, along with 1,500 others, because in 1912, the pocket watch belonged to a steward on the *Titanic*.

There have been worse sea disasters – the Philippine ferry tragedy, for example, where double the numbers died. Unlike the *Titanic*, that disaster is largely forgotten: there is certainly no Philippine Ferry Society, whose members swap memorabilia and build models of the death-ship in every material from matchsticks to margarine; no Philippine Ferry Convention along the lines of the one organized in Southampton by the British *Titanic* Society. As I stood in the maritime museum – one of the visits on the convention's schedule – I was asking myself why people were still intrigued by the *Titanic* disaster, eighty years after it happened. Why *do* people bother learning every fact they can about a sunken ship? And I mean *every* fact, from the colour of the carpet in the first mate's cabin to the contents of the cargo hold.

Maybe superstition is the reason. Travelling on the train to Southampton, I had been engaged in conversation by a man who noticed I was reading a copy of the *Titanic* Society's journal, *The Atlantic Daily Bulletin*. Although not a member of the society, he had read a great deal about the subject. He told me about the novel *Futility*, published in 1898, which predicted the disaster with uncanny accuracy. In the novel, a ship called the *Titan*, of virtually identical tonnage to the *Titanic*, strikes an iceberg, with great loss of life. 'I believe the sinking of the *Titanic* was God's will,' he said. 'The book was a prophecy.' I wondered why God would want to kill so many people. My companion had a ready answer: 'Pride goes before a fall.'

In 1912, there was good reason to be proud of the *Titanic*. The ship was seen as mankind's finest engineering achievement – the largest vessel ever built, a symbol of industrial power. 'Man had come to the conclusion that he was better than nature, that he could do anything,' said George Connor, one of the *Titanic* Society's leading members. 'Man was proved wrong.'

We were now travelling around Southampton on a bus, looking at *Titanic*-related sites, like the hotels where the passengers stayed on the eve of departure and the pub frequented by the *Titanic*'s captain. George told me that his *Titanic* obsession had led him to travel to the Arctic and Antarctic, just to get a better understanding of icebergs. 'People know everything about the *Titanic*,' he said, 'but not many people bother about the iceberg.'

At Southampton Docks we boarded a boat. If the *Titanic* disaster was God's will, then we would be following the first part of the Via Dolorosa, from the bollards where the ship was tied up to the edge of the open sea. 'We're doing exactly the same line as the *Titanic*,' said the voice on the Tannoy. If anyone thought this a trifle morbid, they didn't let it show.

Later that day, on dry land, I was introduced to the society's guest of honour – a *Titanic* survivor, Edith Haisman, who was sixteen in 1912. 'I remember when my father walked up the gangway to board the ship,' she told me. 'He turned very pale. My mother said, "Are you ill?" "No," he said, "I'm all right."'

The arrow on the pocket watch pointed towards ten to two.

CONTACT
Bob Pryor
The British *Titanic* Society
9 Guildford Lawn
Ramsgate
Kent CT11 9AY
Tel: 0843 594213

Toe-wrestling

Ye Olde Royal Oak Inn at Wetton in Derbyshire is approached by a sheep drovers' ancient trail – mile after mile of dry-stone wall, leading to this 300-year-old alehouse set in the heart of the Peak District. The Royal Oak is the type of watering hole that travellers encounter when St Christopher is in one of his better moods. Approved by Egon Ronay and the *Good Pub Guide*, the Royal Oak has friendly staff, seventeen brands of fine malt whisky and comfortable accommodation. Oh yes, and it is also the only pub in England with an active tradition of toe-wrestling.

Just how, and when, toe-wrestling began at Wetton is a mystery. The Royal Oak's current landlord, George Burgess, knows only that two years ago, when he bought the pub, the estate agent's particulars said that the Royal Oak was famous for the sport. Sure enough, behind the bar, George found a board setting out the rules, as well as a pewter cup engraved with the words 'Toe-wrestling Champion'.

At the Royal Oak, George led me to a side room and his son Kevin brought in the board of rules. It was obvious that this piece of painted wood was no antique – I would guess it was less than ten years old, including, as it did, a 'No steroids' rule. It also gave an approved cry of surrender – 'Toe much' – so you could begin to wonder whether toe-wrestling is just a spoof, an imaginary event along the lines of indoor hang-gliding or underwater choral singing.

But you must put such suspicions aside. For when George took

256

over, locals confirmed that they had actually witnessed toe-wrestling contests; they told of how sheer force of ankle power could throw a grown man off his chair. Having used my tootsies for other things that you can read about in this book – flounder tramping, fire-walking, origami (see pages 99, 123 and 181) – I felt I'd be OK at foot-to-foot combat. George picked up the gauntlet (or sock), and he and I were soon sitting facing each other, ready for the barefoot showdown.

Now, human beings can fit their bodily parts together in a number of different ways. It is a remarkable fact that two big toes slot together very well, like clips. Perhaps evolution designed them for this purpose. If you have not tried toe-linking before, I would recommend that you experiment at home with your partner.

As soon as we were interlocked, George and I started to wrestle. Toe-wrestling resembles arm-wrestling, in that the idea is to pin down your opponent, but there are differences. Under the rules, the non-participating foot has to be lifted off the floor, which makes it difficult to gain any sort of purchase – and it also looks exceedingly silly. Howls of pain are soothed by the balm of belly laughs.

George had victories over me in left- and right-foot contests. Encouraged by his success, he is now considering hosting the first-ever toe-wrestling world championships. 'Only approved talcum powders would be allowed,' he said. And the referee would check for verrucas.

CONTACT
George Burgess
Ye Olde Royal Oak Inn
Wetton
Nr Ashbourne
Derbyshire DE6 2AF
Tel: 033 527 287

(The Institute of) Totally Useless Skills

A good example is the trick that Eric Morecambe often performed: up would go the invisible, non-existent ball – his eyes following the trajectory – and the ball would be 'caught', with the appropriate sound effect, by flicking the back of a brown-paper bag. It was a kind of sub-conjuring, fooling no one, and yet in my time I've copied it and I wouldn't be surprised to hear that you have too – just as you probably pretended at primary school that your wooden pencil was made of rubber by moving it in a wobbly way; and I expect that, at some point, you've pressed your arm against a doorframe, moved and been amazed that the arm rises of its own accord. These are all phenomena of interest to the Institute of Totally Useless Skills.

The institute was established by an American, Rick Davis, who has a library of 500 of such tricks, with new ones being added all the time. When I wrote to him, he sent me some literature and I learned a few new techniques. First, there is arm-stretching: if you stretch both arms out in front of you and then with one arm make a vertical circle, stretching it first down, then behind, then over the top and back to the beginning, then . . . whaddayaknow, the arm is a bit longer! (Circle back the other way and it'll go back to its original size.) There is also arm-shrinking: stretch both arms out in front of you, scratch the back of your head with one hand, then stretch that arm out in front again. Sure enough, it's just that bit shorter! Or you might attempt the two-noses trick: cross your fingers, place them at the tip of your nose, close your eyes and lightly rub.

Rick has formulated a definition of a useless skill: 'It must be fun, easy to do, contribute nothing of practical value to society, rely on no special equipment, be safe and non-competitive.' It is a definition that encompasses advanced eye-crossing, yodelling, playing the spoons and making puppets out of napkins. 'I actually regard many of these things as a folk art, passed from person to person,' he says, 'so if anyone wants to learn or share a skill, they should contact me.' He sees his campaign to teach useless skills as a way of fighting back against the pressures to be serious. 'You need to be a contributing member of society and play by the rules so you can function. But you need to give it a break sometimes.'

Recently, when I spoke to him on the phone, he told me that his latest research was on totally useless *office* skills: tricks with paperclips, music with telephones, antics with fax machines. I couldn't think of much you could do with the latter, so he told me about the stretched fax, where you hold on to the paper you're sending and allow it to go through only as hand pressure permits. This leads to long, stretched-out letters. He also mentioned games at water-fountains, including the art of spinning around in a 360-degree circle without spilling a drop of water from the cup. 'Totally useless skills,' he said, 'are the antidote to being totally responsible.'

And his first totally useless skill? 'Taking a degree in philosophy,' he said.

CONTACT
Rick Davis
The Institute of Totally Useless Skills
PO Box 181
Temple
NH 03084
USA

Train Spotting

The 8.30 am from London Victoria to Ashford in Kent does not appear on the BR timetable. One Saturday morning, a train with just such a route left the platform at just such a time – I suppose that made it a collector's item – for this was an excursion train, chartered by railway enthusiasts. I was on board, because I was spotting the train spotters.

What is the collective noun for train spotters? Before you say an 'anorak', I must point out that most of the 200 people on board were not in the traditional livery – though some were, and then it was difficult to resist a smile. Of the 200, all apart from a handful were men, but I managed to speak to one woman, who said she had been obsessed by trains ever since she was carsick as a child. After she'd enthused about the power, the noise, the dirt, the excitement, I asked whether she ever became bored with trains. 'My problem is not getting enough of them,' she said.

The excursion, scheduled to last for eleven hours, appealed to different sorts of railway enthusiasts. For people into traction, we would be travelling on three trains: a 319 (a standard train), a 465 (state of the art) and an EPB (standing for electric-pneumatic brakes, which have been virtually phased out). Regardless of the train, whenever we stopped at a station, a hard core of spotters would dash outside to take photographs, front and rear, from every angle.

To many others on board, the route was the thrill. Track enthusiasts build up mileage travelled along certain lines; they can even be annoyed if the train stops more than 2 inches from the bumpers. Furthermore, British Rail had given permission for the excursion to go on a few short sections of rare track, normally not seen by the public, like siding no. 28, near Grove Park Station. There was also the excitement of stopping at the rarely used back platform at Blackfriars.

So, we passed Clapham Junction, Brixton, Bromley South, Paddock Wood, Lewisham, Gravesend and much of the rest of Network South East. There really wasn't much to do except talk about trains. I heard how spotters spend a fortune travelling from Penzance to Aberdeen, collecting the full set of 4,000-odd locomotive numbers; some spotters will try to tick off the lot within a year and then start again.

The more extreme of the spotters, I discovered, are known as 'bashers', and in the extremest of extreme cases, there are bashers obsessed by *one individual locomotive*, which they follow all over the country. The train in question might be the last one spotted in a particular class, loved especially because it was so difficult to find. Or maybe it has some minor modification which distinguishes it from the rest. Whatever the reason, I am told that in railway magazines there are articles like 'My Favourite is Number 12'. Bashers become terribly upset if their favourite train is withdrawn or goes to the breaker's yard.

Then there are 'shed bashers', obsessed by depots. Or people into timetables. And some people on the excursion were using stopwatches to calculate the precise speed of the train. As for me, I looked at my own watch. It was 12.30. I realized I had another seven hours to go.

CONTACT
Southern Electric Group
12 Dorchester Gardens
Grand Avenue
Worthing
West Sussex BN11 5AY

Tug-of-war

Fit men get into sport for the love of competition; unfit men have a go at sport and find they've had an experience. This is the story of an experience of mine, when this flabby frame travelled to Seale in Hampshire, to participate in what has been described as the toughest of all non-combat sports: tug-of-war. If you want to try it yourself, be prepared to ache. I did. The next day, I could barely sit down. I found it hard to stand up. And trying to lift my foot to step into underpants was a form of purgatory for hell-fire priests to admire.

At the Seale gathering of pullers, I met Peter Craft, the secretary of the Tug-of-War Association. 'When you're going back on the rope,' Peter told me, 'it's one of the greatest feelings you can have. Tug-of-war gets into your blood.'

Body fluids, indeed, are something you have to get used to at a tug-of-war contest. The first I encountered was the dried snot on the sleeve of the Rugby shirt I had borrowed. Then your own sweat flows like a river. And if you have any aversion to the sight of men spitting phlegm, this isn't the sport for you. Oddly enough, all this sits side-by-side with a certain gentility. In the rulebook of the Tug-of-War Association there is an emphasis on politeness, reminiscent of Enid Blyton's Famous Five: 'Tug-of-war teams should have their hands clean before accepting awards ... Punctuality is the basic ingredient of good organization and discipline. We should accept as our maxim, "To be punctual is to be efficient, and what is more it is a mark of courtesy."'

The time for my own appointment with the rope was due. I was to take position no. 4 in the eight-man team. The judge gave the order to take the strain and then we were away.

The others were away and I did my best. In pulling, there are no individual stars, just the concerted efforts of everyone – and I emerged as an individual only because I was so out of harmony with the general heaving.

Often it seemed to me that tug-of-war was like rowing on land, with boots for oars and absolute coordination the key. And just as there is a cox in a boat race, so there is a coach in tug-of-war who shouts encouragement such as, 'I've seen more effort in pulling back a foreskin.' He might just as easily have said to me, 'You look like you're being circumcised from the expression on your face.'

Everyone, apart from one person, dug their heels into the dirt and pulled harder. For my partners, it seemed the suffering was soothed by loyalty to the team. 'We may be in agony,' said one, 'but at least we're in agony together.'

Imagine twelve contests. One was a marathon lasting six minutes and thirty-four seconds – that may not sound much, but it's almost a minute longer than the longest pull in the entire 1990 national championships. At the end of the afternoon, I was reduced to nothing. I had no arms – they had dropped off long before the last contest – and although my legs were still hanging there, I wished they weren't. My torso? Let's say an open wound – and there was more than enough salt to rub into it, with all my sweat. Peter Craft came up to me, smiled and remarked that, in spite of physical distress, I hadn't given up. 'And that,' he added, 'is what tug-of-war is all about. You did really well.'

As Enid Blyton might have said, Peter's kindness made the whole day seem worthwhile. She was an author not noted for her realism, of course.

CONTACT
Peter Craft
57 Lynton Road
Chesham
Bucks HP5 2BT
Tel: 0494 783057

The Tychonian Society

As wheel is to axle, so earth is to sun. Thus did Copernicus put man in his place.

There were those at the time who disagreed, of course – like the Catholic Church. But for several hundred years, no one has disputed what goes around what.

Well, almost no one. Because there are still a few people who say, 'Stop the world, I want to get off.' These are the members of the Tychonian Society, subscribers to the geocentric view of the universe, the belief that the sun orbits the earth. Taking its name from Tycho Brahe, the sixteenth-century scientist who opposed Copernicus, the Tychonian Society is an international organization with its headquarters in the United States. And just before you shout, 'Oh, American lunacy' – moon madness – I must tell that the society was established by a man who holds a doctorate in astronomy from a legitimate university.

I wrote to the Tychonian Society, in the hope that they had some contacts in Britain. I was eventually referred to a professional engineer whom (for reasons of confidentiality) I shall simply call Malcolm.

I must make it clear that Malcolm is not an out-and-out supporter of geocentrism. He was recommended to me because he is fully *au fait* with the reasons for believing that the sun goes around the earth. His opinion is that geocentrism should not be ridiculed or dismissed out of hand, that it might possibly be correct. 'When I started to look at it,' he told me, 'I realized that there was more going for geocentrism than I had thought.' With that, he passed me a copy of the Tychonian Society's journal.

You can be blinded by the sun and you can be blinded by science. I am tempted to say that the two come together in the journal of the Tychonian Society. I was immediately struck by the complexity of the articles and their erudition – or their apparent erudition. 'The mathematics of this model [of a geocentic universe],' I read, 'is arduous though straightforward to one acquainted with the conformal mappings of functions of complex variables.' There followed astronomical terms whose meanings I did not understand, lots of physics and advanced mathematics, plus plenty of references to academic papers supposedly supporting the view that Copernicus got it wrong. I didn't have the technical knowledge to refute – or even comprehend – the arguments within the journal, but I was highly suspicious, as anyone born after the sixteenth century has a right to be. I turned to Malcolm and asked him why the Tychonians should be given any credence.

'Every attempt to detect the speed of the earth going around the sun has failed,' he said. He reeled off a list of experiments. I heard about a scientist called Mascart, who tried to measure the twisting effect that movement of the earth through the ether should have upon polarized light. No effect was found. Another scientist called de Coudres tried to measure the effect that movement should have upon a pair of transformer coils in the inductance of current. No effect was found. Two more scientists, Troughton and Noble, tried to measure a similar effect upon a pair of capacitance plates. Again, no effect was found.

The earth, it seems, does not move. It does not even spin on its axis. We live on a planet that is absolutely fixed in space, while the rest of the universe turns around us. As I heard all this, I kept thinking: this has to be wrong. What about space travel? Mission Control at NASA would have surely missed the moon if their underlying astronomical models were in error?

Malcolm had a reply. 'The Apollo moonshots actually assumed that the earth was the centre of the universe,' he said, 'so as to simplify the mathematics.'

I wasn't beaten yet. Even I, with my limited knowledge of science, had heard of one test that *proves* the earth moves: the Foucault pendulum. This is a pendulum whose angle of movement changes over time because the earth is moving beneath it. But Malcolm told me that geocentrists remain unconvinced. They argue that the change in the angle could be explained by the forces of the rest of the universe (which to them is turning) acting upon a stationary earth.

I doubt whether anything could persuade a geocentrist that he is wrong. For, ultimately, geocentrists believe that there is biblical support for their science. As the Catholic churchmen who persecuted Galileo would have agreed, the earth has a special place in the universe and so it *must* be at the centre. To emphasize this, the society recently changed its name to the Association for Biblical Astronomy. Yet even amongst fundamentalist Christians who support the Genesis account of creation, geocentrism remains the extremest of extreme views. Malcolm, himself a fundamentalist, cannot quite go along with the Tychonians. 'Geocentrism is a hot potato amongst creationists,' he said. 'We have enough difficulty opposing evolution.'

CONTACT
The Association for Biblical Astronomy
4527 Wetzel Avenue
Cleveland
OH 44109
USA

UFOs 1: BUFORA

He meets people who claim to be in contact with aliens from all over the universe, or who claim to be in contact with Christ, or who even claim to be Christ. 'I don't put myself in a position where I don't believe people,' he said, 'but there does come a point where you want *something* tangible.'

John Spencer is the vice-chairman of BUFORA, the British Unidentified Flying Object Research Association. He specializes in the study of so-called close-encounter cases. 'There are people who tell me that they can make a craft land,' he said. 'I went to Sweden on a case like that and stood in a snow-covered field for hours. Nothing happened. I was told that it was because I was wearing metal-framed glasses.'

To its credit, BUFORA always tries to find an everyday explanation for a UFO sighting. 'We successfully explain about 98 per cent of sightings,' he told me. 'Things like aircraft can look very strange at certain angles. Or high-altitude fog can distort a plane's lights.' There was also the case of the man who saw an object drift by that was clearly one of the half-silvered balloons sold at fairs. 'But there are about two or three sightings a year,' said John, 'which are very mysterious.'

In the 'very mysterious' file we would have to include the case of the twelve-year-old girl, mucking out her pony, who heard a loud roar, looked up and saw a teabag-like object with four aerials and a stench of bad eggs. There is also 'the metallic wasp' that entered a house and buzzed about – the witness failed to dent it with an axe. Lights in the sky can be very peculiar too. 'There was a valley in Norway,' said John, 'and over a period of three years there were these unexplained lights. It was captured on video.' I suggested that it might be some natural phenomenon like Saint Elmo's fire or the aurora borealis. 'But the thing is,' said John, 'people found that if they shone a torch into the valley, there would be a response. Two flashes of the torch would lead to two flashes from the valley. And if you did three flashes, you'd get three back, and so on.'

But John took up my point about Saint Elmo's fire. Unlike many within BUFORA, he does not think that UFOs are alien spacecraft. Over the years, he has come to believe that they are a natural phenomenon, but of an unknown type. In a culture nurtured upon *Star Trek* and *Dr Who*, people interpret this mysterious force (or whatever it is) as a vehicle from outer

265

space. In extreme cases, a witness to the phenomenon may become traumatized and claim to meet aliens.

John showed me a photograph of a man holding a piece of pancake. 'He's known as "Pancake Joe",' he told me. The gentleman in question said that a UFO landed in his back yard and that he went for a meal inside the craft – the pancake was on the menu.

'He described the aliens as resembling Italians,' said John.

CONTACT
BUFORA
Suite 1
The Leys
2c Leyton Road
Harpenden
Herts AL5 2TL
Tel: 0582 763218
No personal callers, please

UFOs 2: The International Raelian Movement

Sometime between now and 2025 they will come down.

'Do you expect to meet them?' I asked Dr Marcus Wenner.

'Yes,' he said, 'when they come to the embassy.'

The members of the International Raelian Movement believe in UFOs. What distinguishes the Raelians from organizations like BUFORA is their campaign: they would like to see diplomatic immunity granted to extra-terrestrials – they want to build the aliens an embassy.

'Without an embassy,' said Dr Wenner, the group's organizer in Britain, 'they would be breaking several laws, invading our airspace and territory. But they're not invaders. The embassy would be our invitation. It's the least we can do.'

The Raelian Movement was founded by a Frenchman, Claude Vorilhon, who in 1973 claimed to have been visited by a 4-foot alien in the Clermont Ferrand region of France. After this encounter, Vorilhon gave up his job as the editor of a sports-car magazine, took on the name of Rael, and started spreading the message that mankind owed its existence to a race called the

Elohim and did not evolve, but were genetically engineered by beings from another world. It might seem, therefore, that the Raelian Movement is offering a variation on the God-was-an-astronaut theme of Erich von Daniken, but actually Rael is altogether different from the author of *Chariots of the Gods*.

Soon after he'd met the alien, Rael announced that he was part alien himself: he said that his mother had been inseminated on board a UFO – she had been specially selected for this role by the Elohim – and afterwards her memory was wiped clean so as not to unbalance her psychologically. He also started to sell books and tapes about the technique of sensual massage, supposedly taught to him by the aliens. (I have tried one of the audio-cassettes: you are asked to lie naked on your bed and feel the part of your skin between the sex organs and the anus – all to the accompaniment of ocean sounds and synthesizer music.) Most important of all, Rael began the campaign to build the embassy where the aliens would meet earth's political and scientific hierarchy and give them the benefit of their wisdom. In other words, these aliens would not say, 'Take me to your leader'; the leaders would be taken to them.

Dr Wenner sketched a ground-plan of the embassy which the International Raelian Movement wants to build near Jerusalem. I asked whether they would be hiring contractors to do the bricklaying. 'Within the movement we have architects and builders, so we'll probably put it up ourselves,' he said.

In Dr Wenner's sketch there were several connected circles representing eating and living quarters, and, as you would expect, a landing pad for the aliens' spacecraft. But there was also another area that seemed isolated from the rest. I was curious. 'What's that?' I asked.

It was the swimming pool.

CONTACT
The International Raelian Movement
BCM Minstrel
London WC1N 3XX
Tel: 081 840 3946 or 0272 237447

Variant Chess

You may have heard of the Möbius strip, a mathematical curio consisting of a long piece of paper, twisted and joined at the ends, which makes a loop that starts at the beginning, derails itself, re-rails itself and goes back to the beginning again.

What I doubt is that you will ever have considered, let alone played, a game of chess on such a surface. Yet here am I, fingering pawns, shifting knights, trying out loopy gambits, all the while twisting the board as Möbius-ly as I am able within the limits of my imagination. Because in the game known as Möbius chess, pieces move off one side of the board and reappear on the other, as if travelling upon the strip. Exactly *where* they reappear takes some skill to know. I have been making Möbius strips out of paper, to act as template for my thoughts, and I'm still not confident enough to play anyone.

However, there is one man who is something of a grandmaster on Möbius boards: George Jelliss, the editor of the magazine *Variant Chess*, a journal devoted to exploring unorthodox ways of playing the game.

To give you an idea of the scope of George's magazine, let me quote some examples of chess variants. We might begin with rotation chess, in which the centre of the board is a rotating wheel. Or stereo chess, where the centre is a raised 4 × 4 stack. Then there's kamikaze chess, where capturing a piece necessitates a sacrifice. Or zombie chess, where pieces rise from the dead, but in the colour of the captor. There are variants which introduce new pieces, like the zebra, a sort of lengthened knight, which does a 2,3 leap instead of the traditional 1,2. Indeed, for the animal lover, there is a menagerie of additional pieces: antelopes, spiders, octopuses, squirrels, even wildebeest – each species having its own distinctive move. Or perhaps progressive chess is more to your taste? It demands great imaginative powers, for in this variant white has one move, then black two moves, then white three moves, and so on. Overall, there are *hundreds* of chess variants, and new ones are being invented all the time: random chess, teleportation chess, checkless chess, losing chess, and not forgetting chess with reduced boards and chess with infinite boards . . .

What sort of person plays variant chess? George admits that he finds normal chess boring. 'To get anywhere in the orthodox rankings,' he told me, 'you really have to begin at a very early age and absorb an awful lot of opening theory.' The joy of variant chess is that you start with a clean slate. Set against this, there is one minor problem: finding a partner to play against. George told me that he recently arranged a meeting to bring variant players together. It was not a success – no games being played. 'Unfortunately,' he said, 'we couldn't agree on the rules.'

The dearth of partners means that variant chess players tend either to be attracted to solving problems – there are entire specialist magazines on variant problems of the mate-in-two-moves kind, a subculture of a subculture – or they invent further variants. One of George's creations is curtains chess, inspired by the gunfight at the OK Corral: a screen is lowered which cuts the board in two and stops the players from seeing each other's pieces. Both parties move simultaneously, then the curtain is lifted and there is a shoot-out. 'Perhaps it's what I'll be remembered for in a hundred years' time,' he said.

And I wondered if it wasn't time to wave a chequered flag, for where does all this stop? What exactly is a legitimate chess variant? Surely some variants are so unlike orthodox chess as to be a different game altogether? For example, is draughts a chess variant? Most people would say no, but there is a lack of unanimity on the matter. 'I've even met some draughts players,' says one writer in George's magazine, 'who consider chess to be a draughts variant.'

George points out that orthodox chess is itself a variant, evolving from an Arabic game called *shatranj*, which was derived from still earlier Persian and Indian games. He believes that one day orthodox chess could lose its position as king of the variants. 'Why not?' he said. 'It's happened before. And if grandmasters start losing to computers, they may change the rules.'

Meanwhile, I have invented my own variant: poker chess. In it you leave the pieces in the box and have a game of cards instead.

CONTACT
P Wood
Variant Chess
39 Linton Road
Hastings
East Sussex TN34 1TW

Ventriloquism

When he was in his teens, there were those who doubted his sanity. 'All my friends were going to football matches,' he said, 'and I was saying, "Who's a pretty boy, then?" every time I passed a mirror.'

You do wonder about ventriloquists. Is a vent-act pure showbiz or is it schizophrenia? I asked Nigel Harvey, one of the country's very few teachers of ventriloquism, whether there was any truth in the film *Magic*, about a vent being controlled by his dummy? Nigel admitted that he did know of one ventriloquist who seemed to have a problem or two. 'He puts the dummy in the front seat of his car, and after the show the dummy will say things like, "You were fucking crap tonight." I used to think it was just an act, but it's not. He always takes the dummy out with him. And they're always arguing.'

With that, he introduced me to Benjamin. Benjamin has a large round head and orange hair.

'Benjamin,' said Nigel, 'this is Stephen Jarvis.'

'Never heard of him,' came the reply.

For Nigel, the most important part of ventriloquism is the way the artiste interacts with the dummy. 'Even I move my lips sometimes,' he said, 'but if you can convince the audience that the dummy is real – even if only for a second – you've done your job.' Nigel then pulled off Benjamin's head – there was a yell of 'Owww!' – and the dummy asked politely, 'Could you scratch me in there?' Nigel scratched inside Benjamin's neck. I think I understood the point about interacting with the dummy.

But how do you talk as much as Groucho while seeming to talk as little as Harpo? Obviously, you practise. So, Nigel had me in front of a mirror saying, 'The vicar is in the vestry,' again and again, except that I was actually saying, 'The thicker is in the thestry,' for 'v' is one of those letters that are the lips' invitation to dance. I saw some vibration (or thibration) but not enough to make me feel, shall we say, a dummy. Another exercise was the infamous 'bottle of beer', except that this is not pronounced 'gottle of geer' but 'dottle of deer'. I wasn't doing too badly for a first attempt, but if only I'd started when I was younger.

Nigel began throwing his voice at the age of twelve, when most boys are waiting for theirs to break. Now, only twenty years old, he is a very fine professional vent. Indeed, he has been single-minded about his career ever since hearing Keith Harris and Orville sing 'I Wish I Could Fly'. He played truant from school to practise, and became the runner-up in the final of *Saturday Superstore*'s search for a star. 'Though I was extremely raw, I was extremely good for a twelve year-old,' he said.

We were drinking coffee, and that reminded me: what about the old favourite of reciting the alphabet while drinking a glass of water. 'It's nothing,' he said with contempt. 'It's just a trick glass.' He sipped his own coffee.

'I notice I didn't speak while you were drinking that,' said Benjamin.

CONTACT
Who Said That Productions
Tel: 0226 287107

(They can also give help on designing dummies and getting them made)

The Wallpaper History Society

The paste is ready, you've got the scissors and the brush, the trestles are in place, it's just that . . . well, would it *matter* if you didn't bother stripping off that old wallpaper? It would save time. If there's the odd bump, well, that's nothing. Absolutely nothing.

Isn't that right?

Argue it out with yourself all you want, you'll have misgivings if you fail to peel the walls. I must tell you, though – relax, it's OK, you don't have to strip. There are people who will thank you for pasting ply upon ply, building up the layers over the years, making an artefact as significant as rock stratification to a geologist. To quote from an article in this group's magazine: '[From old buildings] we often remove thick layers of paper, sometimes as many as twenty layers stuck one on top of the other. Once separated, they reveal important evidence of fashions in interior decoration.' I refer to the work of the Wallpaper History Society.

Two of the society's leading members are Joanna Banham, the chairman, and Lesley Hoskins, the executive secretary. When we met, I wanted to know whether the society was genuinely interested in *all* wallpapers or just the arty ones, such as William Morris's designs. What about novelty papers? I've seen wallpaper based upon *Thunderbirds*.

'The society is for people who are interested in any aspect of the history of interior décor,' said Joanna. She mentioned a James Bond paper, showing vignettes of Sean Connery; then a Disney paper with Snow White and Mickey Mouse; and finally, a 1960s Batman paper. The latter revived a memory, for as a child I myself had had Batman wallpaper in my bedroom. 'I should put you in touch with one of our members,' she said. 'She'd be very interested in the socio-economic circumstances of families that had that type of decoration.'

'Part of the fascination of wallpaper,' said Lesley, joining in the discussion, 'is how it reflects society's tastes and values. Wallpaper is very quick to respond to changes in fashion.' Consider the 1950s when people were just starting to go abroad: papers showed exotic vegetables, like garlic and aubergines, as well as bottles of wine. 'The 1950s papers were also a celebration of being able to get food again after the rationing of the Second World War,' Lesley added.

The war ... I saw a reference in the society's magazine to a wartime paper: a sad, simple thing, home-made, just plain paper spotted all over with pink paint. Lesley said that most wallpaper factories were turned over to munitions production, making camouflage for aircraft hangars. Admittedly, there was blackout paper for windows, and sometimes this was double sided: dark on the outside, chintz on the inside. 'And they do say that anaglypta saved the country from Hitler,' said Lesley. 'It's supposed to have held together the bricks of the houses that were bombed.'

As Joanna and Lesley took me backwards and forwards in wallpaper history, I discovered that the oldest surviving paper is an English fragment of 1509, featuring a black and white split-pomegranate pattern. Yet not until the middle of the eighteenth century did wallpaper truly flourish, with the advent of colour printing as well as another major innovation: small sheets of paper were finally joined together to make rolls. Then came the Industrial Revolution and, in 1839, the invention of the wallpaper-printing machine. At last there was the possibility of producing low-cost wallpaper for a mass market. Since 1900? The invention of pre-trimmed and ready-pasted papers, as well as the development of vinyl.

'Wallpaper is a very accessible subject,' said Joanna. 'Anyone can have an opinion on it. When we go on visits to museums to see wallpaper collections, people are always saying, "God, that's awful," or, "I wouldn't have that in my house."'

Yes, anyone can have an opinion. All one's fears of being thought a philistine go out of the window when asked to pass judgment on wallpaper. For example, I am not an expert on modern art and I would feel out of my depth – a little anxious – to comment on the work of someone like Andy Warhol, but in the society's magazine I noticed a wallpaper that he had designed. Called simply 'Cow', it features a bovine head and shoulders in fluorescent pink on a yellow background.

Philistine? Call me what you like, I wouldn't have it in my house.

CONTACT
Lesley Hoskins
Executive Secretary
The Wallpaper History Society
c/o Arthur Sanderson and Sons Ltd
100 Acres
Oxford Road
Uxbridge
Middlesex UB8 1HY
Tel: 0895 238244

The Westerners' Association

It was high noon in Bingley, West Yorkshire. I had strapped on the gunbelt and was practising my draw in the lounge of Allen Ambridge, one of the leading members of the British Westerners' Association.

'I knew you'd want to try,' he said. In between spinning a gun on his trigger finger, he treated me to a display of the two methods of fast draw: thumb-busting, when only one hand is used, and fanning, when the other hand shifts across the body to cock the hammer. Allen is fast: he can pull his reproduction 1872 Colt out of the holster and fire in $^{33}/_{100}$ of a second. But there are faster: he has seen a man achieve $^{25}/_{100}$ – the quarter-second draw. To reach that standard would require hours of practice every day, in front of a mirror, in a showdown with your reflection. 'Fast draw is one of the legends of the West,' he said, 'and everyone in the Westerners' Association does it. Though it never actually happened. Face-to-face fast draw is pure Hollywood.'

Along with fellow Westerners, Allen goes to weekend camps, dressing up in full cowboy gear and eating beans and beef. Clothing is entirely authentic, so there are no modern contrivances like zips. 'I even put on red long johns,' he said, 'though I do wear underpants for hygienic reasons.' Some members take authenticity a degree further: they don't bother to wash.

The British Westerners' Association caters for anyone who

275

wishes to re-enact the culture of the Wild West: its members dress up not only as cowboys but as trappers, Civil War soldiers and Native American Indians, with all the appropriate skills. Allen's love is rope throwing, so he put on his deerskin gloves and took me into the garden for a demonstration and lesson.

'It has a tendency to go stiff in cold weather,' he remarked, concerning the genuine Mexican rope, with cactus fibres bound into the hemp. He stood at my side and, with his hand cranking my wrist, I had the rope in a circle above my head: I managed to lassoo, if not a steer, then a stool.

A stool doesn't satisfy Allen. 'I'd love to do it for real and work on a ranch before I die,' he said. 'I've got the work permit.'

When you've been with him for a while, his accent starts to change; as he becomes more enthusiastic, he starts saying 'sherf' instead of 'sheriff'. 'I live it, I don't play it,' he told me. He did add, though: 'In every man there's a little boy, and every little boy wants to be a cowboy. I never grew up.'

CONTACT
Allen Ambridge
British Westerners' Association
6 Primrose Bank
Gilstead
Bingley
West Yorks BD16 4RB
Tel: 0274 560286

(The International Association of) Whistlers

You've got to be dedicated to fly to the other side of the world just to whistle. Reg Moores told me how he travelled from Brighton to North Carolina to perform 'The Cuckoo Waltz' at a Whistlers' convention. 'I was given that special plaque,' he said, pointing to his mantelpiece, 'for the greatest distance travelled by anyone attending.' He went on to explain how he blows both the melody and the accompaniment by skilful use of his tongue.

The International Whistle-Off, organized by the International Association of Whistlers, takes place annually in America and features contests in classical and contemporary music, and is 'open to any individual, group or family who can whistle a tune with some degree of skill without a musical contrivance in the jowls or under the tongue'. Beyond that, anything goes: standard pucker, fingers in the mouth, or even the rare hand whistle, which involves cupping the hands so that movement of the fingers lets the air out. There is a separate contest in non-human noises; at this, with any luck, you might witness a performance by the famed imitator Dr Horatio Q Birdbath, who can do 300 birds and 700 animals. There also *used* to be a contest for highest decibels, but it was stopped because it got too loud. Some people could do 125 decibels – like a jet taking off.

Reg's own interest in whistling goes back to his teenage years. He is retired now, but he can still recall the blind man who lived near his parents' house. This man was a wonderful whistler – you could hear him way down the road. 'He sounded like an early Roger Whitaker,' said Reg, 'and I remember thinking, "I wouldn't mind whistling like that."' 'Though,' he added, 'I didn't want to go blind.'

Reg demonstrated his technique. He showed me how vibratos can be accomplished by rapidly shifting the tongue. Well, I tried. It's just one of those things I can't do. I was never much good at the leg movement in front crawl, and this was something similar inside the mouth. Reg told me that, as with any musical instrument, I would have to practise. 'At least your teeth don't leak,' he said. He explained how people with a gap in the front, like Terry-Thomas, have problems; a chipped incisor can ruin a whistler's career.

After meeting Reg, I got in touch with the International Association. In their newsletter, *Whistlers' Notes*, I saw an advertisement for an intriguing book, *Mouthsounds*, by Fred Newman: 'How to whistle, pop, click and honk your way to social success.' Not content with written material, I decided to phone up the association's president, Bob Larson. I asked him how long he'd been whistling. 'How long have you been talking?' he said. 'I don't know how long,' he continued. 'I've just always done it.'

CONTACT
Robert Larson
The International Association of Whistlers
3201 North Bryant Avenue
Minneapolis
MN 55412
USA
Tel: 0101 612 521 2640 or 0101 612 540 9507

Witchcraft

'Could you give my son a mention when you write the piece, please?'

When interviewees try this, it's normally time for a polite, 'Yes, of course,' while quietly forgetting the request. But not on this occasion, for the son is called Taliesin, after the first and greatest of the druids, and though just a few weeks old, he already wears the sign of the pentagram, the five-pointed star. It hangs from a chain around his little neck. You see, his mother, Shan, is the high priestess of a group called the House of the Goddess. His mother is a witch.

In London, not far from the Telecom Tower, the House of the Goddess were holding a meeting – the ceremony of the Pagan Moon – that was open to outsiders. So off I went, to see how wicked these witches were.

The meeting began in the afternoon, with Shan leading an informal discussion on initiation rites. She spoke thus: 'Imagine an auditorium with a seat for every living thing. A seat for every person, every animal, every blade of grass. In the centre of this vast hall is a tripod. Overhead are laser beams. Being initiated means leaving your seat and going down to sit on the tripod – where you will be struck by all the lasers.' Sounds a bit like a Pink Floyd concert, I thought – the dark side of the pagan moon?

As the discussion proceeded I was struck by two things. First was Shan's lack of reverence when talking of the Creatrix, the almighty Goddess. She said that there had been times when she had asked the Goddess, 'What the fuck are you doing with my life, you silly old cow?' Second was the humour amongst the witches, playing upon the fairy-tale and Sunday newspaper stereotypes. There were several calls of, 'Cor! Let's have an orgy!' and, 'When do we take our clothes off?' One witch told me that at Hallowe'en they often wear traditional fairy-tale dress – conical hat and black cloak – as a seasonal jape. Yet I couldn't help feeling that the stereotypes were not too inaccurate and that behind the laughter lurked the truth. Shan *did* appear naked in a photograph in a book I saw. And the traditional symbols of broomstick and cauldron *were* present in the meeting-room. In another photograph, Shan was even shown cuddling a black cat.

At seven o'clock the doors were shut, the windows blacked out and electric light gave way to candles. The rites were about to

begin. By each of the four walls were altars, representing the
elements of fire, earth, air and water. We were instructed to go
to the altar of our choice. I liked the look of fire, so I sat down
with some others in a circle and a bowl of water was brought
forth. The circle leader added salt and the bowl was passed
around. Every person in turn dipped in their finger and cast
their anxieties into the brine. Big worries, small worries –
thoughts about dying, concerns about passing exams. I added
whatever was bugging me – probably, did I have enough for the
train fare home – and the bowl was taken away.

Everyone from the four elemental altars now gathered
together. We all lit long wax candles and formed one large circle,
carrying our candles in front of us. The circle rotated, faster and
faster. A song began with the chorus, 'We are the witches who
will never be burned.' Frenzied dancing started around a
cauldron of fire, with Shan holding Taliesin high above her head.
There was a ritual in which we took a partner of the opposite
sex, sat opposite each other on the carpet and, holding hands,
rocked back and forth. A story was told of the Goddess 'coming
from the battlefield, covered in blood, with the scythed heads of
foes hanging from her belt, going to the bedchamber where she
tingles with desire . . .'

And an accident was announced. A male witch had apparently
been kneed in the crotch during the ceremony and had started
urinating blood. Like anyone else with such an injury, he was
rushed to hospital, but a witch stood up and made an interesting
statement: 'A sacrifice must always be made . . . and this
sacrifice was not in vain.'

Finally, an eight-year-old girl was brought forward. Her
parents, both witches, said with pride that they were bringing
her up in the ways of the craft. 'You worked some magic
recently, didn't you?' her father said. The girl nodded. 'Tell
everyone what you did.' It turned out that she had sat an exam
for public school, and to bring her success, she had buried a corn
dolly. Her father asked her if she'd succeeded. 'Yes,' she said.
There was a cheer from the audience.

At this point, I felt disturbed by the proceedings. In twentieth-
century England, *surely* we shouldn't teach children to believe
in the power of corn dollies? But another side of me can't quite
dismiss witchcraft. I want to tell you about what I experienced
some years ago. For Shan's witches were not the first I had
encountered. At university I knew a chap who claimed to be an

adept in the craft. He said that it was possible to make anything happen as long as you willed it, believed it and imagined it. I told him that this was a load of rubbish, and he told me to try it out. He suggested that I attempt to make some little event take place. Nothing too big, but just enough to prove the point. Well, one night I was lying in bed and I thought I'd give it a go. On my wall was a poster and I decided that I'd try to make it fall down. For about an hour I willed, believed and imagined ... and nothing happened. I thought to myself what absolute nonsense this all was. I turned over in bed, and the next instant the poster tumbled down.

CONTACT
Shan
Tel: 081 673 6370

The X-Men Fan Club

Puberty's tough. And how much tougher if you're the only kid on your block who's sprouting feathers as well as body hair.

It was to help such 'genetically challenged' individuals – to use the politically correct term for mutants – that Professor Charles Xavier, a bald, wheelchair-bound telepath, opened his School for Gifted Youngsters. And in 1963, in the pages of Marvel Comics' *The Uncanny X-Men* issue no. 1, writer Stan Lee and artist Jack Kirby gave the world its first glimpse of the pupils at Xavier's superhero academy: the Angel, a rich kid with wings; Iceman, a human fridge; Marvel Girl, able to move objects simply by thinking about them; the Beast, something of a human monkey; and Cyclops, who wore shades all the time – not because it was cool, but so as to put a damper on his deadly optic blasts. Thirty years on, sales of *The Uncanny X-Men* are higher than ever, higher than the Angel could ever hope to soar. When a new comic was launched in 1991 (simply called *X-Men*, without *The Uncanny*), sales for the first issue reached 8.8 million copies – a world record for a single comic. The X-Men have become the most successful comics characters in history.

Now, I had heard rumours of an X-Men Fan Club, supposedly in existence since 1978. Managing to track down an address for this organization, I wrote them a letter. I waited months and there was no reply. In desperation – I wanted all the leisure activities that I could find that begin with the letter X, not including the all-too obvious xylophone – I met up with Phil Hall, the former proprietor of a comics shop called Squonk.

I should tell you straight away that Phil knows *everything* about the X-Men. He is planning to write a book about their history and he has considered applying to *Mastermind*, with the Marvel mutants as his specialist subject. As we sipped coffee from X-Men mugs, we began our discussion.

SJ: Why are the X-Men so successful?

PH: It's like a soap opera, like *EastEnders* or *Coronation Street*, but with mutants – and you have to get your monthly fix. The plots are incredibly complicated and there are so many loose ends. People read it to see if they can make sense of it.

SJ: Give me an example of how complicated the plots can be.

PH: Well, when Christopher Summers – who is Cyclops's son

by a clone of Jean Grey – was transported into the future, knowing he would never see his father again.

SJ: OK. Let's talk about Wolverine.

PH: Oh, he's a nasty little sod. He's got these claws made of adamantium, which is supposed to be the hardest substance in the world, so he can slice through solid steel. Basically, he's got very little conscience and is a bit of a psycho, but the fans love him. When he joined the line-up in 1975, the X-Men really took off.

SJ: And Nightcrawler? Is he popular? He looks a bit odd.

PH: Well, he's come to terms with the fact that he's blue and furry, got a tail and is German. He can live with it now. And women find him very attractive.

SJ: I notice that female characters play a very important part in the comic.

PH: Yes, female characterization is certainly strong – and the women are drawn amazingly sexily, incredibly busty. That's probably one reason why a lot of adolescent boys buy the *X-Men*. In fact, I've always said that the biggest-selling comic of all time would be *X-Babes at St Tropez*, where the X-women get to show their mams. Marvel would make a mint.

SJ: But what about romance?

PH: Well, the longest-running saga has been the affair between Cyclops and Jean Grey. But Cyclops is very shy. It took him forty issues to tell Jean that she's rather nice.

SJ: Jean Grey died, didn't she?

PH: Yes, but she was brought back to life. I thought that was handled far better than some of Marvel's resurrections.

SJ: What about the super-villains? We surely have to mention Magneto and his magnetic powers.

PH: Magneto's a very honourable villain. He's not a criminal, it's just that he had a breakdown and became a super-powered megalomaniac. Not so long ago, he reformed, but now he's evil again. If I had my way, he'd stay a good guy . . .

The conversation continued – for five and a half hours – always getting sidetracked as Phil and I explored the tortuous lives of a bunch of outcasts. At one point the phone rang. It was another *X-Men* collector, who had suffered the disaster of having his mint condition *Uncanny X-Men* numbers 1–25 stolen. All the other comics in this chap's collection were untouched, so the burglar knew exactly what he was looking for.

That is how this piece on the *X-Men* would have ended. Except that months after I met Phil, I received a letter from Geoff Lamprey, who runs the X-Men Fan Club. Apologizing for the delay – he said that he works on Marvel time, where twenty years can slip by with no one noticing – his letter summed up the appeal of the *X-Men*: they are popular because of the parallel between the mutants (who are outsiders in society) and the comic fans (also outsiders in society). 'Odd attracts odd,' he said.

If that sounds like a law from some branch of physics, then that's not surprising. For when I gave him a ring, Geoff described himself as a 'reality specialist', which means that he tries to work out, scientifically, how mutant powers work. He believes that he has an explanation for how Cyclops's optic energy beam defies Newton's laws – in other words, he can tell you why, whenever the beam is used, the hero isn't hurled backwards. 'The force doesn't really come into its own until it leaves the eyeball,' he told me.

I wonder what xylophone players are like?

CONTACT
Geoff Lamprey
The X-Men Fan Club
74 Gloucester Road
Bridgwater
Somerset TA6 6EA

Xenophon

When I first saw his alias in print, I assumed it was his real name – I know it's unusual to be called Regor Nagrom, but it sounded vaguely East European – belonging to a Hungarian émigré, perhaps. Anyhow, once I had uncovered the secret of Regor Nagrom's identity, it was easy to track him down, and he agreed to a meeting. I waited for him by a fountain, in an arcade, somewhere in west London. It was the first stage in entering the shadowy world of Xenophon, a society interested in the recreational study and use of secret codes and ciphers.

Well, I use the word society somewhat loosely. Xenophon is

Regor's *hope*: he hopes that in time it will become a British counterpart to the American Cryptogram Association. At the moment, though, Xenophon has a total membership of one. On the positive side, that meant I could engage the whole society in discussion at a table in the corner of a wine bar. We began by talking about the British and American attitudes towards codes.

'In America, lots of newspapers carry cryptogram competitions,' he said, 'but there's nothing like that over here.' He asked me whether I'd heard of 'The Unsolved Cipher of Thomas Jefferson Beale'. I hadn't, so he told me all about it. In 1880, in Virginia, a pamphlet was published claiming that the author had partially decoded a message left in a box by one Thomas Jefferson Beale. The decoded part said that if the rest of the message could be deciphered, it would give the location of a cache of gold and silver, buried somewhere in the Blue Ridge Mountains. 'To this day,' he said, 'there are people in the States who are trying to crack the code. It could be a hoax, but there's always a lingering doubt . . .' At one time, there was even a club whose members were *solely* devoted to cracking the Beale cipher.

This isn't the only code to remain unsolved. There is also the Voynich Manuscript, believed to date from 1350, which is written in a completely mysterious language. By chance, I had read about this manuscript a few days before meeting Regor, and I remarked that I thought someone had solved it. 'People *say* they're getting somewhere,' he said.

Regor then opened up a plastic carrier bag and took out a book he had written himself. I had never seen its like before – it was a word-pattern dictionary. He explained its usefulness to the code-breaker by writing down the word 'apple'. That word has a particular pattern, which it will retain even if transformed by a letter for letter cipher: that is to say, the second letter is the same as the third, with all the other letters being unique. So, if you find yourself confronted by a five-letter cipher in the apple pattern, the dictionary will enable you to look up all the five-letter words it could possibly be, including apple. Regor hopes to find a publisher for this book, but thus far has not been successful. 'It's a bit of a specialist market,' he said.

I wanted to know more about his plans for Xenophon. He thought it would be nice to have a club magazine, either in code or in back to front writing which could be read by holding it up to a mirror. However, he wanted to attract only people of the right sort. So his name and address appear in this book *in code* – and only those who are successful in deciphering it can be considered worthy potential members of Xenophon.

CONTACT
85XV8 358XR4
QPV TR3S8ZUXV XR8UV49
254U54 DIH NY9

(Advanced) Yo-yo

What is a yo-yo? It's a bucket in a well, a butterfly's tongue, an anchor weighed, Cleopatra in a carpet, a tight curl. But no matter the gloss you put on it, you're going to get bored with basic rolling and unrolling, the old up down. To get variations on the theme, you need to meet Don Robertson, the only man in Britain who can teach you advanced yo-yo skills.

He'll walk the dog and rock the baby, via a windmill, then spaghetti, a loop-the-loop, a flying saucer, and finish by catching the yo-yo in his pocket. The only person who could rival his skill was his son Mark, who tragically died last year. 'He was better than I am,' Don told me. The difference was Mark's ability to do a double fountain.

Don showed me a single fountain: the yo-yo shoots up to the front, high above your head, then does the same behind you, a sort of spray. A double fountain requires this to be done with a yo-yo in both hands. 'I used to say that a double fountain was impossible,' said Don. 'I reckoned you needed another pair of eyes to watch the second yo-yo. But Mark did it.'

Don's interest in the yo-yo began in the 1950s, when there was a nationwide revival of the craze. 'It's one of those things that comes and goes,' he said, meaning the craze and not the yo-yo itself. At the time, he was working as a magician and was taken on by Butlins because they needed someone to demonstrate and sell yo-yos. 'I don't know how I got the job. I couldn't use a yo-yo at all,' he said.

But after a lot of practice, Don won the European yo-yo championship. There was a qualifying round consisting of tricks, followed by an endurance session, where competitors had to loop-the-loop as many times as possible without making a mistake. Since then, Don has appeared many times on TV as a yo-yoer.

'About the time of Watergate,' he reminisced, 'there was a newsclip which featured President Nixon with a yo-yo. So I made a yo-yo out of a large tape-recorder spool. The BBC wouldn't let me show it on TV. But it was a sensation on TV in other countries.'

Don proceeded to 'tune' his yo-yo. 'Only experience can tell you what the right tension for the string should be,' he said. I watched, but it is one of those operations that the brain cannot take in straight away. He showed me the separate moves for tightening and slackening the string, and I saw the yo-yo trace two separate loci in the air, but don't ask me what they were. I wish the human eye had a freeze-frame facility.

Don tried to teach me the simplest trick of all – making the yo-yo stay at the bottom of the string, until, with a simple tug it comes back up again. The technique is to give the yo-yo a hard throw and then let the hand go limp. As with most things in this book, I didn't succeed. But the yo-yo is like a flea of the mind. So the next day I went off to the shop and bought myself a toy.

When you walk the dog for the first time, you realize that if you had a tail, you'd wag it.

CONTACT
Don Robertson
1 Tara Court
Princes Road
Buckhurst Hill
Essex IG9 5DT

Postcript

Yo-yo Times is the essential newsletter for yo-yo enthusiasts. Though aimed at yo-yoers in the USA, much of the contents will appeal to British readers – for instance, tips on new tricks. My favourite is sled dog, which is walking the dog when there's snow on the ground. The yo-yo digs a neat hole, but if you give a tug, it comes flying out.

CONTACT
Yo-yo Times
PO Box 1519-BL
Herndon
VA 22070
USA
Tel: 0101 703 742 9696

Zen Archery

Once, a master of the Japanese art of Zen archery travelled west, and further west, until he came to England. Upon studying the native language and history, he learned that the English longbow of Agincourt fame owed its power to the wood of the yew tree. 'How right and truly appropriate,' he said 'that this English word "yew" sounds exactly like their word of identity, "you". It is as if to confirm that whenever an arrow is released, its path depends entirely upon one person – you, yourself and no one else.' A small, bow-shaped smile came to his lips as he realized how easily the English might have discovered the essence of his Japanese art ...

I wrote that mock parable after travelling to Dartford in Kent, to the headquarters of the British Association for Japanese Archery. There, wearing his kimono, was Don Slade-Southam, the Association's president. He bade me take off my shoes and we stepped on to the dojo, the practice-court – in fact, the only permanent archery court in England which is equipped to traditional Japanese standards. But what exactly is Japanese archery?

In *kyudo*, the Way of the Bow – or Zen archery, as it is often called – hitting the target is of secondary importance; what counts is the archer's state of mind. Ideally, the archer should be empty of intention and filled with the pure awareness of the present moment. There should be no desire to succeed. It is the paradox of releasing an arrow without being interested in hitting the target that captures the Zen essence of this sport-cum-philosophy-cum-art.

'*Kyudo* begins where other martial arts end,' I was told by John Carder-Bush, one of the association's leading members. 'After you've done karate or judo for ten or fifteen years, you come to realize that your only opponent is yourself. In *kyudo*, you are up against yourself from the word go. You cannot run away.'

Other members agreed that *kyudo* is about you versus you. If you miss the target, you look inwards and ask, 'Why?' – always to be reminded that internal attitude is the key to success or failure.

Like the Japanese tea ceremony (see page 139), Zen archery is entirely ritualized. There are no random movements, so if, in the course of conducting a ritual, you drop an arrow, there is yet another ritual for picking it up. I watched as the members demonstrated *yawatashi*, a ceremonial shoot involving a master and two assistants. First the master moves, then the assistant, then the second assistant, like a wave. It is all very slow, a confrontation with your own impatience; but eventually an assistant draws down the master's kimono to bare a shoulder and a breast, and only then is an arrow released . . .

It is said that a master of Zen archery can tell if a shot has been successful simply by listening to the sound of the string.

Don beckoned to me and handed me a bow. In no sense can this Zen weapon be called user-friendly. Unlike the English longbow, the Japanese bow is asymmetrical, with the lower limb much shorter than the upper. This perversion of shape means that the arrow will veer off target, to the right – unless, that is, the archer has mastered the Japanese technique of simultaneously spinning the bow-shaft in the hand to the left. I thought I'd leave that for a later lesson. The important thing was to get an arrow in the air.

I found that I couldn't even draw back the string. The archers smiled. 'There's a secret to it,' they said. Muscle power alone will never draw back the string of a Zen bow.

I think I am too impatient by nature to learn Zen archery. Don admitted that there was one female member who trained for *eight months* before she released her first arrow. Part of her problem was fear – for the bowstring is drawn back a long way indeed, way behind the head, and as that string comes twanging forward, there is always the possibility that it will strike the archer, and even maybe *slice* the archer, turning him or her into an instant Van Gogh.

I am reminded of the old Zen koan, or riddle, which asks: 'What is the sound of one hand clapping?' Perhaps the answer is: 'Well, there were really two hands, but the master was a bit hard of hearing following his archery session.'

CONTACT
Don Slade-Southam
7 Barn End Drive
Wilmington
Kent DA2 7BX
Tel: 0322 222145